HOW TO DESIGN AND CONSTRUCT
PERIOD FURNITURE

Early Georgian desk.

HOW TO DESIGN AND CONSTRUCT PERIOD FURNITURE

by Franklin H. Gottshall

BONANZA BOOKS

NEW YORK

To My Mother,

who bought my first set of tools and
encouraged the early efforts which make
this work possible, this book is
affectionately dedicated

CONTENTS

FOREWORD

This book, with its principles of design directly related to furniture of the important periods, is presented with the hope that it is a step toward improvement in a field where improvement is desirable. Good taste in furniture design, as in all arts, may be cultivated. The acquisition of fine judgment and good taste is seldom the result of chance. Definite rules, of a type that do not confine the designer within limits that are too narrow, will be of material assistance in laying the foundation for designs that are consistently superior in beauty and merit.

The material and information is presented so that illustrations and descriptions are as near together as possible. This makes the assimilation of vital facts and information easier than where more turning of pages is necessary. Dimensions have been given in every case where this was possible or desirable. While it is frankly admitted that these cannot fit every case or problem that will come up, they are, however, sufficiently accurate to form sound bases for the type of experiments that will be necessary to formulate original designs. The author's aim, throughout the book, has been to aid the designer who wishes to do original work. For this same reason, a rather lengthy and complete glossary has been added, which, with its references and cross references, together with references constantly given in the text, makes the finding of valuable information and definite facts easy.

In addition to the large number of illustrations whose scope is limited to the presentation of information of a general character, definite projects too have been included. We refer to the projects shown on Plates 7, 8, 13, 15, 20, 25, 27, 31, 36, 37, 42, 46, 49, 50, 53, 55, and 60. Most of these projects have been built from the drawings herewith presented, and photographs and all other essential data are given. This was done with two aims in view. One was to show the student the correct manner in which to work up his designs, and the other aim was to tie the information given in each chapter definitely to a case problem.

A great deal of the information appearing in this book has never been presented in a single volume before. In order to make the presentation of such a large amount of information possible it was necessary to do two things. First, the necessary and desirable facts and characteristics concerning each style had to be collected. Secondly, they had to be presented in such a manner that authenticity would not be impaired or lost. This, it is believed, has been accomplished by working up new and original designs in most cases, in which this information is clearly shown in its proper forms and combinations. Many authors have tried to present information on the important periods, resulting in exhaustive works, usually in several large volumes. One author, for example, in presenting the characteristics of American furniture alone, took three large volumes and several thousand photographs and a great number of line drawings. By adopting the method of presentation used in this book, the prohibitive expense of gathering many photographs is not necessary. The essential characteristics of a large number of chairs, for instance, may be combined in one illustration, which presents, perhaps more information than ten or more photographs, on which it is difficult or impossible to show pertinent facts relating to the project. The styles and techniques of drawing have also purposely been varied, to aid the draftsman who lacks experience.

The book is intended for three classes of people: (1) For schools and teachers, to use as a text or reference book. (2) For professional men, including furniture designers, draftsmen, architects, and interior decorators. (3) For amateurs who design and build furniture as a hobby. The need of each class has been definitely kept in mind when the material was being assembled.

The author wishes to thank the following people for material assistance and suggestions:

William Ball, Sr., of Hope Manor, West Chester, Pa., for permission to make drawings of hardware which he manufactures, shown in Figures 2, 7, and 10, Plate 6; Figures 2, 4, 5, 6, 7, 8, 9, 11, 12, 13, 14, and 15, Plate 12; Figures 1, 2, 3, 4, 6, 7, 8, 9, 10, and 12, Plate 21; Plate 26; Figures 1 to 12, Plate 38; Figures 1 to 9 and 11 to 18, Plate 54.

The Berry Schools, Mt. Berry, Ga., for photographs of Figures 46, 103, 126, and 235; Queen Anne hall table, page 95; Sheraton chair, page 151; mirror, page 153; Brothers Adam armchair, page 163.

The Grand Rapids Brass Co., Grand Rapids, Mich., for permission to make drawings of hardware which they manufacture, shown in Figures 1, 3, 9, 11, 12, and 14, Plate 6; Figures 1, 3, and 10, Plate 12; Figures 5 and 11, Plate 21; Figures 13 to 19, Plate 38; Plate 47; and Figure 10, Plate 54.

The Metropolitan Museum of New York for photographs of important pieces in their collection, shown in Figures 41, 61, 67, 86, 144, 172, 190, 241, and 252; the Queen Anne settee, page 97; Chippendale wing chair, page 125; and the chest of drawers, page 229.

Wallace Nutting, and The Old America Co., of Framingham, Mass., for photographs of Figures 81, 94, 122, 165, 274, 275, 281, and 286; the Sheraton bedstead, page 154; the chest on chest, page 227; and Figures 6, 8, and 13, Plate 6.

The F. Schumacher Co., of New York, for photographs of Figures 47 to 55 inclusive and of the American Federal chair on page 229, and for permission to use printed material relating to fabrics, formerly published by them.

The Elgin A. Simonds Co., of Syracuse, N. Y., for photographs of Figures 66, 107. 108, 223, 226, 243, and 256; the

William and Mary table, page 82; Queen Anne chair, page 95; Sheraton wing chair, page 153; and the Spanish table, page 196.

Mr. L. Day Perry, Editor of *Popular Homecraft,* for permission to use material published by the author in a series of articles on principles of design.

Mr. John J. Metz, Editor of *The Industrial Arts and Vocational Education Magazine,* for permission to use material published in a series of articles on principles of design.

Mr. Nelson Grofe, artist, of Boyertown, Pa., for material aid in working up the chapter on Color.

To all others, who may have been missed in the foregoing list, but whose encouragement and assistance the author gratefully acknowledges.

FRANKLIN H. GOTTSHALL

CHAPTER 1

THE DIVISION OF SPACE AND AREAS

The observance of definite principles will materially aid the craftsman in formulating a design for a piece of furniture. Whether these rules are consciously or unconsciously applied to the problem is a matter of no moment. It is quite reasonable to suppose that in the beginning, when the novice is adventuring into the field of design, rules such as are given in this and the following chapters will be of great value. After some experience many of these rules will be applied as a matter of habit, though they are of a type that allow the designer a considerable amount of choice in the use of his own judgment. Does the beginner need to learn rules in his pursuit of good design or would it not be just as well to leave the matter up to his good judgment entirely? This question may be answered by asking another. Does one who studies arithmetic for the first time need rules to go by? He does, and for the same reason that the designer needs rules to follow. Without them he would be at a loss as to the most practical method of procedure, resulting in a waste of effort, and in most cases a very poor product.

The mechanics of cabinetmaking is a science understood by many, since most of the emphasis has been placed on this phase of the work, in the trade and in schools. The principles of good design, and the ability to use them intelligently is a science of which comparatively few can claim to be the masters. The novice, when attempting to design a piece of furniture will want to know how to divide masses effectively, how to secure good proportions, and the type of ornament most suitable for his creations. Some of these things may be determined by trial and error methods, but the chances for success are far greater if definite rules are applied to the particular problem.

Most of the designer's problems have already been solved by designers of past generations, and the rules and laws governing the solutions are pretty well defined, and available, if one but knows where to look for them. Most of the rules are simple to follow and easy to use. The results obtained by applying them to the individual problem will depend for their success upon the skill of the craftsman. No two designers will interpret a design in the same manner. The best rules for the designer are those that allow him considerable option in the solution of his problem; variety being the very essence of design. The great furniture styles, especially those of the eighteenth century, are richly indicative of conscious planning, and any-

1

one who wishes may learn most of the things he needs to know about good design from them. They form the basis of our present study; they hold the answer to all that we need to know.

Three things are of primary importance to secure a good design: Utility requirements must be met, and not sacrificed for other considerations. The construction should be of the best possible kind. Beauty of the final product should be the constant aim of the designer; it being an end worthy in itself, and one that is seldom, if ever, inimical to usefulness.

Utility and sound construction need little if any discussion here. These two will be touched upon from time to time in later chapters. First of all, until the individual periods are studied in detail, beauty, and the means for securing it will be our chief concern. A casual examination of a beautiful piece of furniture may not reveal the secret of its beauty. Upon analysis it will be found that the following things are among the important factors that make it attractive: Spaces properly divided, an attractive outline, good proportions, properly balanced elements, appropriate ornament, materials of fine quality, harmonious color combinations, and fitness to surroundings.

THE PRIMARY MASS. All furniture may be divided into two groups: that in which the primary mass is a vertical structure, and that in which it is a horizontal structure. The primary mass may be a cabinet, a chair, or a desk. It is usually composed of several design units. A table, for example, has a top, two ends, and two sides. Long tables, sofas, and similar pieces are examples of horizontal primary masses; while tall secretaries, cabinets, and similar pieces are examples of vertical primary masses. All good designs will fall definitely into one class or the other. For this reason (Rule 1) *Dominant lines should lead the eye in a vertical direction on a vertical primary mass, and horizontally on a horizontal primary mass.* We have all seen the incongruous effect that results when a tall person wears a sweater that has prominent horizontal stripes. The effect is inharmonious because it disregards the principle laid down in Rule 1. A similar lack of harmony will result if horizontal lines are too prominent on a vertical piece of furniture.

MAJOR AND MINOR DIVISIONS OF A PRIMARY MASS. Since every piece of furniture has several sides, there will be several design units, each of which will have to be considered individually when working up a design. All of these units will not, however, be of equal importance. Thus (Rule 2), *Every primary mass should be composed of major and minor masses, or areas; these in turn may be composed of subdivisions which may or may not be of equal size and importance.* The principle of giving dominance to certain areas, in the division of the masses, is one of the most important to be found in effective design; and once this has been realized, an important step has been taken toward achieving desirable results.

DIVISION OF A PRIMARY MASS VERTICALLY — TWO DIVISIONS. For the most practical solution of the problem, con-

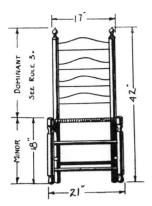

Fig. 1. Ladder-back
side chair.

Fig. 2. Small table.

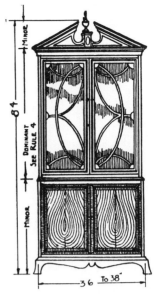

Fig. 4. China cabinet
with French feet.

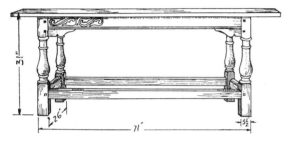

Fig. 3. Refectory table.

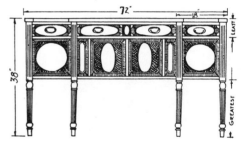

Fig. 5. Sideboard.

sider the divisions of a mass vertically first of all, and then later, horizontally. Vertical divisions come first in dividing most areas, so this procedure will be logical.

A mass is divided vertically by horizontal lines or elements, such as moldings, borders, and the like. A mass may be divided vertically as follows:

(Rule 3) *When a mass is to be divided into two parts vertically, one part should be greater than the other. The greater area may be above or below the minor area.* Chairs are good examples with which to illustrate this rule. In Figure 1, for instance, the dominance is in the upper part. On the table in Figure 2 the dominance is in the lower part. In no case is it desirable to have the two areas equal.

THREE DIVISIONS VERTICALLY. When the mass is to be divided into three parts vertically, two methods of treatment are possible. (Rule 4) *To divide a mass into three divisions vertically, the areas should be all unequal, with the largest one between the other two.* This method is followed in the design of many beautiful pieces of furniture. Good examples are shown in Figures 3 and 4. By another method: (Rule 4a) *The lowest area may be the greatest, and each succeeding area may be smaller.* This is the method employed in Figure 5, and in the spacing of the drawers in the central area of Figure 6. Rules 3, 4, and 4a are particularly applicable to the design of good turnings. The application of Rule 3 is shown on the foot of Figure 7. Rule 4 has the widest application of any to turnings; in fact, it applies to most of the best designed turnings. (See the column in Plate 36.) Figure 8, shows a turning designed by Rule 4a.

MORE THAN THREE DIVISIONS VERTICALLY. (Rule 5) *If a mass is to be divided into more than three parts vertically, the piece should first be divided into two or three major areas of unequal size, using the rules already given (3, 4, or 4a), and then each of these should be treated individually to determine necessary subdivisions.* Figure 9 shows a highboy which illustrates this principle admirably. In this piece there are a great number of divisions, but they are grouped in a manner so as to make the design reasonable and orderly. By first separating it definitely into three major areas, the chances of having the problem become too complicated are reduced. The divisions immediately become interesting design units which may be attrac-

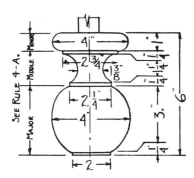

Fig. 6. Late Sheraton chest of drawers with mirror.

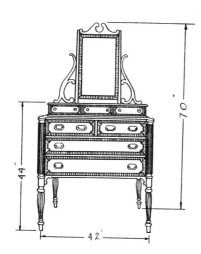

Fig. 8. Ball foot.

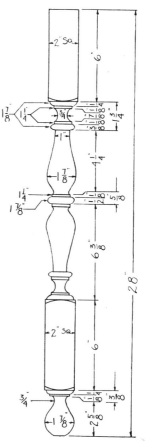

Fig. 7. Type of leg used on gate-leg tables and turned small tables.

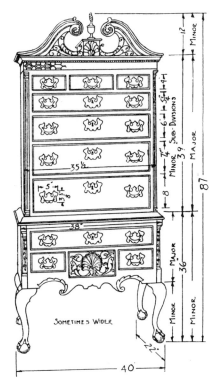

Fig. 9. Highboy.

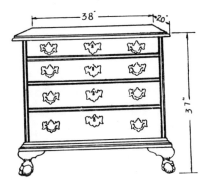

Fig. 10. Chest of drawers.

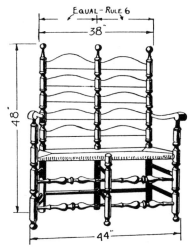

Fig. 11. Love seat.

tively subdivided. The central major division of the primary mass is subdivided according to the method given in Rule 5a:

In the case of a chest of drawers, or a similar structure, the lowest area should be the greatest, with each succeeding area smaller in size. (See also the upper section of the Welsh Dresser, shown in Plate 9 and in the chest of drawers shown in Figure 10.)

DIVISIONS OF A MASS HORIZONTALLY. TWO-PART DIVISION. A mass is divided horizontally by vertical lines or elements. When a mass is to be divided into two parts horizontally, one of two methods may be followed, depending upon utility requirements.

(Rule 6) *When a mass is divided into two parts horizontally, the parts may be made equal in size and area.* This rule is illustrated in Figure 11. It is the most common method of dividing a mass into two parts horizontally. By this method the two areas are bisymmetrically balanced.

(Rule 7) *Some masses may be divided into two parts horizontally by making one area greater than the other, but the two areas should be balanced* (See Fig. 12). This method is the most effective two-part division, but more skill is required to make it satisfactory. The smaller area is made to balance the greater area by properly subdividing it so as to give it greater weight. This is

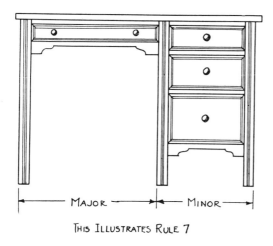

MAJOR ———— MINOR

THIS ILLUSTRATES RULE 7

Fig. 12. Two balanced areas.

known as occult balance. The principle for securing an occult balance is the same as that used when balancing a beam on a fulcrum which is closer to one end than the other. By placing a greater weight on the short end than on the long end, the beam will be balanced.

THREE-PART HORIZONTAL DIVISION. A mass may be divided into three areas horizontally in three different ways.

(Rule 8) *A mass may be divided horizontally into three equal areas* (See Fig. 13). This is the least interesting of

the three methods, and should not be used except where utility requirements admit of no other treatment. The very fact that there are as many as three areas, however, often provides enough interest to make the scheme possible. Sometimes the central area may be made more important than the other two by added emphasis in the way of ornament (See Fig. 14).

(Rule 9) *A mass may be divided into three parts horizontally by making the central area greatest, and placing it between two smaller areas of equal size.* This is the most effective method of the three. A beautiful example illustrating this rule is the one on Plate 46. It is the principle employed in the design of sideboards, and many other well-designed pieces by master craftsmen such as Sheraton and Hepplewhite.

(Rule 10) *A mass may be divided into three parts horizontally by placing the smallest area between two larger areas of equal size.* Panels on chests (See Fig. 15), are often arranged in this manner. A scheme of this kind is shown in the lower section of the Welsh Dresser on Plate 9, and also the arrangement of the areas on

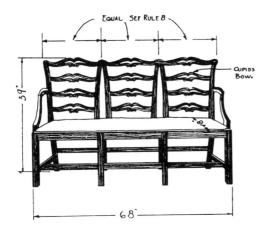

Fig. 13. Three-back, ladder-back settee.

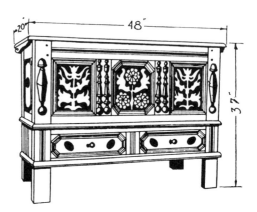

Fig. 14. Tulip-and-aster chest.

Fig. 15. Chest with small panel between two larger panels.

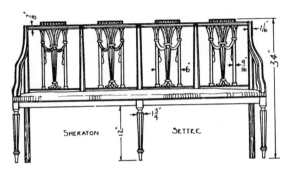

Fig. 16. Four-back settee.

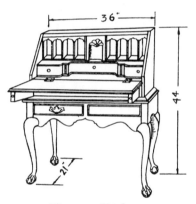

Fig. 17. Desk.

the cabinet of the Spanish Vargueno, in Plate 50.

MORE THAN THREE DIVISIONS HORIZONTALLY. (Rule 11) *When more than three areas horizontally are desired, or necessary, they may be of equal size and importance* (See Fig. 16). Rule 11a gives another possible solution. (Rule 11a) *When more than three areas horizontally are desired, a large area may be placed between a number of smaller areas. The small areas on one side should balance those on the opposite side* (See upper section of cabinet in Fig. 17). The small areas on either side of the large one, in this scheme, need not all be alike, but they must be balanced.

QUESTIONS FOR REVIEW

1. Why is it necessary to study rules of design before drawing plans for a piece of furniture?

2. What three things are of primary importance to secure a good design?

3. Define the term *primary mass*.

4. In what direction should dominant lines run on a horizontal primary mass? On a vertical primary mass? Why?

5. What composes a design unit on a piece of furniture?

6. What is meant by vertical division of a mass? Horizontal division?

7. Is a mass usually divided first in a

vertical direction, or in a horizontal direction?

8. State the rule for dividing a mass into two parts vertically.

9. What two rules may be followed in dividing a mass into three parts vertically?

10. What is the most effective method of procedure to follow in dividing a mass into more than three areas vertically?

11. What two methods may be followed in dividing a mass into two parts horizontally?

12. How many effective methods are there for dividing a mass into three parts horizontally? What are they?

13. What are the most effective methods for dividing a mass into more than three areas horizontally?

SUGGESTED PROBLEMS

1. Design a bedside table using the principle of design given in Rule 3.

2. Design a stool, 18 in. high using the principle of design given in Rule 4.

3. Design a Colonial bookshelf to hang upon the wall, using the principle of design given in Rule 4a.

4. Draw the design of a paneled chest using one of the principles of design given in Rules 8, 9, or 10.

CHAPTER 2

CURVED LINES AND ELEMENTS, AND THEIR APPLICATION TO OUTLINE ENRICHMENT

In the first chapter, rules 1 to 11a inclusive were given to show effective methods of dividing large areas on a primary mass to enhance its beauty and usefulness. The importance of dividing large areas, in a manner to make them more attractive, becomes self-evident when one sees objects having little or no appeal because of the lack of such planning. The sins of improper space division are many, but they are as nothing when compared to the transgressions practiced against beauty by improper outline enrichment. Therefore, the second phase in the study of good design will very properly be about curved lines and elements, as they apply to outline enrichment.

Pieces of furniture on which straight lines are used exclusively may be beautiful, if well proportioned, properly ornamented, and constructed of fine materials. The Chinese have designed some remarkable cabinets, and other pieces, from which curves are entirely absent on outline structure. There is very little new about ultramodern design, except a few new materials which take the place of wood occasionally. It follows rules and precepts that are, in some cases, thousands of years old. We will admit that

pleasing form is possible when straight lines alone are used, but the field of possibilities is greatly enlarged if curved lines are used as well.

On a piece of pottery, metalwork, or jewelry, it is sometimes possible to use curved elements exclusively, and make an object of utility and refinement. In furniture design this is not always possible. Pieces in the Louis XV style, particularly chairs, were sometimes designed so that not a single straight line was found in their entire composition (See Fig. 20). In Plate 32 is shown a Hepplewhite chair, designed after the manner of Louis XV chairs, in which this has been done. This is high art, and the piece has exquisite grace and refinement. The eye derives pleasure from beautiful curves, especially when they are used for the enrichment of outlines. They endow a design with a freedom and grace not possible when straight lines alone are used. The straight line imposes too many restrictions upon a designer, who, if he is a real artist, will use firm, free-flowing curves to enhance the beauty of his creations.

A desire to use curves for the enrichment of outlines is apparent in the work of every amateur. This desire is some-

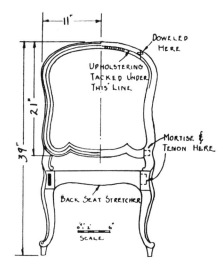

Fig. 20. Louis XV chair-back detail.

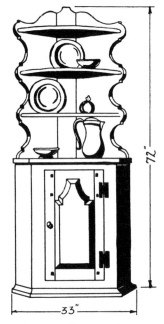

Fig. 21. Corner dresser.

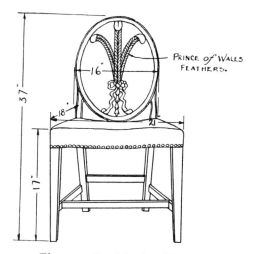

Fig. 22. Oval back with straight
taper legs.

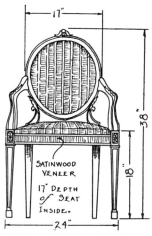

Fig. 23. Armchair.

times expressed in the meaningless scrolls of an apron on a stool; or what is worse, with mechanical curves drawn with a compass or some other device. The lack of ability to design beautiful outlines is due to improper thought in some cases, but more often lack of proper training. Mechanical curves have their place in design, but should be sparingly used. They lack the essential element found in all good design, which

is interesting variety. Poor design is the result of monotony brought about by mechanical effects, in many cases — mechanical curves, mechanical repetition of identical elements, mechanical proportions, and the like. Good design avoids these things.

An examination of the curves used in the enrichment of outlines, as well as in surface enrichment, which is treated in

Chapter 4, will reveal four distinct types of curves. They are: the compass curve, the freehand one-direction curve, the reverse curve, and the compound curve. Each of these with the exception of the compass curve offers opportunities for a great deal of variety.

THE COMPASS CURVE AND ITS APPLICATIONS. (Rule 12) *Compass curves may be used to round corners, and occasionally in colonial or provincial designs, to secure certain quaint effects. They may also be used with freehand curves which will relieve their mechanical severity.* An example of a piece in which this was done is shown in Figure 21. Here it results in a quaint effect frequently found on Colonial designs. This was due in great part to the lack of training of early craftsmen in principles of design. This very fact often gives Colonial pieces a peculiar charm not found in the better designed styles.

THE ONE-DIRECTION CURVE AND ITS APPLICATIONS. (Rule 13) *The most beautiful curves are firm freehand curves graceful and rhythmic in unfolding themselves.* The one-direction freehand curve, which is also the simplest curve, has great possibilities. The limits of its possible variation are the straight line on the one hand, and the circle on the other. It is the curve found in the oval, a motif used with such excellent effects by Sheraton and by Hepplewhite and the Brothers Adam on some of their finest chair backs (Figs. 22 and 23). It is the curve used in the design of the scroll found on the Ionic column; an element of great renown and refinement, especially as used by the Greeks. This scroll may be adapted to many decorative uses

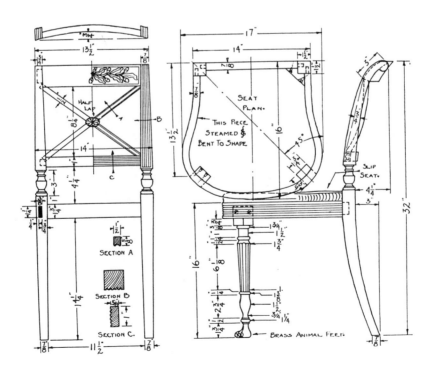

Fig. 24. Details of typical Duncan Phyfe side chair.

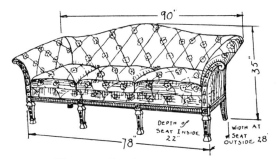

Fig. 25. Brothers Adam sofa.

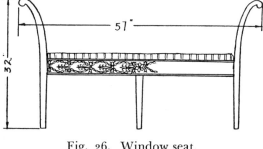

Fig. 26. Window seat.

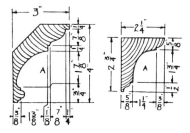

Fig. 27. Beautiful compound moldings.

Fig. 28. Bow-back Windsor armchair.

as shown in Plate 28, where it is used on the apron of the desk, and in Plate 60, where it forms a prominent feature in the design of a Windsor chair. A very important one-direction curve is the one known as, "the curve of force." This curve is shown inside, on the curve of the chair back in Figure 24 (side view), and on the upper parts of the legs on the window seat and sofa, Figures 25 and 26. The curve of force always begins with a gentle sweep, and ends with a quicker, though rhythmic, curl. It is a supporting curve, and is found on beautiful turnings and moldings in its pure or modified form. (Rule 14) *A beautiful one-direction curve has no straight line in its composition.* Although the curve is at times very elusive, Rule 14 should never be broken.

THE REVERSE CURVE AND ITS APPLICATIONS. Reverse curves, even though poorly formed, usually appeal to our sense of beauty. This is seldom true of any other curve used in design. The designs of the legs shown in Plate 17, prove this, because the reverse curves used on the legs have straight lines in the center, but they nevertheless appeal to one's sense of beauty almost as much as others that do not have this fault. This use of straight lines as parts of reverse curves was a common failing on pieces of the authentic Queen Anne style. Even Chippendale sometimes transgressed in this respect. The applications of the reverse curve to furniture designs are innumerable. It is found on Queen Anne furniture most of all; being in this case the chief form of enrichment. It also is found on beautiful turnings, and on fine carvings. (Rule 15) *The reverse curve is most beautiful if the curve has no straight line in its composition, and is sharper on one bend than on the other.*

THE COMPOUND CURVE AND ITS APPLICATIONS. The compound curve is the one with which the designer will have the greatest difficulty. It is compounded of two or more of the simple curves. If well executed it is very effective, and using it on a design requires a great nicety of judgment. Its use, more than any other element found in design, will reveal the true ability of a designer. (Rule 16) *A compound curve, to be effective, must not be a meaningless scroll, but must express its function in a definite manner.* This rule is clearly illustrated in the design of the chair in Plate 32. It is a rule often broken in the design of a scroll-sawed apron, or other outline structure of poorly designed furniture.

TURNINGS AND MOLDINGS. Turnings that are designed with beautiful curves, according to the rules just given are superior to the haphazard designs which one so often finds. (Rule 17) *Good turnings always have beautifully formed curves.* Among the things that make turnings beautiful are: (Rule 18) *The curves on turnings must be full and well rounded out, rather than scant and flat.* This gives an impression of richness and sufficiency of material, not found in thin cheap turnings. (Rule 19) *Curves in turnings, moldings, or other outline structure should connect with fillets at as nearly a right angle as possible.* This makes the change in direction definite, and leaves a clean-cut satisfying profile. Another thing to avoid in turnings and moldings is monotonous repetition of identical elements. On beautiful compound moldings, such as the one shown in Figure 27 this is avoided. The same is true of beautiful turnings. The beauty of objects such as the Windsor chair, in Figure 28, is often due almost entirely to the observance of these rules.

The moldings shown in Figure 29 are the simple moldings found in architectural design. Those shown in Figure 30

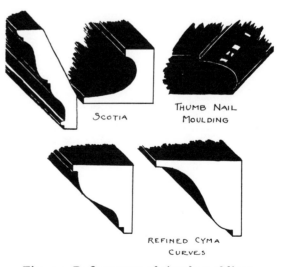

Fig. 30. Refinements of simple moldings.

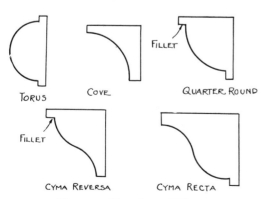

Fig. 29. Simple moldings.

have been refined by redesigning the curves, or combining several curves to make them more interesting and serviceable.

QUESTIONS FOR REVIEW

1. Give several reasons why it is desirable to use curved lines and elements on outline structure?

2. Why is it impractical to design a piece of furniture, using curved lines exclusively? Can it be done successfully?

3. Under what conditions are compass curves desirable in a design?

4. What are the four types of curves used in furniture design?

5. What are the conditions necessary to make curves beautiful?

6. Name one important function of the "curve of force."

7. What is the most effective method for designing elements upon which reverse curves are used?

8. Which one of the four curves that have been studied is the one most difficult to use successfully? Why?

9. Name at least two things that are necessary to make a turning beautiful.

SUGGESTED PROBLEMS

1. Design a turned candlestick, making use of the principles of design found in Rules 13 and 14.

2. Design a low Queen Anne coffee table, using the principles of design suggested by Rule 15.

3. Draw the design for a Colonial gate-leg table, or for any of its turned parts, using the principles of design given in Rules 17, 18, and 19.

CHAPTER 3

PROPORTION IN FURNITURE

A third important factor necessary to make a piece of furniture beautiful is good proportion. It is a subject about which one hears a great deal, mostly in a general sort of way, and one which deserves the best thought and judgment of which the designer is capable. Good judgment is absolutely necessary to determine good proportions. Rules can be given that will be of material assistance when solving problems of proportion, but after all, they are only the tools of the craft, and are subject to the limitations of the designer who uses them.

Good proportions are as important for securing pleasing form as proper space division, or proper outline enrichment. The proportion of a mass is a factor that must be taken into account when solving the problems suggested by the first two chapters. (Rule 20) *The division of masses, the planning of curved lines and elements for outline enrichment, and the determination of proper proportions, are closely related problems which must be solved simultaneously.* To keep the subject of pleasing form and how it may be secured as simple as possible, the three problems are discussed separately. In actual practice they cannot be considered separately.

Good proportions are the result of a proper relation of lines and masses. Certain relations of length to width are beautiful, while others differing only slightly may lack interest. By observing a few simple rules when planning space divisions, and in the solution of various other problems that arise while formulating a design, most of the errors resulting in clumsy graceless objects may be avoided.

An object that has good proportions, has unity and harmony, because the different elements are properly related to each other. Objects on which the elements are identical, such as a square panel, might upon first thought seem to be well proportioned, because of this relationship. Identical elements produce neither harmony nor beauty, but only mechanical effects. Pleasing proportions result from more subtle relationships. The eye finds greater pleasure in a rectangle, or a figure on which the relationship of elements is not quite so obvious. The same is true of curved and other figures. An oval is more beautiful than a circle, and an isosceles triangle more beautiful than an equilateral triangle. (Rule 21) *Good proportions result from subtle relationships of length to width, or relationships which may not be too easily analyzed.* In Figure 33 are shown several simple geometric figures that have interesting proportions. It is upon similar principles that the designs of

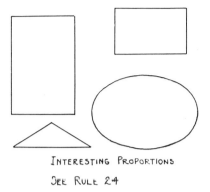

INTERESTING PROPORTIONS
SEE RULE 24

Fig. 33. Simple geometric figures.

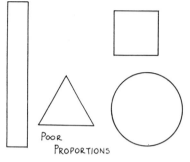

POOR
PROPORTIONS

Fig. 34. Proportions that should
be avoided.

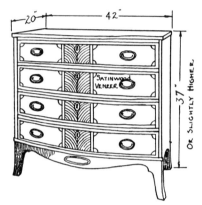

Fig. 35. Chest of drawers.

primary masses and their subdivisions should be based. An oval or a rectangular table top is always more interesting than a round or a square one. Figure 34 shows proportions that should be avoided whenever possible. Since most of the objects that a designer will wish to plan may be bounded by lines forming either rectangles, ovals, or triangles, he may solve most of the problems of proportion by properly planning the proportions of simple figures of this kind.

(Rule 22) *To secure good proportions, the contrast between the length and width of a mass should not be too great.* This is a rule that is of particular importance when planning long narrow elements such as drawers. Ugly proportions on masses of this kind may usually be avoided by proper subdivision. The designs of Sheraton and Hepplewhite are particularly well planned in this respect. Poorly proportioned areas of this kind were usually subdivided to make them more attractive (See Fig. 35).

(Rule 23) *Masses on which the proportions are about 2 to 3, 3 to 5, 5 to 8, and similar relations, are interesting.*

Proportions of this kind are beautiful in ovals and triangles as well as rectangles. Even in cases where the length is exactly twice the width, the relationship is not as interesting as when proportions are used that are more difficult to determine. An equilateral triangle is the least interesting triangle that one can draw. Pediments for cabinets, highboys, and similar pieces are never based on the proportions of an equilateral triangle.

Thus in planning the major and minor divisions of a piece of furniture, or any other object, one should always try to choose the most subtle relationships possible, consistent with the utility requirements of the object. Where only a single area is under consideration this will be a simple matter. Most of the difficulties will arise while planning pieces in which there are several areas, some of which may have to be subdivided. A great deal of the furniture designed by the later eighteenth-century cabinet-makers, especially Sheraton, gives evidence that they had mastered the difficulties of proportion. Particular attention may be directed to the pieces shown on Plates 29, 33, 34, 39, and 40, for special merit in this respect. Attention might be directed to Figure 35, for example, for the manner in which the minor masses have been handled to improve the proportions of what would under ordinary methods of treatment have resulted in poorly proportioned elements. Instead of long narrow areas in which the contrast of length to width would have been too great, the drawers have been subdivided to enhance their beauty. This has been done without any sacrifice of utility, such as would have been the case if the drawers had been made smaller to produce the same effect.

(Rule 24) *Experiments with rectangles, or other geometric figures, whose limits will be similar or identical to those of a proposed design, should result in getting good proportions.* To make the illustration of the rule as clear as possible, the method of procedure has been shown on Plates 9 and 28.

(Rule 25) *When there is a fixed or limiting element in a design, it must be the starting point in working out proper proportions.* In the case of a chair design, one must begin with the height of the seat. If it is to be 18 in. high, then a rectangle 18 in. high must be drawn, and various widths experimented with until one is found that seems to be satisfactory. Next the same experiment may be tried with the upper part of the chair by extending the vertical lines above the seat, and stopping them with a horizontal line representing the top of the chair, at the proper elevation, which will be determined by the judgment of the designer. This rule is illustrated in Figure 36. Three scale drawings were made for comparison. The seat on each one is the same height, but the backs vary. The proportions of the design in the center

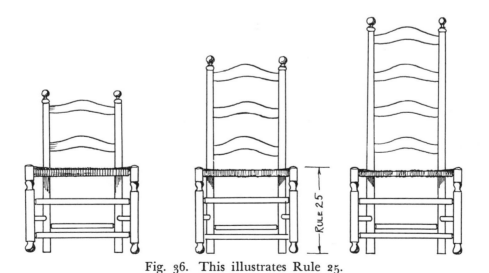

Fig. 36. This illustrates Rule 25.

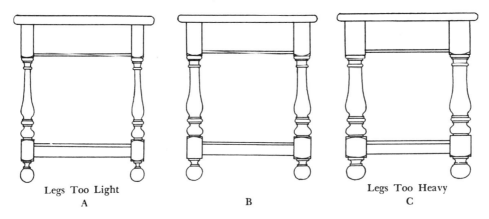

Legs Too Light   B   Legs Too Heavy
A   C

Fig. 37. Proper proportions may be determined by comparing several
scale drawings of an object.

are the best of any. This gives us another rule of proportion: (Rule 26) *The proper proportions for a design will be finally determined by comparing a number of scale drawings of the proposed mass or object.*

A great deal of confusion often exists in the mind of the novice, when designing a piece of furniture, as to the best method of determining proper proportions for legs or similar elements, to make them suit the rest of the design. A simple and effective method of procedure for overcoming these difficulties is to make a scale drawing of the proposed object, designing the members in question as heavy or light as his judgment or inclination dictates. Then to the left of it draw a similar design, but make the members lighter. To the right of it draw a third elevation and on this make the members in question heavier. It should now be possible, by comparing the drawings, to select the most desirable design, or to make further corrections that will make it entirely satisfactory (See Fig. 37).

Questions for Review

1. What elements of design must be properly related to secure good proportions?

2. Under what conditions may a mass be said to have good proportions?

3. Name several ratios that are desirable in planning the proportions of a mass.

4. What is the proper method by which good proportions may be secured in a furniture design?

5. What must be the starting point in designing the proportions of a chair?

6. How will the proper proportions for a design be finally determined?

Suggested Problems

1. Design a handkerchief box or a stationery box, using the principles of design suggested in Rules 21, 22, and 23.

2. Design a Cromwellian chair, using the principles of design suggested in Rules 24, 25, and 26, to secure good proportions.

CHAPTER 4

THE SOURCES AND KINDS OF ORNAMENT, AND ITS APPLICATION TO FURNITURE DESIGN

It has been shown how to secure beauty in an object by careful planning and arrangement of masses, outlines, and proportions. If the rules suggested in the first three chapters are thoughtfully carried out, great improvements should be noted in the structure and form of almost any object one may wish to design. The elements of structural form are the fundamental requirements of a design, and their proper planning and arrangement is of the greatest importance. These elements are the framework of design, while ornament constitutes the finish and trim. Ornament, more especially that which is intended for surface enrichment, is something we can do without, and still not impair the utility of an object. If a piece of furniture has pleasing form it does not necessarily need ornament to make it beautiful. This is proved by the handsome designs shown on Plates 16, 56, and 57.

The desire for ornament is, however, older than written history. Evidence of this is found in every archeological excavation. Ornament of excellent design is found painted upon walls, carved upon stone, molded into pottery, and engraved upon metals. This desire is as apparent today as it was several thousand years ago, though as civilization progresses there are improvements in materials, and in the technique of their application to design. Despite this fact the important methods by which objects may be ornamented now are still those that were practiced in days of antiquity. They are four in number, and speaking in broad terms may be classified as (1) contour enrichment, (2) carving, (3) painting, (4) inlaying. Contour enrichment has already been treated in the second chapter, though a few additional aspects of it will be touched upon in this chapter. The remaining three methods of ornamenting furniture, together with rules for their application to design, will be treated in this and the following chapter.

(Rule 27) *The sources from which ornament for furniture should be chosen are three in number: abstract forms, naturalistic motifs, and artificial objects.*

Abstract motifs are derived from geometric sources, and consist of borders, moldings, inlaid bands; or applied ornament such as bosses, lozenges, dentils, etc., found especially on furniture designed before the eighteenth century (See Plate 5). They may consist of geometric allover patterns, either carved or painted on panels as on the chest design, Figure 40. This shows a form of orna-

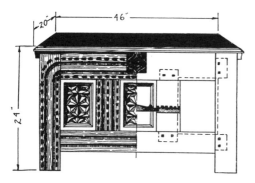

Fig. 40. Seventeenth-century chest.

ment known as chip carving, which has great possibilities if well handled. Ovals, and other figures, formed by inlaid bands, as used by Sheraton, are very pleasing forms of abstract ornament. Gothic tracery of the type shown on the drawer fronts and grilles of the Spanish vargueno, Plate 50, constitute still another form of abstract ornament. It would be difficult to mention all of the interesting possibilities of this source of ornament, and its applications to furniture design. A great deal of the hardware illustrated throughout the book falls into this class.

Naturalistic motifs are derived from things found in nature. They may be divided into several groups. Under the first group we have those of human or animal origin. These consist of busts (Fig. 41); animal heads and feet, such as spread eagles (Fig. 42); ball-and-claw feet (Plate 22); griffins, cherubs (Fig. 43); and the like.

A second group of naturalistic motifs consists of ornament derived from plant life. This consists of carved leaves, especially the acanthus leaf; palm or olive branches (Fig. 44); the honeysuckle (Fig. 45), and others. Most of these are conventionalized to make them suitable for ornament. The beautiful and appropri-

Fig. 41. Louis XV Table. This table is well proportioned and richly but tastefully decorated. Chippendale adapted many of his designs from pieces such as this.

Fig. 42. Mirror.

Fig. 43. Louis XVI
painted panel.

Fig. 44. Louis XVI
detail.

Fig. 46. Ball-and-claw feet, when well
executed, are elements of remarkable
beauty; when poorly executed are
vulgar and hideous.

Fig. 45. Anthemion or
honeysuckle.

ate carving on the knees of the desk (Fig. 46), give ample evidence of the wonderful possibilities of motifs of this class. Leaves and flowers are always favorite motifs on upholstering materials, as shown in Figures 47 to 55 inclusive. During the period of Louis XV, French designers let their imaginations run riot, and attempts were made to copy nature as it was found, and in some cases to outdo it. The outcome, in extreme cases, was a bewildering maze of ornament that degenerated into bizarre effects, and resulted in objects of little or no beauty. In some cases the ceilings, walls, woodwork, and furniture were carved, gilded, painted, and otherwise ornamented to such an extent that people of good taste rebelled against the extravagance of the display. Too much ornament, no matter how beautiful individual elements comprising it may be, is far worse than none at all, and is a thing to be avoided. A little ornament, carefully chosen for its appropriateness, and well executed at the right place, will result in furniture of distinction and elegance.

The third group of naturalistic ornament consists of rock-and-shell motifs, or rococo ornament, as it is commonly known. This was brought to great heights of development by French designers, being first used toward the end of the reign of Louis XIV, and with greater frequency by designers during the reign of Louis XV. Chippendale was influenced by it, using motifs of this kind, on what he called, his best furniture. It is a form of ornament peculiarly suited to design using the principle of occult balance, and where very rich effects are desired. Figure 56 shows a

Fig. 56. Piece of hardware
with rococo motif.

piece of hardware on which this motif has been used with interesting results. It is a type of design that should not be attempted except for the very richest pieces of furniture, which are to be placed in appropriate settings.

The third major source of ornament for surface enrichment comprises artificial objects, and includes motifs such as vase forms, musical instruments, ribbons and love knots, and a large assortment of kindred subjects. Many of the motifs shown on Plate 41, such as the lyre, are of this class. Most elements of this nature are of classic origin, and were used with considerable skill by the Brothers Adam, and contemporary designers in the latter part of the eighteenth century. They are especially suitable for inlays and painted designs. The Brothers Adam introduced the vogue for classic

ornament, bringing it to England, whence it spread to France and America. In America, Duncan Phyfe used motifs like the lyre, Prince of Wales feathers, and others of a similar nature to excellent advantage. The advantages of using inlaid ornament were that it permitted a much lighter, more graceful structure, colorful artistic effects, and, of course, satisfied the desire for something new. Where a saving of expense was necessary, the designs were painted instead of inlaid.

When a piece of furniture is being designed, certain places will naturally suggest themselves as suitable to be enriched with ornament. (Rule 28) *Places which are particularly well suited to be ornamented are: outlines, borders, panels, and shaped or modeled surfaces.* These include places such as doors of cabinets, drawer fronts, table aprons, chair backs, chair and table legs, panels, pediments and tops of tall pieces, bed-

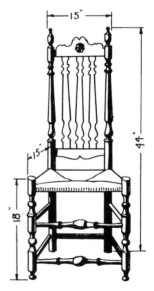

Fig. 57. Banister-back
side chair.

posts, and outlines around important openings.

All ornament falling under the heading of outline or contour enrichment is composed of straight and curved lines. This ornament comprises scroll-sawed patterns, examples of which are shown in Figures 21 and 57; turnings and moldings, as in Figure 58; carving in bold relief, as in Figure 59; and scrolled

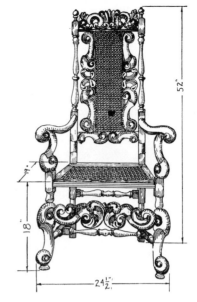

Fig. 59. Carolean chair.

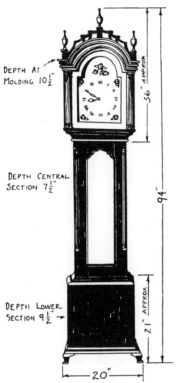

DEPTH AT MOLDING 10½"

DEPTH CENTRAL SECTION 7½"

DEPTH LOWER SECTION 9½"

Fig. 58. Tall clock.

metalwork as in Plate 50. The rules that should be observed for the proper solution of problems of this type have already been pretty well covered in Chapter 2, and will not need repeating here. Several additional rules are given, however, which take up considerations not adequately covered before.

(Rule 29) *Outline enrichment must not destroy logical structure, but must*

help to support and strengthen it, and unite individual members into a unified whole.

(Rule 29a) *Surface enrichment must not destroy or hide logical structure, but must become a definite part of it.*

The chair shown in Figure 59 could be severely criticized, because it breaks these rules. A much finer type of structure on which these rules have been closely observed is the tall clock, Figure 58. This structure is based upon rules similar to those observed in the design of a fine column. There is an adequate base, a slender shaft, and then the important upper part, similar in some respects to the entablature above a column. The structure has a roof, just as an architectural structure has a roof. The individual members are unified in a logical manner by means of beautiful moldings. The quarter columns serve to give support to the structure at points which might otherwise seem weak. Outline enrichment is not complicated, but simple and appropriate; and this brings us to the next rule.

(Rule 30) *Outline enrichment must not be so complicated as to destroy the unity and dignity of an object, but because of its grace, refinement, and simplicity, should emphasize the parts of the structure upon which it is found.* Rules 29 and 30 are frequently broken, and for this reason the very ends which the designer wishes to achieve by the use of ornament are defeated. The observance of Rule 16 will aid the designer in also observing these two.

(Rule 31) *Outline enrichment of a*

subordinate mass should never destroy the harmony which exists between it and the parent mass of which it is a part.

(Rule 31a) *Surface enrichment of a subordinate mass should never destroy the harmony which exists between it and the parent mass of which it is a part.*

The apron of the cabinet shown in Figure 60 breaks Rule 31 to some extent. One has a feeling that the design would be improved if the lines were straight to harmonize with the mass above it. The tall cabinet (Fig. 61), serves as an excellent example with which to illustrate Rule 31a. Turned drawer pulls of the

Fig. 60. Lacquered cabinet.

Fig. 62. Drawer pulls.

Fig. 61. Tall cabinet which lacks only appropriate hardware to make it an aristocrat. Birds-eye maple veneer on mahogany.

Fig. 63. Louis XIV cabinet.

type and scale of those that appear on this piece have no place on a design that is in all other respects such a fine example of its type. What an improvement there would be if pulls were used like those shown in Figure 62. The ones shown are entirely out of harmony with the parent mass.

THE ENRICHMENT OF BORDERS. Under the general classification of borders will be found members such as table aprons, seat rails, friezes, rails and stiles on doors, borders enclosing panels, picture frames, and sometimes drawer fronts.

(Rule 32) *The ornament on borders*

should be dynamic; that is, it should cause the eye to move in the direction taken by the border itself. The frieze under the cornice of the Louis XIV cabinet (Fig. 63), does this. Various other examples of borders that are designed according to this rule may be found on Plates 5 and 41.

(Rule 33) *None of the elements of the design on a border should destroy the movement in an onward direction by introducing contrary lines of sufficient prominence to break the continuity of the foward movement.* Study the borders on Plates 5 and 41, and see the distinct forward movement because of the manner in which the ornament is arranged. The designs have a slight contrary motion, especially those shown in Figure 64. This contrary movement in a vertical direction, on what is known as the inceptive axis, gives added interest to the design.

The inceptive axis is a definite or imaginary line about which design elements are grouped in symmetrical fashion to form a design unit. In simpler words, it is the starting point, or line, about which the design unit is constructed. The vertical center line of the palmated leaf is the inceptive axis on Figure 65. A number of design units may be connected by other elements of minor importance, known as links. The small bell-shaped flowers are the links on this border. These links are important, for the continuity of the design is often due to them. They help the eye to easily bridge what would otherwise be a gap. This arrangement also serves to illustrate once more the dominance of one unit over another, a principle always to be found in effective design.

Inlaid bands are favorite mediums of decoration on borders. They should be-come a natural part of the parent mass which they decorate, and to do this they must not be too prominent. They must be consistent in scale and color with the mass on which they are found. Carved ornament should never be glued or tacked to a surface, but should always be carved from the solid wood. Tacked-on ornament is easily detected, and always cheapens the product.

PANEL ENRICHMENT. (Rule 34) *The ornament enclosing a panel should cause the eye to move in the direction of the outline of the panel, and should be of such a character as to strengthen this outline.*

(Rule 34a) *The ornament found on the bordering members of a chair back should cause the eye to move in the direction of the outline of the chair back, and should be of a character to strengthen and support this outline.*

Panels are usually minor masses enclosed by borders of some kind. They are rather large plain surfaces, which lend themselves particularly well to decoration. They are of the utmost importance in a design, being logical centers of interest. Chair backs, because of their evolution from panels, and their

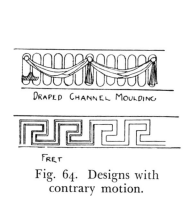

DRAPED CHANNEL MOULDING

FRET

Fig. 64. Designs with
contrary motion.

THE DESIGN ON THIS APRON MAY BE PAINTED OR CARVED

Fig. 65. Table with painted or carved apron.

Fig. 66. Louis XVI chair. A beautiful example classical in its conception.

Fig. 67. The refined ornament on this chair back is worthy of most careful study.

great similarity to them, are subject to the same rules of design as panels so far as ornament is concerned. Note the excellent character of the ornament on the chairs shown in Figures 66 and 67; how it strengthens and supports the outlines of the chair backs in each case, and its appropriateness to the design. In both cases the chair backs have more character because of the ornament. This is not the case in the chair back shown in Figure 59.

(Rule 35) *If border ornament on a panel has important centers of interest, they should be placed at the corners, or at points in the center of the border, or they may be at both of these places.* The picture above the desk in the frontispiece, partakes of the nature of a panel, and the frame is an excellent example of this rule. The corner is a natural place for ornament, since the eye, in following

the lines of the design, must come to a temporary stop at that place before it can continue on its journey around the frame. Figure 68 shows a border on which the centers of interest are at the corners. Figure 69 shows them placed at the centers of the border, and in Figure 70 they are found at both places. Sometimes interest may be centered only at the upper border (See Fig. 71).

(Rule 35a) *If border ornament on a chair back is to have important centers of interest, they should be placed at the center of the top rail, or the junctions it makes with the back legs, or at both of these places.* Important ornament is often placed at the junction of the legs and stretchers to emphasize this important place on a design (See Fig. 66). The same is true of table designs, as shown in

Figure 72. Many chair backs have important ornament at the top, at the center of the rail, this being a logical place to which to call special attention (See Fig. 73).

(Rule 36) *If a panel is square, or round, the center of interest may be in its center. Minor centers of interest, or elements of ornamentation may radiate from this chief center of interest, but must not destroy the balance of the design.* The design of the Gothic tracery on the carved chest (See Fig. 15), illustrates this rule. The end panels are square, but they also partake of the nature of round panels, because of the nature of the design. This design illustrates many fine principles used in panel enrichment, and it is for this reason that the photograph has been included, since

Fig. 68. Geometric panel with a lozenge ornament.

Fig. 69. Geometric panel with a boss ornament.

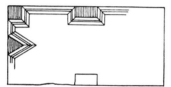

Fig. 70. Painted geometric panel.

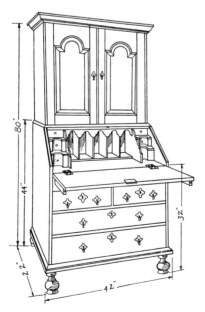

Fig. 71. Straight-top secretary.

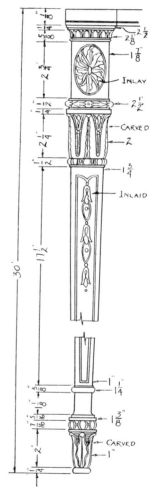

Fig. 72. Detail of square Adam table leg.

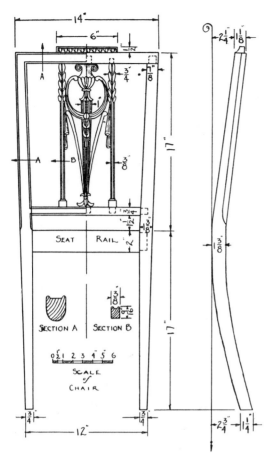

Fig. 73. Detail of chair with oval-shaped scroll near top of splat.

Fig. 74. Cabinet.

it represents a style of furniture of much earlier date than any treated in this book.

(Rule 36a) *On square panels, centers of interest may be concentrated on lines leading from the center of the panel to the corners.* (See panel on the right, Fig. 15.)

(Rule 37) *When a panel is rectangular, and is placed in a vertical position, the center of greatest interest should be on the vertical center line at a point above or below the center of the panel; preferably above it.* The beautiful panel in the center of the chest in Figure 15, shows interest concentrated on the center line, near the top of the panel. This is a very effective method of treatment, and is found on many fine panels. The end panels on the upper part of the cabinet (Fig. 74), are treated in a similar manner, though here the ornament is painted instead of carved.

(Rule 37a) *Minor ornament on either side of the vertical center line should not destroy the balance of the design.*

(Rule 38) *Centers of interest on the vertical splat of a chair back should be concentrated near the top of the splat.* A chair splat is very similar to a panel, and should be treated in much the same manner. The center of greatest interest in the chair back shown in Figure 73 is the oval-shaped scroll near the top of the splat.

(Rule 39) *When a rectangular panel is placed horizontally, interest may be centered at the following places: in its exact center; on the horizontal center line at points equidistant from the center; above or below the center on the vertical center line.* Figure 74 shows small end panels with ornament in which interest is concentrated at the exact center of the panel. Figure 75,

Fig. 75. Carved panel.

shows a panel on which there are points of interest between the center and the ends of the panel. In Figure 76 the center of greatest interest on the panel enclosing the cabinet of the Spanish vargueno, is at the lock, illustrating the third part of Rule 39. There are several minor centers of interest, to be sure, but the important one is the lock, slightly above the center of the panel on the vertical center line.

(Rule 40) *Any ornament carved on a chair back should become a definite part of the mass without obscuring or weakening the structure, and should be of such a character that comfort is not sacrificed because of it.* Chair backs on chairs designed by Chippendale were nearly always carved in some manner. In some cases, on his ornate chairs, of which he made a great many, this rule was disregarded, since the chairs were made largely for show.

THE ENRICHMENT OF A MODELED SURFACE. The enrichment of modeled surfaces is a more difficult task than the enrichment of flat surfaces. To do it properly requires the technique of a sculpturer. Modeled surfaces include objects such as cabriole legs, human or animal forms, such as spread eagles, turnings

that are to be carved, etc. Because of the varied nature of the outlines and levels on such objects, they require types of ornament that must in each case be adapted to the individual structure under consideration.

(Rule 41) *Carving is the most proper form of ornament for a shaped or modeled surface.* It may be painted or gilded, to be sure, but the basic ornament on objects of this kind will be carving (See cabriole legs on the desk in frontispiece, and in Fig. 46.) Inlay or painted ornament on structures of this kind would be entirely out of place.

(Rule 42) *Any ornament carved on a modeled surface must become a definite part of that mass without obscuring its structure, and if properly executed should give added emphasis and elegance to the structure.* This rule is clearly illustrated in Plate 28, where a comparison may be made on a piece of furniture. Here the front legs are very beautifully

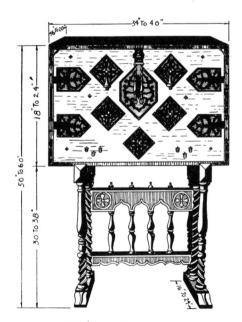

Fig. 76. Vargueno.

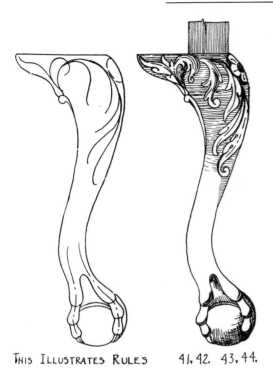

THIS ILLUSTRATES RULES 41. 42. 43. 44.

Fig. 78. Leading lines which form skeleton of design, and completed carving.

carved. The back legs have been left plain. The fact that the ornament gives added distinction to the modeled surface on which it appears cannot be denied after a glance at this drawing. The ornament on the front legs has become a definite part of the design (See Fig. 46).

(Rule 43) *To design free ornament, or ornament for a modeled surface, first draw suitable leading lines. These should be in the form of an inceptive axis, a beautiful curve or curves, or radial lines.* By free ornament is meant ornament that is not subject to the rules of bisymmetric balance, such as shown in Figure 56. To give a practical demonstration of how the ornament for a modeled surface may be designed, cabriole legs are shown in which the leading lines are drawn according to the principles given in Rule

43 (See Fig. 78). The first leg shows the leading lines which form the skeleton of the design, and the second leg shows the design for the carving completely drawn.

(Rule 44) *Centers of interest on shaped or modeled surfaces should be concentrated at points which are meant to be of superior importance.* Make a study of the legs on the desk in the frontispiece, and of other objects that are subject to this rule, to see how it may best be accomplished.

QUESTIONS FOR REVIEW

1. What elements may be considered fundamental requirements of all design?

2. What are the four principal methods by which furniture may be ornamented?

3. How many sources of ornament for furniture design are there? Name them.

4. Define abstract ornament; naturalistic ornament.

5. Into what three groups may naturalistic ornament be divided? Give an example of an element from each group.

6. Name two places that will naturally suggest themselves as suitable places for ornament on a Chippendale chair; on a Hepplewhite card table.

7. What rules should be observed in regard to the relationship of outline enrichment to structure?

8. What rules should be observed in regard to the relationship of surface enrichment to structure?

9. What members, or elements of a design, are generally classified as borders?

10. What important principles of design should be observed in order to design effective border enrichment?

11. Define the term *inceptive axis*.

12. What is a panel, and what is its relative importance in a design?

13. Name three places where border ornament for panels or chair backs may be emphasized to make this design unit effective.

14. If a panel is square or round, where should emphasis be placed?

15. Where should emphasis be placed on a vertical rectangular panel?

16. Where may emphasis be placed on a horizontal rectangular panel?

17. Where should the center of interest on the vertical splat of a chair back be placed?

18. What rule should be observed when designing the ornament for a chair back, so as not to destroy its usefulness?

19. What kinds of surfaces are the most difficult to enrich? Why?

20. How should one proceed in designing free ornament for a panel? For a modeled surface?

21. Where should emphasis be placed in designing ornament for a modeled surface?

Suggested Problems

1. Design a picture frame with carved ornament, observing Rules 32, 33, and 34.

2. Design a Sheraton side chair, observing Rules 34a, 35a, and 38, in the design of the chair back.

3. Design a square collar box, making use of the principles of design suggested by Rules 36 and 36a.

4. Design a carved panel for a Spanish Renaissance chest, observing Rules 37 and 37a.

5. Design a cabriole leg for a Louis XV chair, or for a Chippendale chair, observing Rules 41, 42, 43, and 44.

CHAPTER 5

COLOR IN FURNITURE

The designer having mastered the first four chapters on design, should now have a set of practical ideas concerning effective methods of treating design elements, in order to promote beauty in a piece of furniture, as regards structure and ornament. It may be that he will occasionally find it necessary or desirable to use color in his creations. The use of color may be limited to furnishing a proper background for his pieces. It is true that furnishing backgrounds may not be strictly a furniture designer's problem, but it is a problem that should be considered. (Rule 45) *A scheme of furnishing cannot be successful unless the relation between the furniture and the background is harmonious.* Since a relation always exists among colors when they are used together, be it harmonious or otherwise, it is only proper that the designer should make it his business to see that proper relations will exist, so far as lies within his power. (Rule 46) *Properly colored walls, woodwork, floors, ceilings, and draperies, are essential to a successful scheme of furnishing.* Much of the success of the Brothers Adam, as designers, was due to the fact that they were very careful to have the scheme of furnishing in accord with the background.

It will be necessary for the designer to select proper upholstery materials, if not to design them, for his creations. Painted furniture, of good design, if properly colored is desirable, and there is a demand for it. Color is once more being appreciated in proper relation to its importance as a factor in design.

Some of the finest Italian and French furniture was painted and decorated by artists. Louis XIV induced artists to come to France, and paid them well to decorate fine furniture in his workshops. William and Mary cabinets, and Queen Anne highboys were sometimes lacquered in oriental fashion by trained craftsmen (See Fig. 60). More recently, in America, dower chests of singular beauty and artistic merit have been painted, particularly in Pennsylvania German communities (See Fig. 81). Hepplewhite and Sheraton pieces were frequently painted, especially chairs and small tables. Painting of this kind is done with artist's colors. For backgrounds such as walls and woodwork, cheaper pigments are used.

Leonardo Da Vinci, one of the greatest artists of all time, is said to have remarked that seven years should be spent by the prospective artist, in learning to mix colors, before he is properly fitted to paint pictures. The textile weavers in the world-renowned Gobelin Tapestry Works of France, spent long periods as apprentices before they were thought

33

competent to accurately judge the fine gradations of color necessary to compose the masterpieces of the weaver's art.

A designer of furniture cannot, perhaps, hope to become sufficiently expert by learning the few simple rules given in a short chapter. These rules will be of value in starting him on the right road to a better understanding of color and harmony. Experiments and practice should bring a large measure of success to him who applies the rules. The discussion of color will cover two phases of the subject. The first will concern itself with pigments and some of their properties, and the second will deal with principles of color harmony.

Assuming that the reader has had no previous knowledge about color, a few of the terms will be defined here so that he may acquire a correct nomenclature of the subject. To begin with there are three *primary colors:* red, yellow, and blue. All other colors come from mixtures based on these three. For instance, mixing yellow and red produces orange, yellow and blue produces green, and red and blue produces violet. The results of these mixtures are known as secondary colors. These secondary colors may also be mixed with each other to get the *tertiary colors* olive, citrine, and russet.

PROPERTIES OF COLOR

(Rule 47) *All colors possess three distinct properties: hue, value, and chroma, or intensity.*

(Rule 48) HUE *is another name for color, the two being identical.* For our purposes we will select twelve equally graded hues, from an unlimited number of possible variations of the color spec-

Fig. 81. Pennsylvania German hand-painted pine chest.

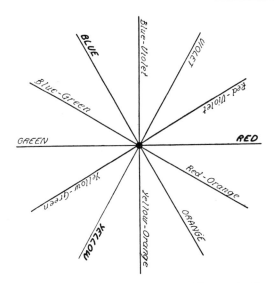

Fig. 82. Complementary hues diametrically opposite each other.

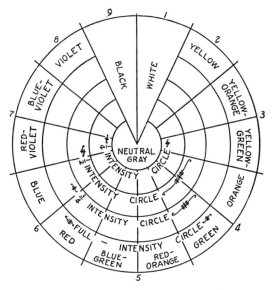

Fig. 83. Hue, value, and intensity clarified.

trum. They are: Red, orange-red, orange, orange-yellow, yellow, yellow-green, green, green-blue, blue, blue-violet, violet, and red-violet.

(Rule 49) VALUE *is the quality by which light hues are distinguished from dark hues.* Its divisions are known as tints and shades. The term *tint* covers the gradations from white to middle value of colors. Shade means the gradations from middle value to black. There are an infinite number of color values ranging from white to black, but for the sake of practicability we will limit our value scale to nine. They are white, high light, light, low light, middle, high dark, dark, low dark, and black.

(Rule 50) *The quality of* INTENSITY *relates to the brilliance or purity of a color.* The intensity, or *chroma*, as it is sometimes called, may have many gradations, but a scale of four will suffice for ordinary purposes. They may be designated as full intensity, three-fourths intensity, one-half intensity, one-fourth in-

tensity. A hue having less than one-fourth intensity verges into neutral gray. The intensity of a color may be reduced by mixing it with its complementary color. Theoretically we do not reduce the intensity of a color by the addition of thinners, white or black. Actually, when mixing pigments, we may reduce the intensity by such additions.

(Rule 51) COMPLEMENTARY COLORS *are colors which when mixed together neutralize or gray each other.* In the mixing of pigments, green is the complement of red, violet is the complement of yellow, and orange is the complement of blue. Red-violet and yellow-green are complementary hues, because they are composed of hues that are complementary. For the same reason orange-red is the complement of green-blue, and orange-yellow the complement of blue-violet. To make the above as clear as possible we show a chart on which complementary hues are diametrically opposite each other (See Fig. 82).

The chart shown in Figure 83 is presented to clarify hue, value, and intensity. It is composed of five concentric circles. These are divided into fourteen sectors, each one representing a hue; and black which is the limit of color on the dark side, and white representing the opposite extreme. On the outside of this color wheel, beginning with the number 1, and going in a clockwise direction, are the nine color values, given in their proper order. Within the outside circle are shown the hues at their full chromatic or color strength, and each in its proper *value* sector. Orange-yellow and yellow-green are both found in the *light value* sector. If standard yellow-green is darkened with black it may become a hue of the same value as standard green, or darker as still more black is added. The circles represent degrees of intensity. If one part of green is mixed with four parts of red it gives us a red of three-fourths intensity. This hue will be found in the red sector and the three-fourths-intensity circle. In the same manner, two parts green and four parts red will give a red of one-half intensity; three parts of green and four of red will produce a red of one-fourth intensity. If equal parts of red and green are mixed, the hues should entirely neutralize each other, forming gray.

COLOR HARMONY

To use colors properly in a color scheme, there are several methods or systems that may be followed. The results obtained by the application of these principles will depend for their success largely upon the skill and judgment of the individual craftsman. Color charts, systems, and similar aids are necessary, only as steppingstones to an understanding of principles, or for exact reproduction of numerous identical hues. An artist, once he has "arrived," generally discards all such devices, for he no longer needs them.

A great deal of the effectiveness and harmony of furniture in a room will depend upon the treatment of the walls, ceiling, floor, and trim. Mathematically correct relations of hue, value, and intensity may exist, but trying to work them out would be more likely to confuse the amateur than to help him. There are several things the beginner may safely do in treating backgrounds, and be sure of satisfactory results. The first is to make ceilings light. Pure white is not always best, especially if the room is normally bright, because it may cause a glare. Very light ivories or gray may be more satisfactory. The walls should be darker than the ceiling, but not darker than middle value. This is a rule that has been successfully broken by a few decorators, but only in unusual cases. The trim may be of slightly different hue and tint than the walls, but the difference is usually not great. A rule covering this may be stated thus: (Rule 52) *Ceilings should be lighter than walls; walls should not be darker than middle value; trim and walls should vary only slightly, if at all, in value and intensity; and floors should be darker than either walls or trim.*

(Rule 53) *The greater the area to be colored, the less intense the colors should be.* This makes it possible for people and decorative objects, such as furniture and pictures, which are more intensely colored, to be seen to greater advantage. A brilliantly hued, or overdecorated background cries out for recognition so loudly, that everything else may be lost in the scheme. Modern art sometimes disregards this rule, and tries interesting schemes using bright-hued backgrounds. Nevertheless this is hardly safe practice for the novice, and is to be recommended only for experienced decorators. It is well to key a decorative scheme to one dominant hue by making it a common element in all the hues used. This will result in a satisfactory relationship of all the elements in the room.

There are two important systems for securing color harmony, that may, with a little practice and judgment, be used with good results. One set is known as *related harmonies* and the other is known as *harmony by contrast,* or complementary arrangement. There are two related harmony groups. One is known as harmony by analogy, and the other is known as the *one-hue harmony.*

(Rule 54) HARMONY BY ANALOGY *is secured by relating all the colors in the scheme to one major color.* That is, all the hues used in the scheme contain one color element. For example, violet, red-violet, and red would form such a relationship, because all of these colors contain red as the common element. Green, yellow-green, and yellow is another possible analogous relationship, each color containing yellow. The schemes need not be limited to three hues, but may contain more. (Rule 54*a*)

Complementary colors are not used in the analogous scheme. Colors used in the analogous schemes should preferably be used in varying values or intensities, or should differ in both.

In the *one-hue harmony,* only one color is used, and variety is achieved by varying the value, intensity, and texture of the hues. This scheme is apt to be monotonous if carried too far. A bright spot of color introduced as an accent will relieve this condition. (Rule 55) *Black, white, gray, silver, or gold, are neutrals which may be used in any color scheme.* Any of these will introduce interesting variety in a color scheme.

(Rule 56) CONTRASTED HARMONIES *are secured by using (1) complementary colors; (2) double complementaries; (3) split complementaries; (4) triads.*

A *complementary harmony* is one using complementary colors. A complementary harmony may be handled in several ways. One method is to use the hues in varying intensities. The larger the area covered by one hue in the scheme, the less intense it should be. Another method is to separate the hues by areas of neutrals, such as gray, black, browns, or even gold or silver. The brightest spots of color should be used where interest is to be the greatest. If too many bright colors are used in any scheme they may destroy harmony. The principle of dominant and minor arrangement applies in color composition as well as to design.

The *double complementary harmonies* are brought about by using two adjacent hues, such as are found on the complementary chart, with their complementary colors. In such a scheme there should be one outstanding hue, used in the greatest amount, but it should be the dullest color in the scheme. The color used in the next greatest amount may be brighter, and so on, until the smallest amount is the brightest.

Split complementary harmonies are composed of a primary and the colors found on either side of its complement on the complementary color chart. Blue, orange-red, and orange-yellow, is an example of such a scheme. One cannot start such a scheme with a secondary color, because the opposite primary color cannot be split.

The *triad schemes* are made up of combinations of three hues that are equidistant from each other on the complementary color chart. There are four possible triad schemes. They are:

1. The primary triad, or red, blue and yellow.

2. The secondary triad, or green, orange, and violet.

3. The intermediate triad, orange-yellow, blue-green, and red-violet.

4. The intermediate triad, yellow-green, blue-violet, orange-red. The triads require careful treatment. The greatest area of color should be almost gray. The next greatest should be at least one half neutralized, and the third, if bright, should cover only small areas.

Questions for Review

1. Why is a study of color desirable for a furniture designer?

2. Why is it desirable to have properly colored backgrounds for furniture?

3. What kinds of pigments are used for decorating furniture?

4. Define the term *primary color; secondary color.*

5. Define the following terms commonly associated with a discussion of color: Hue, value, intensity, tints, shades, complementary colors.

6. Of what value are color charts in selecting proper color schemes for a piece of furniture?

7. What is a safe method of treatment for backgrounds, such as walls and woodwork, in order to secure harmonious relations between them and furniture?

8. Name the two systems for securing color harmonies.

9. Define the term *harmony by analogy*

10. Name and define the two methods of securing harmonies by analogy.

11. Define the term *harmony by contrast.*

12. Name and define each of the four methods for securing harmonies by contrast.

13. Why should large areas of color be less intense than smaller areas?

14. What are neutral colors, and of what importance are they to a color scheme?

15. How is emphasis of an important part on a design brought about by the proper use of color?

Suggested Problems

1. Make a color chart on a piece of artist's board, and with good grade water colors, fill in graduated scales of values and intensities for each hue.

2. Design a small box to hold gifts, and for the design work out a harmo-

nious color scheme, using either the analogous or the contrasted harmony system.

3. Design a chest, and divide it off into panels, and work out a proper color scheme for the design.

SUMMARY OF RULES ON PRINCIPLES OF DESIGN

DIVISION OF SPACE AND AREAS

1. Dominant lines should lead the eye in a vertical direction on a vertical primary mass, and horizontally on a horizontal primary mass.

2. Every primary mass should be composed of major and minor masses, or areas; these in turn may be composed of subdivisions, which may or may not be of equal size and importance.

3. When a mass is to be divided into two parts vertically, one part should be greater than the other. The greater area may be above or below the minor area.

4. To divide a mass into three areas vertically, the areas should all be unequal, with the largest one between the other two.

4a. The lowest area may be the greatest, and each succeeding area may be smaller in a three-part division vertically.

5. If a mass is to be divided into more than three parts vertically, the piece should be divided into two or three major areas of unequal size, using Rules 3 or 4, and then each of these should be treated individually to determine necessary subdivisions.

5a. In the case of a chest of drawers, or a similar structure, the lowest area should be the greatest, with each succeeding area smaller in size.

6. When a mass is to be divided into

two parts horizontally, the parts may be made equal in size and area

7. In some cases a primary mass may be divided into two parts horizontally by making one area greater than the other, but the two areas should be balanced.

8. A mass may be divided horizontally into three equal areas.

9. A mass may be divided into three parts horizontally by making the central area greatest, and placing it between two smaller areas of equal size.

10. A mass may be divided into three parts horizontally by placing the smallest area between two larger areas of equal size.

11. When more than three areas horizontally are desired, or necessary, they may be of equal size and importance.

11a. When more than three areas horizontally are desired, a large area may be placed between a number of smaller areas. The small areas on one side should balance those on the opposite side.

CURVED LINES AND ELEMENTS

12. Compass curves may be used to round corners, and occasionally in Colonial or provincial designs, to secure certain quaint effects. They may also be used with freehand curves which will relieve their mechanical severity.

13. The most beautiful curves are

firm freehand curves, graceful and rhythmic in unfolding themselves.

14. A beautiful one-direction curve has no straight line in its composition.

15. The reverse curve is always most beautiful if the curve is sharper on one bend than on the other, and has no straight line in its composition.

16. A compound curve, to be effective, must not be a meaningless scroll, but must express its function in a definite manner.

17. Good turnings always have beautifully formed curves.

18. The curves on turnings must be full and well rounded out, rather than scant and flat.

19. Curves in turnings, moldings, or other outline structure, should connect with fillets at as nearly a right angle as possible.

PROPORTION

20. The division of masses, the planning of curved lines and elements, and the determination of proper proportions, are closely related problems which must be solved simultaneously.

21. Good proportions result from subtle relationships of length to width, or relationships which may not be too easily analyzed.

22. To secure good proportions, the contrast between the length and the width of a mass should not be too great.

23. Masses on which the proportion is about 2 to 3, 3 to 5, 5 to 8, and other similar relations, are interesting.

24. Experiments with rectangles, or other geometric figures, whose limits will be similar or identical to those of a proposed design, should result in getting good proportions.

25. When a fixed or limiting element is in a design, it must be the starting point in working out proper proportions.

26. The proper proportions for a design will be finally determined by comparing a number of scale drawings of the proposed mass or object.

ORNAMENT

27. The sources from which ornament for furniture should be chosen are three in number: abstract forms, naturalistic motifs, and artificial objects.

28. Places which are particularly well suited to be ornamented are: outlines, borders, panels, and shaped or modeled surfaces.

29. Outline enrichment must not destroy logical structure, but must help to support and strengthen it, and unite individual members into a unified whole.

29a. Surface enrichment must not destroy or hide logical structure, but must become a definite part of it.

30. Outline enrichment must not be so complicated as to destroy the unity and dignity of an object, but because of its grace, refinement, and simplicity, should emphasize the parts of the structure upon which it is found.

31. Outline enrichment of a subordinate mass should never destroy the harmony which exists between it and the parent mass of which it is a part.

31a. Surface enrichment of a subordinate mass should never destroy the harmony which exists between it and the parent mass of which it is a part.

32. The ornament on borders should be dynamic; that is, it should cause the eye to move in the direction taken by the border itself.

33. None of the elements of the design on a border should destroy the movement in an onward direction by introducing contrary lines of sufficient prominence to break the continuity of the forward movement.

34. The ornament enclosing a panel should cause the eye to move in the direction of the outline of the panel, and should be of such a character as to strengthen this outline.

34a. The ornament found on the bordering members of a chair back should cause the eye to move in the direction of the outline of the chair back, and should be of a character to strengthen and support this outline.

35. If border ornament has important centers of interest, they should be placed at the corners, or at points in the center of the border, or they may be placed at both places.

35a. If border ornament on a chair back is to have important centers of interest, they should be placed at the center of the top rail, or the junctions it makes with the back legs, or both of these places.

36. If a panel is square, or round, the center of interest may be in its center. Minor centers of interest, or elements of ornamentation may radiate from this chief center of interest, but must not destroy the balance of the design.

36a. On square panels, centers of interest may be concentrated on lines leading from the center of the panel to the corners.

37. When a panel is rectangular, and is placed in a vertical position, the center of greatest interest should be on the vertical center line at a point above or below the center of the panel; preferably above it.

37a. Minor ornament on either side of the vertical center line should not destroy the balance of the design.

38. Centers of interest on the vertical splat of a chair back should be concentrated near the top of the splat.

39. When a rectangular panel is placed horizontally, interest may be centered at the following places: in its exact center; on the horizontal center line at points equidistant from the center; above or below the center on the vertical center line.

40. Any ornament carved on a chair back should become a definite part of the mass without obscuring or weakening the structure, and should be of such a character that comfort is not sacrificed because of it.

41. Carving is the most proper form of ornament for a shaped or modeled surface.

42. Any ornament carved on a modeled surface must become a definite part of that mass without obscuring its structure, and if properly executed should give added emphasis and elegance to the structure.

43. To design free ornament, or ornament for a modeled surface, first draw suitable leading lines. These should be

in the form of an inceptive axis, a beautiful curve or curves, or radial lines.

44. Centers of interest on shaped or modeled surfaces should be concentrated at points which are meant to be of superior importance.

Color

45. For a scheme of furnishing to be successful there must be a harmonious relation between the furniture and the background.

46. Properly colored walls, woodwork, floors, ceilings, and draperies, are essential to a successful scheme of furnishing.

47. All colors possess three distinct properties: hue, value, and chroma or intensity.

48. Hue is another name for color, the two being identical.

49. Value is the quality by which light hues are distinguished from dark hues.

50. The quality of intensity relates to the brilliance or purity of a color.

51. Complementary colors are colors which when mixed together neutralize, or gray, each other.

52. Ceilings should be lighter than walls; walls should not be darker than middle value; trim and walls should vary only slightly, if at all, in value and intensity; and floors should be darker than either walls or trim.

53. The greater the area to be colored, the less intense the colors should be.

54. Harmony by analogy is secured by relating all the colors in a scheme to one major color.

54a. Complementary colors are not used in an analogous scheme.

55. Black, white, gray, silver, and gold are neutrals which may be used in any color scheme.

56. Contrasted harmonies are secured by using: (1) Complementary colors, (2) double complementaries, (3) split complementaries, (4) triads.

CHAPTER 6

THE JACOBEAN STYLES
1603–1688

HISTORICAL BACKGROUND AND GENERAL CHARACTERISTICS

There were three distinct styles in the Jacobean period. The first two of these were similar in many respects, while the third produced many distinct changes. The entire period lasted, from 1603 to 1689. The first part of the period, lasting from 1603 to 1649, included the reigns of James I and Charles I. The second part of the period, sometimes known as the period of the Commonwealth, lasted through the reign of Cromwell, from 1649 to 1660. The last part of the period, 1660 to 1689, sometimes known as the Carolean period, lasted through the reigns of Charles II and James II. In its entirety the period is sometimes known as the Stuart period.

Each one of these three periods engendered its individual style of furniture, directly influenced by the spirit of the time, by customs, and by practices of earlier joiners, as well as by Flemish craftsmen who came to England from the continent. In presenting the characteristics of each style, the first period will be referred to as the Jacobean style; the second as the Cromwellian style; and the third as the Carolean style. Since the first two of these are similar in all but a few respects, they will be treated as one.

Exceptional characteristics, wherein one style differed from the other, will be noted from time to time.

THE JACOBEAN AND CROMWELLIAN STYLES

These styles, influenced by the Puritan customs, in the ascendancy at the time, are distinguished for their plainness and for their lack of those fine points of design that distinguished later styles. This period of English history was strongly influenced by religious sects who taught creeds of self-abasement, strict religious discipline, and personal discomfort; these practices being considered essential for the saving of the soul. This spirit influenced the habits of the people to such an extent that it was strongly reflected in the furniture styles of the period. Furniture was stanchly built, but was ungainly in many respects, and one finds few of the elements bespeaking comfort and refinement, so characteristic of later periods. Lines were uncompromisingly straight. Beautiful proportions, if found at all, were more likely the results of chance than of intelligent planning. Ornament was in many cases almost entirely lacking, because it was considered a frivolous and sinful luxury. It reached its full expression during the Cromwellian period.

Not all of the ornately decorated furniture of the Elizabethan period was discarded, or destroyed; but some of it remained as a pattern and guide for cabinetmakers throughout this entire period. It was the Jacobean style which most strongly influenced the early Colonial style in America, because the colonists left England during this period, and brought with them the actual pieces themselves, or at least the ideas upon which the style was based.

The chief characteristics of the Jacobean and Cromwellian styles are: (1) The furniture was essentially straight lined in plan and elevation (See Plate 1). Rectangular and cubical forms are to be found. (2) Many of the pieces were cumbersome, especially at the beginning of the period. This was partly due to the fact that oak, a heavy and coarse-grained wood, was the principal cabinet material of the time; and because the manners and customs of the people demanded solid, substantial furniture. Domestic wood, in sufficient quantities was still available to meet all the demands for the few pieces deemed necessary to meet the requirements of the average family. The more common and cheaper pieces were made of cheaper wood, such as deal, elm, beech, and chestnut. (3) Framed construction was the rule; that is, the frame-

work of the pieces consisted of rails and posts, mortised and tenoned together, and held in place by means of wooden pins driven through the joints (See Fig. 85). Large surfaces were enclosed by panels, either plain or crudely decorated, as shown on Plate 1. (4) Turning, for legs and stretchers was common practice, especially as the style developed, and it served to alleviate somewhat the otherwise rigid austerity of many pieces. (5) Applied ornament was commonly used to decorate pieces, though it was often crude in form, and more often marred rather than beautified the surface to which it was applied. (6) Ball feet came into being late in the period, earlier feet having been straight and square in most cases. (7) Crude types of carving, known as scratch carving, an incised form of decoration; and a flat-faced low-relief carving, were practiced. These together with broad inlays, and some painted designs, formed the principal means of

Fig. 86. Press cupboard illustrating typical ornamentation of the Jacobean period

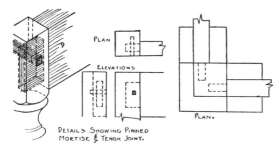

DETAILS SHOWING PINNED
MORTISE & TENON JOINT.

Fig. 85.

decoration. (8) There was little upholstering. The seats in most cases were of wood, though rush seats sometimes took the place of these.

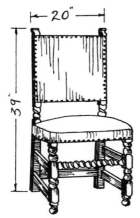

Fig. 87. Cromwellian chair.

Fig. 89. Long form.

In showing the examples on Plate 1, the author made an attempt to choose examples that were characteristic of the style, and at the same time reasonably handsome and adaptable to modern needs. To do this it was necessary to pick and choose those pieces and features most likely to be of value to the designer, and to combine them properly, to make them valuable as guides. No attempt at slavish copy has been made in this or any subsequent style shown in the book. There are a sufficient number of books available in which this has been done.

The pieces of furniture in common use at the time were press cupboards

(Fig. 86), wainscot chairs, Cromwellian chairs (Fig. 87), settles (Fig. 88), long forms (Fig. 89), stools (Fig. 90), chests (Fig. 91), looking glasses, refectory

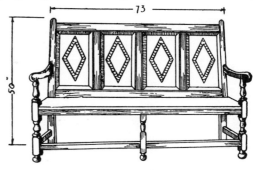

Fig. 88. Settle.

Fig. 90. Stool.

tables, court cupboards (Fig 92), small tables (Fig. 93), cabinets and cupboards of various sorts, sideboards, daybeds, and bedsteads (Fig. 94).

CHAIRS

Up to the time when Cromwell came into power, chairs were not a common article of furniture in the average English home. They were considered seats of dignity, and were pieces of furniture reserved for the privileged class only. Common people used stools and long forms as seats. Even these were sometimes few in number. Due to a more democratic spirit of the times, however, chairs became more common articles of furniture during the Commonwealth

CHEST
FIG. 1

FIG. 2
CHEST ON FRAME

FIG. 3
CHEST of DRAWERS.

FIG. 4
COURT CUPBOARD

REFECTORY TABLE
FIG. 5

SETTLE **FIG. 6**

FIG. 7
CROMWELLIAN CHAIR

SMALL TABLE
FIG. 8

FIG. 10
STOOL

FIG. 9 LONG FORM

Early Jacobean Period

Plate 1.

period, and persisted as such from that time on.

The chairs in common use during the Commonwealth period were: wainscot chairs, similar to the settle (Fig. 88); Yorkshire chairs; Derbyshire chairs; Cromwellian chairs, a name given to small turned chairs. Settles and love seats (so called because they were built for two people, and used as courting chairs), were built similar to chairs. Besides these there were, of course, stools and long forms.

WAINSCOT CHAIRS. Wainscot chairs had square, or nearly square seats of wood. They had fairly heavy stretchers

below the seat, close to the floor, and the front stretcher was used as a footrest. All joints were mortised and tenoned, and further secured with oak pins. These pins were never round, but were either square or roughly octagoned. They were driven into a round hole. The chairs had crudely formed heavy arms (Fig. 6, Plate 1). Legs were heavy, and the front legs were turned with simple shapes. Back legs were generally square. The back of the chair was paneled and carved, similar to the one shown in

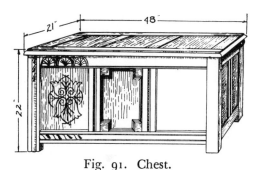

Fig. 91. Chest.

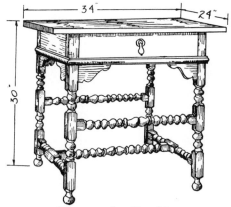

Fig. 93. Small table.

Fig. 92. Court cupboard.

(A Wallace Nutting Reproduction)
Fig. 94. Jacobean bedstead with unusually good carving.

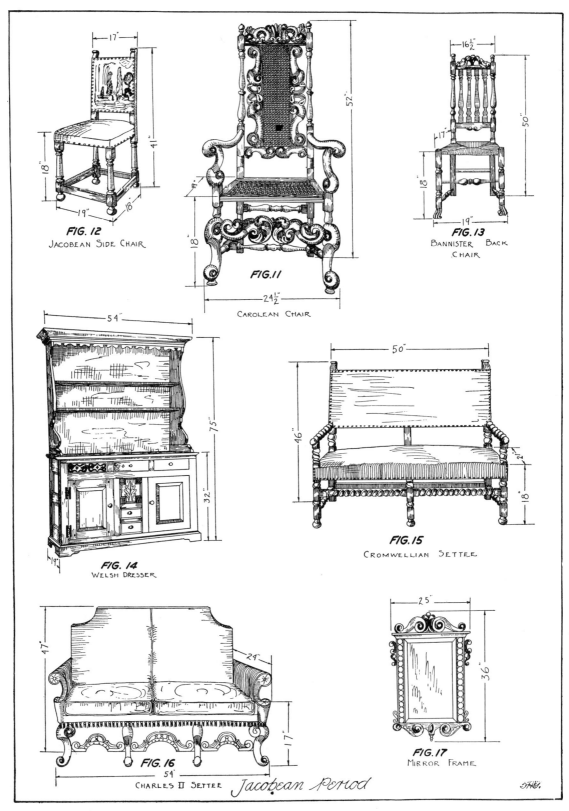

FIG. 12
JACOBEAN SIDE CHAIR

FIG. 11
CAROLEAN CHAIR

FIG. 13
BANNISTER BACK CHAIR

FIG. 14
WELSH DRESSER

FIG. 15
CROMWELLIAN SETTEE

FIG. 16
CHARLES II SETTEE

FIG. 17
MIRROR FRAME

Jacobean Period

Plate 2.

Figure 88, or like Figure 95. The top rail, or cresting, of the chair back, was often carved, and was usually set on top of the legs rather than between them. The chairs as a whole were heavy and

Fig. 95. Carved and arched panel.

cumbersome, and they are seldom copied for present-day use.

YORKSHIRE AND DERBYSHIRE CHAIRS. Yorkshire chairs had square legs in back, and two carved rails, hoop shaped at the top. One of these is halfway between the seat and the top, and the other near the top of the chair. These chairs had square, or nearly square seats, which were rush bottomed or upholstered. The front legs were usually turned, with square places where the stretcher joined them.

Another chair somewhat similar to this was the Derbyshire chair. The chief difference between this and the Yorkshire chair lay in the treatment of the chair back, which had turned vertical spindles, set between two horizontal, carved stretchers, the upper one usually arched between the spindles. Both chairs had carved ears, or finials (See Plate 9).

CROMWELLIAN CHAIRS. The Cromwel-

lian type chair should be designed with turned legs. Turning may be plain or spiraled, with square sections where stretchers are to join them. Stretchers may be straight or turned. The chairs should be well braced, and there may be as many as two or three stretchers on a side, below the seat. The spiral turning was a feature introduced by the Flemish immigrants. Seats on these chairs are similar to those described for Yorkshire chairs. Joints were always mortised and tenoned, and should never be doweled. There was little or no rake to the back on these chairs.

LONG FORMS AND STOOLS

These were the seats used by the common people. Long forms were placed along the sides of long tables, and several people could be seated side by side. Seats of long forms are long and narrow. They are sometimes molded around the edges. The legs should be turned. They may be splayed to prevent the bench from tilting (See Fig. 90). On Plate 3 are shown typical turnings of the type used for long forms and stools. Long forms always had stretchers close to the floor. These were straight, so that the feet might be rested upon them. The construction and ornament of a stool is clearly shown in Figure 90.

SETTLES

Besides the chairs and stools there were settles, built after the manner of chairs. Some of these were built like wainscot chairs, with paneled backs (See Fig. 88). A double-backed chair of this type was called a love seat.

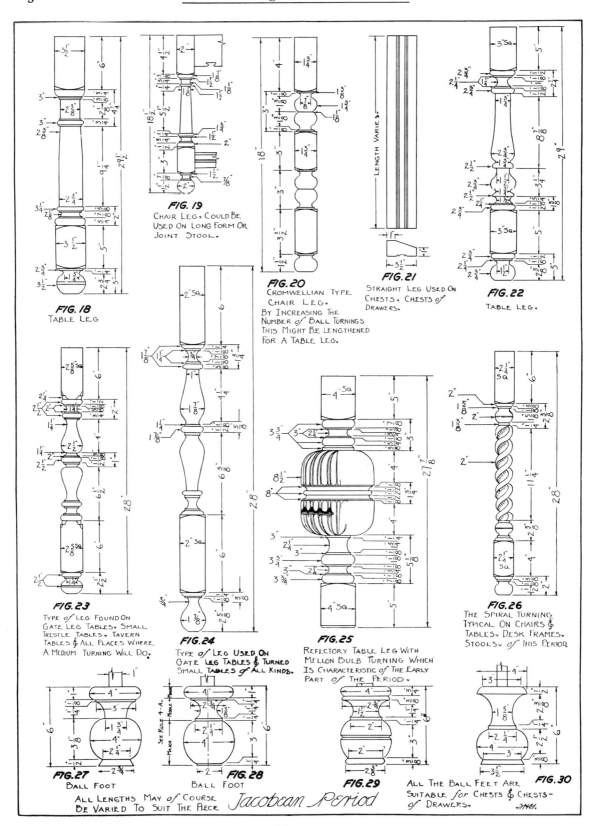

FIG. 18
TABLE LEG

FIG. 19
CHAIR LEG. COULD BE
USED ON LONG FORM OR
JOINT STOOL.

FIG. 20
CROMWELLIAN TYPE
CHAIR LEG.
BY INCREASING THE
NUMBER of BALL TURNINGS
THIS MIGHT BE LENGTHENED
FOR A TABLE LEG.

FIG. 21
STRAIGHT LEG USED ON
CHESTS. CHESTS of
DRAWERS.

FIG. 22
TABLE LEG.

FIG. 23
TYPE of LEG FOUND ON
GATE LEG TABLES. SMALL
TRESTLE TABLES. TAVERN
TABLES & ALL PLACES WHERE
A MEDIUM TURNING WILL DO.

FIG. 24
TYPE of LEG USED ON
GATE LEG TABLES & TURNED
SMALL TABLES of ALL KINDS.

FIG. 25
REFECTORY TABLE LEG WITH
MELLON BULB TURNING WHICH
IS CHARACTERISTIC of THE EARLY
PART of THE PERIOD.

FIG. 26
THE SPIRAL TURNING
TYPICAL ON CHAIRS &
TABLES. DESK FRAMES.
STOOLS. of THIS PERIOD

FIG. 27
BALL FOOT

FIG. 28
BALL FOOT

FIG. 29

FIG. 30

ALL THE BALL FEET ARE
SUITABLE for CHESTS & CHESTS-
of DRAWERS.

ALL LENGTHS MAY of COURSE
BE VARIED TO SUIT THE PIECE   *Jacobean Period*

Plate 3.

TABLES

Dining tables of the better sort, in the Jacobean style, were of the refectory type, and had long rectangular tops. It was, in early times, the custom to sit on only one side of these tables. Food was served from the other side. Among the poor, tables were often merely trestle boards, that is, boards set on trestles (See Fig. 96). Gate-leg tables were invented about the time of the Cromwellian period, and were the pattern for various smaller tables of similar design and construction.

REFECTORY TABLES. Refectory tables should have turned legs. These may be

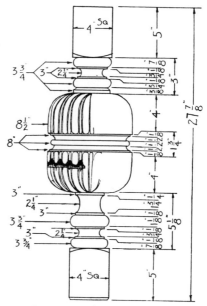

Fig. 97. Refectory table leg with melon-bulb turning.

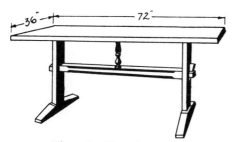

Fig. 96. Trestle table.

turned like huge melon bulbs, as at the beginning of the period (See Fig. 97). These melon bulbs may be decorated with fluting, reeding, or carving. Carved designs may include lunettes, acanthus leaves, and other patterns of conventionalized form. Melon bulbs were a feature of Elizabethan tables. Later in the Jacobean period, turnings took the forms shown in Figures 3 and 98. Stretchers should be square or rectangular in section, with rounded top edges. They should be mortised and tenoned to the legs, and should be placed close to the floor.

These tables may be designed so that they may be lengthened. This is accomplished by making the top in three sections. The central section lies above the other two, and is so arranged that when the end sections are drawn out they will rise to a level with it, or it will lower to

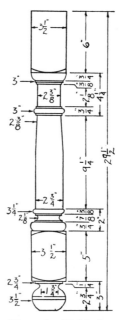

Fig. 98. Table leg.

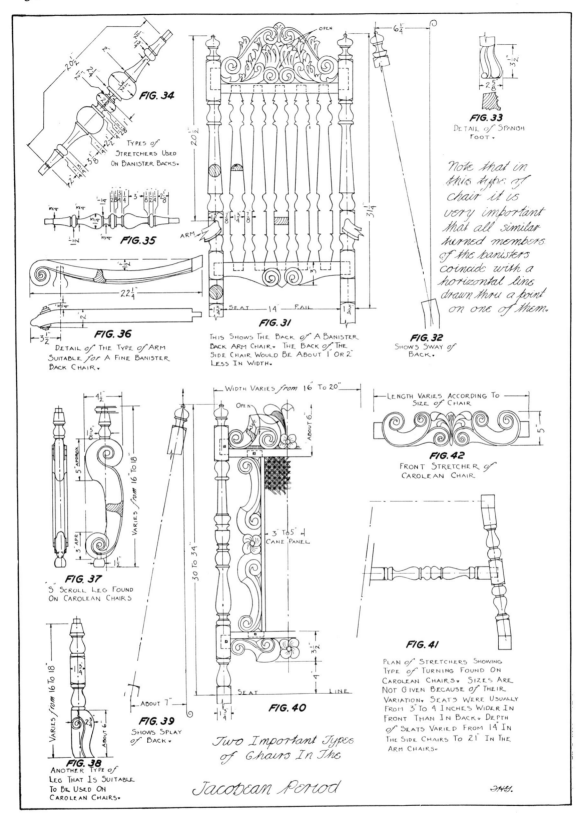

FIG. 34
TYPES OF
STRETCHERS USED
ON BANISTER BACKS.

FIG. 35

FIG. 36
DETAIL OF THE TYPE OF ARM
SUITABLE FOR A FINE BANISTER
BACK CHAIR.

FIG. 31
THIS SHOWS THE BACK OF A BANISTER
BACK ARM CHAIR. THE BACK OF THE
SIDE CHAIR WOULD BE ABOUT 1" OR 2"
LESS IN WIDTH.

FIG. 33
DETAIL OF SPANISH
FOOT.

*Note that in
this type of
chair it is
very important
that all similar
turned members
of the banisters
coincide with a
horizontal line
drawn thru a point
on one of them.*

FIG. 32
SHOWS SWAY OF
BACK.

FIG. 37
S SCROLL LEG FOUND
ON CAROLEAN CHAIRS

FIG. 39
SHOWS SPLAY
OF BACK.

FIG. 38
ANOTHER TYPE OF
LEG THAT IS SUITABLE
TO BE USED ON
CAROLEAN CHAIRS.

FIG. 40

WIDTH VARIES from 16 TO 20"
OPEN
CANE PANEL

FIG. 42
FRONT STRETCHER OF
CAROLEAN CHAIR.
LENGTH VARIES ACCORDING TO
SIZE OF CHAIR

FIG. 41
PLAN OF STRETCHERS SHOWING
TYPE OF TURNING FOUND ON
CAROLEAN CHAIRS. SIZES ARE
NOT GIVEN BECAUSE OF THEIR
VARIATION. SEATS WERE USUALLY
FROM 3" TO 4 INCHES WIDER IN
FRONT THAN IN BACK. DEPTH
OF SEATS VARIED FROM 14" IN
THE SIDE CHAIRS TO 21" IN THE
ARM CHAIRS.

*Two Important Types
of Chairs In The*

Jacobean Period

Plate 4.

Fig. 99. Small tea table.

Fig. 101. Gate-leg table.

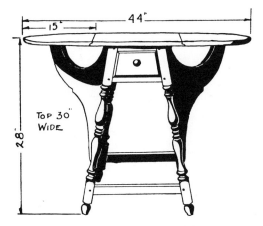

Fig. 100. Butterfly table.

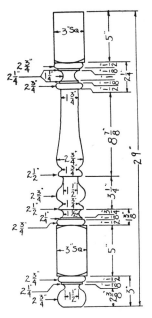

Fig. 102. Table leg.

a level with them. In this way the table may be made twice its ordinary length. The aprons of these tables may be carved with a conventionalized border of some kind as the guilloche, foliated "S" scrolls, strapwork, etc.

GATE-LEG TABLE. Next to the refectory table the gate-leg table was the most important one in the period. From it evolved many smaller occasional tables similar to those shown in Figures 99 and 100.

The legs are usually turned. The curves of the turnings are repeated on each piece (See Fig. 101). The stretchers were also turned. The curves on these

should be sections taken from the pattern of the leg. These curves may be shortened or elongated as the case may require. On early gate-leg tables of the Jacobean period, the legs and other turnings were often quite heavy, and instead of legs like those shown in Figure 101, they commonly had legs and turnings like those shown in Figures 98 or 102. Tables of this kind were often quite large and heavy.

The tops of gate-leg tables should be oval, though occasionally they are found

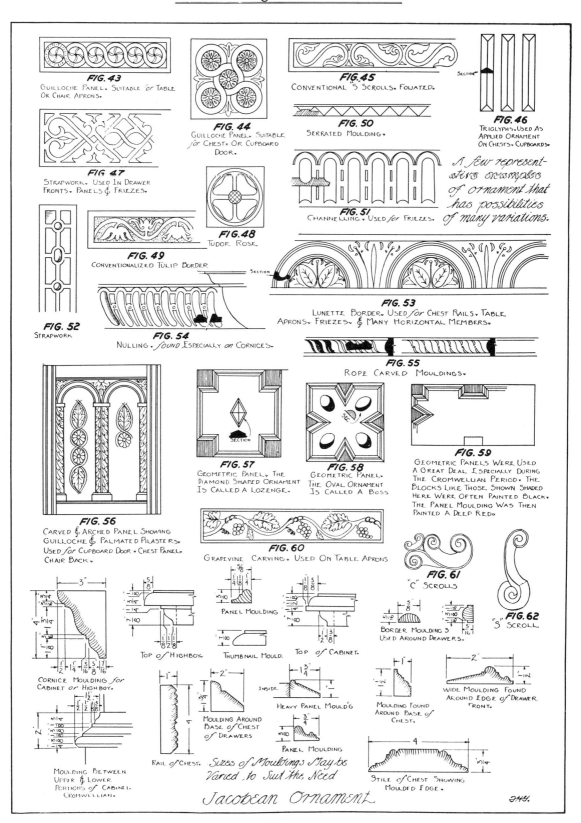

FIG. 43
GUILLOCHE PANEL. SUITABLE FOR TABLE OR CHAIR APRONS.

FIG. 47
STRAPWORK. USED IN DRAWER FRONTS. PANELS & FRIEZES.

FIG. 52
STRAPWORK

FIG. 44
GUILLOCHE PANEL. SUITABLE FOR CHEST OR CUPBOARD DOOR.

FIG. 48
TUDOR ROSE

FIG. 49
CONVENTIONALIZED TULIP BORDER

FIG. 54
NULLING. FOUND ESPECIALLY ON CORNICES.

FIG. 45
CONVENTIONAL S SCROLLS. FOLIATED.

FIG. 50
SERRATED MOULDING.

FIG. 46
TRIGLYPHS. USED AS APPLIED ORNAMENT ON CHESTS. CUPBOARDS.

FIG. 51
CHANNELLING. USED FOR FRIEZES.

A few representative examples of ornament that has possibilities of many variations.

FIG. 53
LUNETTE BORDER. USED FOR CHEST RAILS. TABLE APRONS. FRIEZES. & MANY HORIZONTAL MEMBERS.

FIG. 55
ROPE CARVED MOULDINGS.

FIG. 56
CARVED & ARCHED PANEL SHOWING GUILLOCHE & PALMATED PILASTERS. USED FOR CUPBOARD DOOR. CHEST PANEL. CHAIR BACK.

FIG. 57
GEOMETRIC PANEL. THE DIAMOND SHAPED ORNAMENT IS CALLED A LOZENGE.

FIG. 58
GEOMETRIC PANEL. THE OVAL ORNAMENT IS CALLED A BOSS

FIG. 59
GEOMETRIC PANELS WERE USED A GREAT DEAL ESPECIALLY DURING THE CROMWELLIAN PERIOD. THE BLOCKS LIKE THOSE SHOWN SHADED HERE WERE OFTEN PAINTED BLACK. THE PANEL MOULDING WAS THEN PAINTED A DEEP RED.

FIG. 60
GRAPEVINE CARVING. USED ON TABLE APRONS

FIG. 61
"C" SCROLLS

FIG. 62
"S" SCROLL

BORDER MOULDINGS USED AROUND DRAWERS.

PANEL MOULDING

TOP OF HIGHBOY

THUMBNAIL MOULD.

TOP OF CABINET.

CORNICE MOULDING FOR CABINET OR HIGHBOY.

RAIL OF CHEST.

MOULDING AROUND BASE OF CHEST OF DRAWERS

HEAVY PANEL MOULD'G

INSIDE

PANEL MOULDING

MOULDING FOUND AROUND BASE OF CHEST.

WIDE MOULDING FOUND AROUND EDGE OF DRAWER FRONT.

STILE OF CHEST SHOWING MOULDED EDGE.

MOULDING BETWEEN UPPER & LOWER PORTIONS OF CABINET. CROMWELLIAN.

Sizes of Mouldings May be Varied to Suit the Need

Jacobean Ornament

Plate 5.

with round, and even rectangular tops. There may be a drawer on one or both ends of the middle section of the table, usually having a wooden turned knob for a drawer pull (See Figs. 4 and 5, Plate 6). The leaves are supported by gates, made up of several turnings. These are mortised and tenoned together, and swung on dowels turned on the inside vertical member of the gate. The top and bottom side stretchers have holes into which these dowels fit. In order for the gates to fold up nicely, the legs on the gate, and the stretcher which they join when folded, are half lapped. Thus the outside of the gate and the outside of the stretchers fit flush on square parts of each, when brought together. The table apron and the top of the leg are treated in the same way. The side apron of the table therefore, must be over an inch thick, so that in half lapping, it will not be severed in twain.

The gate must be made less than half the width of the table frame, in cases where two gates are to be put on each side of the table. The outside of the gate must lack several inches of meeting the table leg when folded in. The leaves are joined to the middle table board with a rule joint, and the hinges should have one leaf longer than the other (See Plate 31).

GAMING TABLES. These were small tables, and they may be made with square, round, or octagon-shaped tops. The tops had slight depressions cut into them for coins or tokens. The legs may be turned, square, or spiraled. Brackets may be cut on the lower edges of the aprons, where they are joined to the legs. The aprons may be carved with strapwork, or some other suitable pattern. The legs sometimes have triglyphs, or other ornament applied to them on the square sections where they are joined by stretchers. Tops on these tables were of the double variety, the leaf hinged to lie on top of the table top proper in the same manner as on later card tables.

TAVERN TABLES. These are small rectangular tables, sometimes having a small drawer. The legs may be square, but are more commonly turned (See Fig. 93). The tables should be braced with stretchers which are usually turned. Feet may be square, ball, or pear shaped.

CHESTS

Chests were among the most common articles of furniture, and much labor and expense seems to have been expended on their decoration. They were used to store clothing and all kinds of household articles and valuables. The early ones were made with lids usually paneled. American chests of a similar type were usually made of wide, flat, pine boards. Later on, toward the end of the Jacobean period, chests were put on frames, or the legs were extended and drawers were added below the chest. Thus we find several new pieces of furniture evolving (See Fig. 14).

The chests were generally paneled. There may be two, three, or even more panels in front, three being the usual number. These may be carved, decorated with applied molding, painted or inlaid. Most of the more pretentious

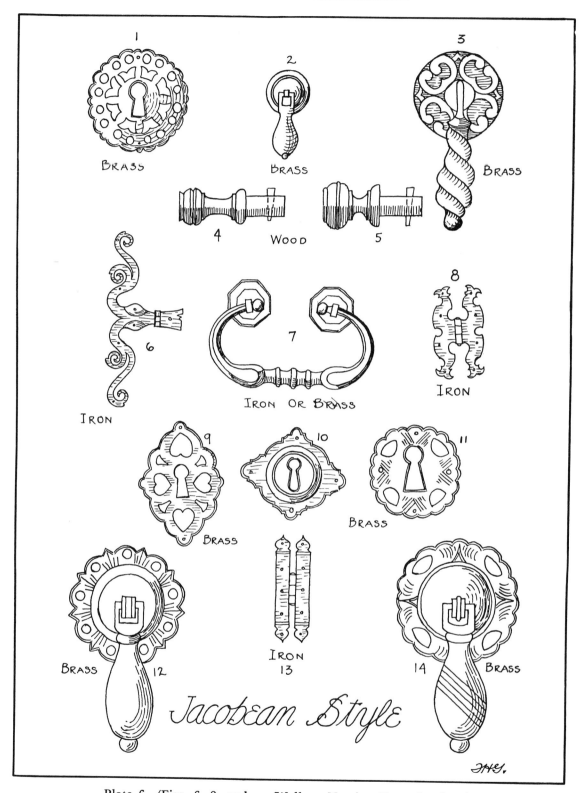

Plate 6. (Figs. 6, 8, and 13 Wallace Nutting Reproductions.)

ones were carved. Straight legs prevailed during the early part of the period. These were sometimes carved, or at least molded down the front. The legs should be chamfered on the inside to dispense with sharp corners on the inside of the chest.

These chests should have a lid that can be raised, and it may be fastened with hinges of either wood or iron. These hinges, if made of wood are in the form of cleats fastened to the bottom of the lid on each end, outside the chest. They are swung on dowels driven into holes bored into the back legs (See Fig. 14). The stiles, legs, and rails of the chests are made up in the form of frames, and mortised and tenoned together. The panels are fitted free, into grooves on the legs and rails; that is, the panels are not glued fast to the frame. The stiles and rails may be molded or carved. Rope carving, lunettes, imbricated (fish scale) carving, strapwork, and other motifs may be used.

The designer may in some cases improve upon the original proportions and methods of space division common to early chests of the period. Very little thought was given to this feature by original builders. The pieces were attractive in a quaint way, and too much "improvement" may destroy a great deal of this charm, thus destroying the very soul of the style.

CUPBOARDS

There were cupboards of many kinds — cupboards to be hung on the wall or on frames to be set against the wall. The most important of these were the press cupboards and court (short) cupboards. These were used as a form of sideboard in the more pretentious homes. Other cupboards were livery cupboards, hutches, Welsh dressers, corner cupboards with open shelves, and the like.

PRESS CUPBOARDS. This was perhaps the most important cupboard of the period. It consisted of a cupboard in the bottom part of a frame, surmounted by another more shallow cupboard in the upper part of the frame. The lower cupboard most generally had only two doors, while the upper cupboard had either two or three. The press cupboards, and the court cupboards were used to store food — bread, cheese, and wine. The press cupboards were always profusely decorated. Sometimes, as in the Metropolitan Museum example shown (See Fig. 86) almost every available inch of surface was carved or decorated in some manner. The method of fastening the lower doors on this cupboard, is an example of marked crudity of design. The turnings also, are not of the best type. The carving and molding, however, are good examples of their type, and for this reason the piece has been selected to be shown here. These cupboards had stout square legs, often molded down the front, and sometimes on the side as well. The sides of the cupboard should always be paneled, and the panels are occasionally carved. The door and drawer pulls on cupboards of this kind are small turned wooden knobs, while the hinges are of iron. Butterfly or rattail hinges may be used.

COURT CUPBOARDS. These are similar to press cupboards. The only difference

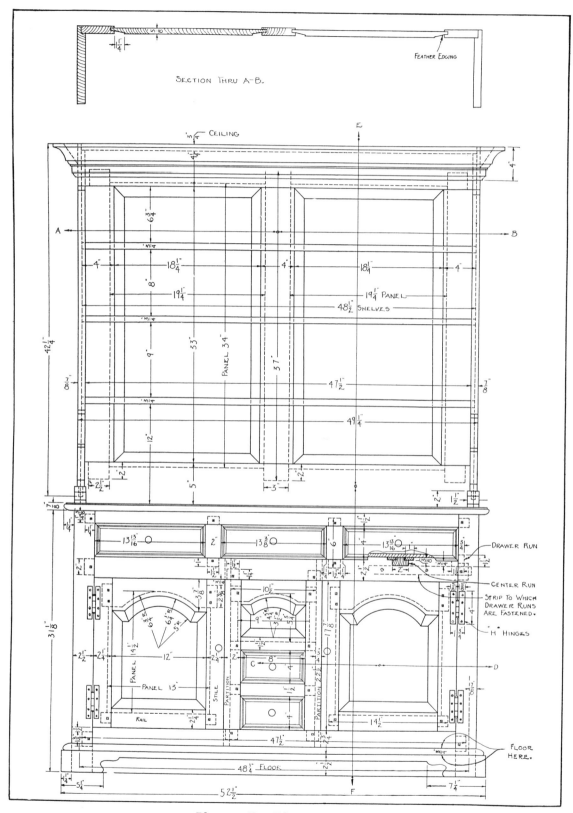

Plate 7. (See Plates 8 and 9.)

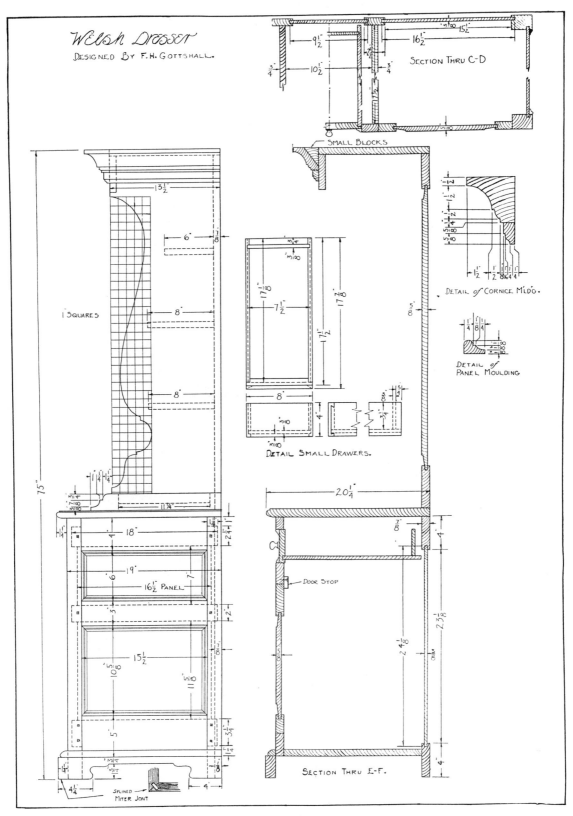

Welsh Dresser
DESIGNED BY F.H. GOTTSHALL.

SECTION THRU C-D

SMALL BLOCKS

DETAIL OF CORNICE MLD'G.

DETAIL OF PANEL MOULDING

1 SQUARES

DETAIL SMALL DRAWERS.

DOOR STOP

SECTION THRU E-F.

SPLINED MITER JOINT

Plate 8. (See Plates 7 and 9.)

lies in the treatment of the lower part, which instead of being a cupboard has only shelves, and occasionally a drawer or two (See Fig. 92). Turned posts on these are usually more than 6 in. in diameter.

LIVERY CUPBOARDS. These were generally designed to stand on the floor. They were used to hold food, and sometimes clothing, arms, or armor. Cupboards of this type may be made in almost any size. They are often high, and rectangular in shape, and have one or two paneled doors in front. These provide for a circulation of air inside the cupboard by means of an opening at the top of the door. This opening may be partly enclosed by a row of turned spindles, sometimes split in half. The cupboards usually had bracket feet. Other cupboards of this type used for the purpose of storing food only were hung on the wall. If made to hang on the wall they were small affairs, and the bottom was finished off with a molding or a scrolled apron.

WELSH DRESSERS

The Welsh dresser was an important piece of furniture that came into use about this time. It was a tall piece of furniture having a cupboard below, and open shelves above. It was used to display pewter and china, or hold various utensils in prevalent domestic use. It was, more than likely, the forerunner of the present-day kitchen cabinet. Several fine examples have been found, however, which lead us to believe that they were sometimes placed in the parlor to give them greater dignity. It is one of

these pieces that has been chosen to illustrate some of the characteristic features of design and construction of the period, as it may be adapted to modern uses. From Plates 7, 8, and 9 many valuable lessons in the design and construction of Jacobean furniture may be obtained. The piece has been designed with special attention to proper space

Fig. 103. Welsh dresser with shelves to hold plates for display.

division and proportion. The end panels, for example, are not of the same size, and the division of masses on the front elevation is worthy of note. On Plate 9 are several figures giving an analysis of the design and the principles involved.

The lower part consists of a cupboard having two paneled doors and several small drawers. The upper part has three shelves, in this case not all of them being

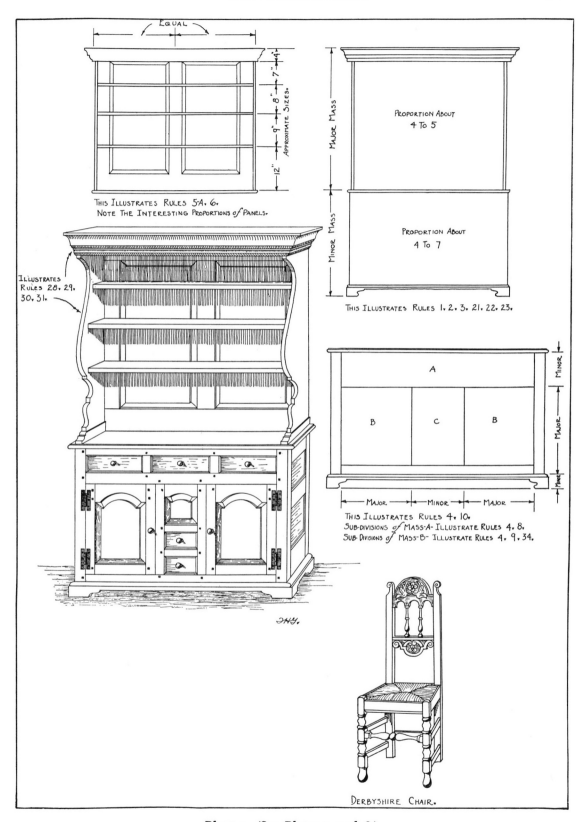

EQUAL

4″
7″
8″
9″
12″

APPROXIMATE SIZES.

THIS ILLUSTRATES RULES 5A. 6.
NOTE THE INTERESTING PROPORTIONS *of* PANELS.

MAJOR MASS

MINOR MASS

PROPORTION ABOUT
4 TO 5

PROPORTION ABOUT
4 TO 7

THIS ILLUSTRATES RULES 1. 2. 3. 21. 22. 23.

ILLUSTRATES
RULES 28. 29.
30. 31.

MINOR
MAJOR
MINOR

A

B   C   B

MAJOR — MINOR — MAJOR

THIS ILLUSTRATES RULES 4. 10.
SUB-DIVISIONS *of* MASS-A- ILLUSTRATE RULES 4. 8.
SUB-DIVISIONS *of* MASS-B- ILLUSTRATE RULES 4. 9. 34.

JHY.

DERBYSHIRE CHAIR.

Plate 9. (See Plates 7 and 8.)

the same width apart. In the lower part, the ends are paneled and bordered with molding. All joints are mortised and tenoned, glued and pinned. The upper section is held in place by means of several dowels fastened to the lower section. The upper section may be lifted off in case the piece is to be moved.

The shelves have a groove, or channel, running along their entire length to hold plates for display. The top has a wide and handsome cornice molding. The ends of the upper section consist of two boards shaped into beautiful vase-like forms, that are good examples of the use of Rules 15 and 19 in design. The back is handsomely paneled.

CHESTS OF DRAWERS

These were of the type shown in Figure 104. They should have paneled ends. The inside edges of the stiles and rails, on the outside of the chest, may be molded. During the earliest part of the period the posts were merely extended below the lowest drawer to form the feet. Later, when ball feet were introduced from Holland, they became the most common type of foot used. Bracket

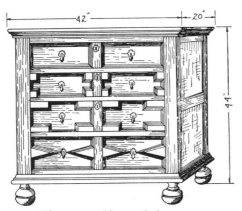
Fig. 104. Chest of drawers.

feet were also used, though these were more common in America than in England. Drawers were ornamented with geometrically applied moldings, and sometimes with bosses and split turnings, though the latter were more often fastened to the posts. Hardware of the type shown on the chest of drawers in Figure 104, is the most suitable for these pieces.

CHESTS ON FRAMES

These consisted of a small chest with one or two drawers below, built on a

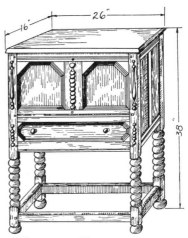
Fig. 105. Chest on frame.

frame. These frames should have turned legs, and stretchers (See Fig. 105).

CAROLEAN OR LATE JACOBEAN, 1660–1689

The last part of the Jacobean period, lasting from 1660 to 1689, was a more extravagant period, due to the restoration of the Stuart line, and to the fact that people had become tired of the restraints placed upon them by Cromwell and his followers. Charles II, who had lived at the French court, where all forms of art were being encouraged by

Louis XIV, naturally tried to imitate him when he returned to England. The furniture not only became richer in design, but was more comfortable. Skillful craftsmen from France were induced to come to England, and under their hands, rich carving in bold relief took the place of the crude carving of the earlier part of the period. Spiral turning almost entirely superceded plain turning. In short, French methods were emulated and encouraged. Oak was still the principal wood used, but walnut began to take its place as it was easier to carve and decorate. By the end of the period it had to a great extent superceded oak as the most important cabinet wood. Rich upholstery fabrics were manufactured or imported from France, for the chairs, sofas, and seats (See Figs. 47, 48, and 49).

MISCELLANEOUS PIECES

The principal articles of furniture, besides those before treated, and which, of course, persisted, were: Carolean chairs; banister-back chairs; upholstered chairs, similar to Louis XIV patterns; sofas; upholstered daybeds; writing cabinets; dainty cupboards; cabinets for the display of china; gaming tables; spiral-turned gate-leg tables; various small occasional tables for serving tea or other beverages; footstools; and clocks.

CHAIRS

CAROLEAN CHAIR. This was a very elegant piece of furniture (See Fig. 59 and Plate 4). It is richly carved with scrolls, foliage, and flowers. The back and seat should be caned. Sometimes the

entire back and the seat were upholstered. While the chair is very rich in ornament it may be criticized for breaking some of the rules of good design, notably Rules 29, 29a, 30, and 40. It must be admitted that the chair is a regal looking piece of furniture despite these inconsistencies.

The back legs are turned above the seat, and the turning should show considerable variation. The top of the leg ends in a turned finial. The back on chairs, during the Carolean period, had little splay, but if one is designed for present-day use, it should be given considerable rake above the seat (See Fig. 106). The front legs are either turned or carved in the manner shown in Plate 4. If carved the legs may be set at almost

ABOUT 7"

Fig. 106.
Splay of back.

Fig. 107. Banister-back
Jacobean side chair.

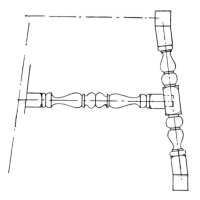

Fig. 109. Plan of stretchers
used on Carolean chairs.

BANISTER-BACK CHAIRS. The banister-back chair is handsome without being overdecorated. Like the Carolean chair it has a pierced and carved headpiece (See Figs. 107, 108, and Plate 4). The headpiece is fastened between the back legs with mortise and tenon, as is the stretcher just above the seat. The back

any desired angle. The carved headpiece, as well as the back and front stretchers under the seat, are pierced, besides being carved. The "S" scroll and "C" scroll are oft-repeated elements on chairs of this type. These are intermingled with foliage, and other naturalistic motifs. The Tudor rose, which was a national emblem, is frequently found, as are the three feathers of the Prince of Wales. These chairs were sometimes made with arms, but since they are now chiefly used for decorative purposes they are usually built as side chairs, and placed where a rich and imposing effect is desired. The upholstered-back types are comfortable, and often have arms. Velvets, velours, and printed fabrics are the proper upholstering materials for this type of chair.

Fig. 108. Banister-back Jacobean
armchair.

legs should be splayed as shown in Figure 106. The banisters are mortised and tenoned to the headpiece, and to the stretcher above the seat. These banisters must be so placed in the back that a horizontal line drawn from side to side will line up with the same detail on each turning (See Fig. 110). The banisters are turnings made exactly like the legs, but split in half. The flat sides of these must be turned toward the front of the chair. The best of these chairs have Spanish feet, as shown in Figure 111, though turned pear feet may be used. The arms for a banister-back chair should be of the scrolled type (Fig. 112). Sometimes, in the best examples, the scrolls are made to protrude from each side like

to them. The front stretcher on the chairs should be boldly turned, while the side stretchers are smaller, but similarly turned. The seat may be rush bottomed or upholstered.

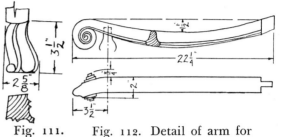

Fig. 111. Detail of Spanish foot. Fig. 112. Detail of arm for banister-back chair.

SOFAS

With greater luxury, and a greater desire for comfort, came upholstered sofas and love seats. They are known as Charles II sofas (See Fig. 113). They

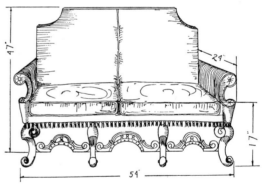

Fig. 113. Charles II settee.

have rather high backs, the top of which is divided as though two or three chairs had been joined together. The upholstering material may be tapestry, velvet, or velour. The legs and stretchers may be designed like any of those found on Carolean chairs.

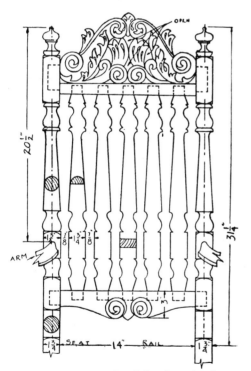

Fig. 110. Back of banister-back armchair.

the twisted horns of a ram's head. Thus the name of ram's-head scroll was given

DAYBEDS

Daybeds again came into great favor after the Commonwealth period, and were much richer than formerly. Legs and underbracing are similar to Carolean or banister-back chair legs and stretchers. The head rest is fastened to the posts with chains in such a way that it may be raised or lowered to any position desired, since this was a reclining couch for boudoirs. The posts to which the head rest is fastened are extensions of the legs, and should be splayed above the seat of the couch. The surface upon which one lies may be caned, rush bottomed, or upholstered.

FOOTSTOOLS

Besides the stools used in the early part of the period, footstools now began to appear. Chair seats were made lower, and instead of resting the feet on the lower stretcher of the chair, footstools were used. Contemporary chair design will indicate the design of footstools.

BEDSTEADS

Bedsteads of the best type, remained similar to those found during the Elizabethan period. These had heavy posts, often with melon-bulb turnings and ornate carving on the posts. The lower part of the posts were square with carved molding. There was a tester, or rather a canopy of wood; framed and paneled on its underside, and with a cornice molding around the outside. Because of low ceilings, common at the time, these bedsteads were usually not very high; though some with very tall posts are known.

The beds of the poor, naturally, were not so rich but were built much like the one shown in Figure 94. They were low posters and were made up of turned spindles and posts. Ropes supported the mattress, and the bed itself was high off the floor to make room for a trundle bed beneath. These trundle beds were common articles of furniture, both in England and early America. They solved the problem of conserving space, which was necessary in the characteristically small cottages of the people.

WRITING CABINETS

Writing cabinets were desks of a type common at the time. Desks as we know them had not yet appeared. At this time cabinets on a tablelike frame served the purpose of our desk. In some cases there were even several drawers beneath the cabinet, and it is from this piece of furniture that our word *bureau,* which means a writing cabinet in France, originated. The frame, at this late part of the period, often consisted of twisted-wood turned legs. The cabinet itself had either two doors enclosing the pigeonholes, or a wide lid, hinged at the bottom, so that it could be lowered to form the writing surface. There was a wide cornice molding at the top, and sometimes on very rich pieces, this was carved in the most approved fashion of the time.

OTHER CABINETS

There were numerous other cabinets in use at the time. They were used for purposes too numerous to mention. Most of the more expensive ones were very ornately decorated and carved. The author has seen several examples that had battle scenes, or scenes from the Bible carved on the panels. Ornate moldings and ornament were the rule of the day.

There is to be found in the Jacobean period a diversity of ornament found in few other periods or styles. Plate 5 shows only a few of the countless variations possible. Oak and walnut were the principal woods used, but many American woods such as maple, birch, ash, and the like may be used as substitutes. It will bear repeating that framed construction and mortise-and-tenon joints, comprise the only correct construction. Drawer sides were usually nailed to the fronts, and sometimes there were grooves in the thick drawer sides, into which drawer runs were fitted, supporting the drawer.

QUESTIONS FOR REVIEW

1. How many distinct styles are represented in the Jacobean period? What are they?

2. What influences were largely responsible for the type of structure and forms of ornament used on Jacobean and Cromwellian styles?

3. Name several of the chief characteristics of the Jacobean and Cromwellian styles.

4. What may be said for the type of construction in use during the entire Jacobean period?

5. How did the quality of ornament compare with that found on more recent styles?

6. Why is it seldom desirable to copy authentic pieces of the Jacobean style?

7. Name several important types of chairs, and give important characteristics of each.

8. What other pieces of furniture were similar in construction to chairs?

9. What were the common types of tables in use during this period?

10. What precaution must be taken when designing the gates on gate-leg tables?

11. How were chests commonly constructed during the Jacobean period?

12. Name several important types of cupboards in use during the Jacobean period, and define their uses.

13. What is a Welsh dresser? Describe the general construction of one.

14. What is the probable origin of chests of drawers?

15. In what ways did furniture of the Carolean style differ from pieces in the earlier part of the Jacobean period?

16. Did designers and cabinetmakers always observe the rules of good design when working up their pieces?

17. What were some of the greatest faults of the designs, and what may modern designers do to correct them?

18. Describe a writing cabinet of the Carolean period.

SUGGESTED PROBLEMS

1. Design a chest in the Jacobean style. Make special efforts to observe Rules 4, 9, 10, 23, and 24, in formulating this design.

2. Draw the design for a dining table in an early Jacobean manner, or an entire dining-room suite. (See Chapter 18.)

3. Design a small writing or desk box with a slanting lid. Design it to be placed upon a small table.

4. Design a banister-back chair, but make it somewhat simpler than the ones shown in Figures 107 and 108. (The design of the top, for example, may be considerably simplified.)

CHAPTER 7

THE WILLIAM AND MARY STYLE
1688–1702

HISTORICAL BACKGROUND AND GENERAL CHARACTERISTICS

The William and Mary style marked a new era in furniture design. The period lasted only a short time, but the changes in style and types were very marked ones. The Carolean style, which preceded it, was French in most of its aspects. The William and Mary style was essentially Dutch in character and feeling. William was the grandson of Charles I, while Mary, his wife, was the daughter of James II, who had abdicated before they assumed the throne. William had been a ruler in Holland before coming to England, and Mary had lived there long enough to become strongly influenced by the habits and customs of the Dutch people. The Dutch were a comfort-loving and domestically inclined race, and had developed a style of furniture that reflected these tendencies.

When William and Mary assumed control of the British government, their field of influence was also extended to domestic affairs. Not only was furniture imported from Holland, but artisans and tradesmen as well. Queen Mary was interested in furniture, china collecting, and needlework; and people who furnished homes during this period were influenced by her taste and example in such matters. Because the style was remarkably well suited to middle-class homes and living conditions, it caught the fancy of the people more rapidly than it might have done had this not been the case. The replacement of oak by the more handsome walnut, a change that had progressed rapidly during the Carolean period, was also partly responsible for the growth in popular favor of the new style; it being a material particularly well suited to the type of design.

Perhaps the greatest appeal of the William and Mary style lies in its simplicity. In the main it has clean, clear-cut lines, that contrast sharply with the pieces in the Jacobean styles. The style retained the rectangular structure and contour of earlier styles.

The chief characteristics of the style are: (1) Trumpet-turned legs or similar shapes (Fig. 116). (2) Crossed or X-shaped stretchers, or others of a similar nature (See Plate 10). (3) Single- or double-hooded tops for cabinets (See Fig. 117) and similar shapes for chair and sofa tops. (4) Ball or bun feet. (5) Beautifully shaped aprons or skirts, carrying out the hooded effect, and also with reverse curves and flat arches. (6) Large unbroken surfaces; either plain (Fig.

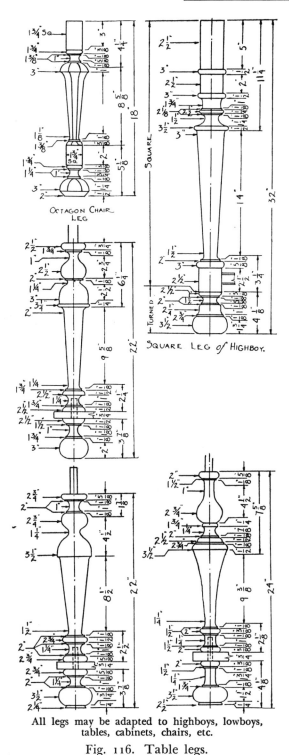

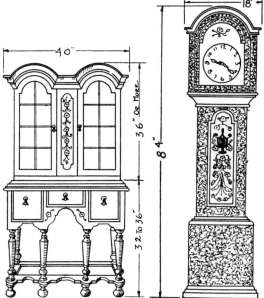

Fig. 117. Double-hood china cabinet
and tall clock.

All legs may be adapted to highboys, lowboys,
tables, cabinets, chairs, etc.
Fig. 116. Table legs.

71), painted (Fig. 60), or handsomely
Much of the painted furniture was
decorated with figured veneer.

lacquered. This form of decoration was
introduced by French workmen, who
got it from the Orient. The fancy,
burled walnut veneers were matched, or
applied in interesting patterns to wide
surfaces. Oystering, a form of veneering
taking its name because of its similarity
in appearance to the inside of an oyster
shell, was one of the many new effects
invented. The framed construction characteristic of the Jacobean style was almost entirely absent from this style. The
furniture, therefore, lost a great deal of
the sturdiness of the former styles. Moldings remained a prominent feature on
this style, but with the advent of walnut
they were somewhat reduced in scale.
Carving was used principally on chair
backs, and then mostly during the early
part of the period.

PIECES. The important pieces were:
chairs, stools, tables, secretaries, sofas,

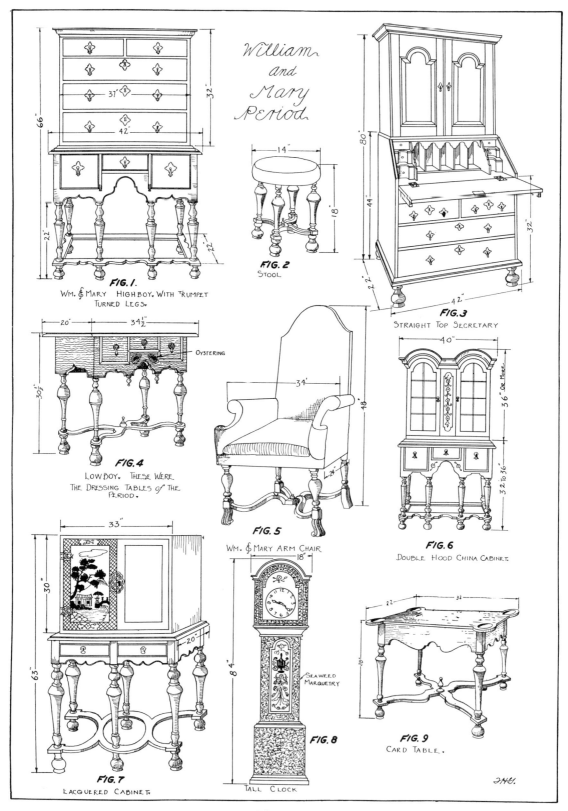

William and Mary Period.

FIG. 1.
WM. & MARY HIGHBOY. WITH TRUMPET TURNED LEGS.

FIG. 2
STOOL

FIG. 3
STRAIGHT TOP SECRETARY

FIG. 4
LOWBOY. THESE WERE THE DRESSING TABLES of THE PERIOD.

FIG. 5
WM. & MARY ARM CHAIR

FIG. 6
DOUBLE HOOD CHINA CABINET.

FIG. 7
LACQUERED CABINET.

FIG. 8
TALL CLOCK

FIG. 9
CARD TABLE.

Plate 10.

love seats, highboys, lowboys, cabinets, chests, chests of drawers, mirrors.

CHAIRS

Chairs in this style should be designed with high backs. The backs may be upholstered, or caned and carved much like the Carolean chairs, with the exception that the cresting should be hood-shaped. Carving on William and Mary chairs is also finer in detail and scale. One does not find so much of the deeply cut scrollwork as on the Carolean chairs. The cresting, when carved, may be fastened between the back posts, or may cap the posts. In the latter case it is fastened to dowels turned on the tops of the posts. Upholstered chairs of this style were sim-

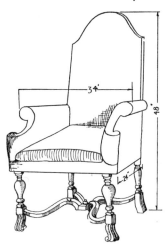

Fig. 118. William and Mary armchair.

ilar to the one shown in Figure 118, though some were straight across the top. On carved chairs the arms may be scrolled, wooden ones, like those found on the banister-back chair (Fig. 112). Chair legs may be any of the types shown on Plate 11. They should have X-shaped stretchers for underbracing. Chairs of this type may have the Dutch

bun or ball foot, or the Spanish foot, as shown in Figure 118. Upholstering materials suitable for the style include velvets, velours, tapestry, needlepoint tapestry, or printed materials in rich colors.

STOOLS

There were many kinds of stools; the most characteristic William and Mary type being the kind shown in Figure

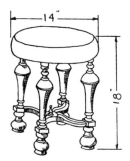

Fig. 120. Stool.

120. Stools may have round or rectangular tops. The same types of legs found on chairs are also suitable for stools. All underbracing should be similar to that found on the chairs.

TABLES

Tables, for the most part, should be of the light turned types used during the Carolean period. In addition to these, however, there were tables like the card

Fig. 121. Card table.

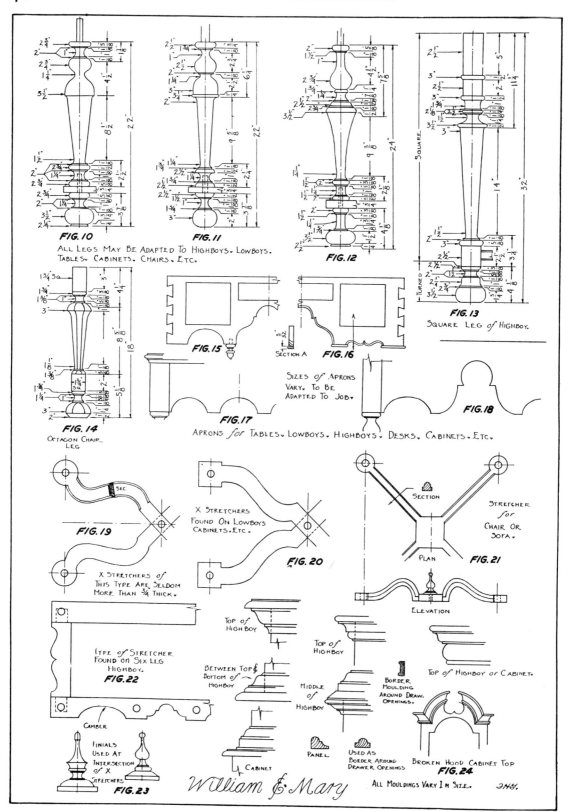

FIG. 10

ALL LEGS MAY BE ADAPTED TO HIGHBOYS. LOWBOYS.
TABLES. CABINETS. CHAIRS. ETC.

FIG. 11

FIG. 12

FIG. 13
SQUARE LEG of HIGHBOY.

FIG. 14
OCTAGON CHAIR
LEG

FIG. 15

SECTION A   FIG. 16

SIZES of APRONS
VARY. TO BE
ADAPTED TO JOB.

FIG. 17

FIG. 18

APRONS for TABLES. LOWBOYS. HIGHBOYS. DESKS. CABINETS. ETC.

FIG. 19

X STRETCHERS of
THIS TYPE ARE SELDOM
MORE THAN ¾ THICK.

X STRETCHERS
FOUND ON LOWBOYS
CABINETS. ETC.

FIG. 20

SECTION

PLAN   FIG. 21

STRETCHER
for
CHAIR OR
SOFA.

ELEVATION

TYPE of STRETCHER
FOUND ON SIX LEG
HIGHBOY.
FIG. 22

CAMBER

FINIALS
USED AT
INTERSECTION
of X
STRETCHERS.
FIG. 23

TOP of
HIGH BOY

BETWEEN TOP &
BOTTOM of
HIGHBOY

MIDDLE
of
HIGHBOY

CABINET

PANEL

USED AS
BORDER AROUND
DRAWER OPENINGS.

TOP of
HIGHBOY

BORDER
MOULDING
AROUND DRAW.
OPENINGS.

TOP of HIGHBOY or CABINET.

BROKEN HOOD CABINET TOP
FIG. 24

William & Mary

ALL MOULDINGS VARY IN SIZE.

Plate 11.

table shown in Figure 121. This type of table may be adapted for card playing, or it may be used as an occasional table, a hall table, and the like.

DESKS

Desks in this style may have slanting fronts. Sizes vary, but a very pleasing adaptation from the style is the desk shown in Figure 122. It is intended as a

(A Wallace Nutting Reproduction)
Fig. 122. A ladies' desk.

ladies' desk. The slanting lid, when opened, forms a writing surface. The desks must be designed so that this surface is the correct height from the floor, which will be about 30 in. The lid is supported by small slides which may be drawn out. Legs should be of the trumpet type, with X-stretchers, having a turned finial at the intersection. Drawer pulls are usually of the pendant-drop type, and may have flower forms

stamped on them. Other suitable hardware is shown in Plate 12. The ladies' desk is built of curly maple, with legs and feet of walnut.

SECRETARIES

These are desks with a cabinet above. This cabinet may be used for books, papers, or documents. The cabinets of this type may be designed with glazed or paneled doors. If glazed, the design of the mirror (Plate 15) will suggest a possible shape for the top of the door around the glass. The tops of these secretaries may have single- or double-arched hoods, or may be straight. Ball or bun feet are proper. Drawer fronts and doors may be veneered with figured veneers. Sometimes the panels were painted with floral designs that were very beautiful.

A different type of secretary, or writing cabinet, was one having several drawers below, and a hooded upper part. The pigeonholes and small drawers, comprising the desk, were in a cabinet behind a wide lid, which could be let down to form the writing surface. This type of cabinet had no slant front, the lid being in a vertical position when closed, and the upper section being as deep as the lower section which contained the large drawers.

SOFAS AND LOVE SEATS

A love seat, as before stated, is a small sofa large enough for two people. Sofas and love seats may be treated as one subject, being similar. The back as well as the seat on these should be upholstered. Sofas, like the chairs in this style, have high backs. These may be straight

William & Mary

F.H.G.

Plate 12.

across the top, but more often they are designed with double-, or even triple-arched backs, just as though two or more chair backs had been put together. Loose cushions, as many as there are backs, may take the place of a single long one. Legs and underbracing are similar to those found on chairs of the style.

HIGHBOYS

A highboy is a chest of drawers on a frame. This form of construction be-

Fig. 123. Broken-hood cabinet top.

came popular during the William and Mary period. Highboys may be designed with straight or hooded tops. In either case there should be a prominent cornice molding. Later in the period, this hood was sometimes "broken" (See Fig. 123), and this paved the way for the new type of hood or bonnet which later became popular.

Drawer fronts may be plain, veneered, or painted. Some have been found that had painted panels set in the midst of figured veneers.

Highboys may be designed with four legs and X-stretchers, but five or six legs are of common occurrence, chiefly for the sake of variety in design. When there are five or six legs, only two are in the back, and the rest are in the front. A special type of stretcher shown in Figure 124 was used in this case.

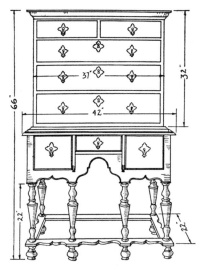

Fig. 124. William and Mary highboy with trumpet turned legs.

Highboys should always have ball or bun feet. There should be a bold molding dividing the upper from the lower section. On English examples this molding was more prominent than on American highboys. The upper section is not quite as wide nor as deep as the lower section.

LOWBOYS

Lowboys were the dressing tables of the period. As such they had a mirror hung above them (See Plate 14). It is this piece, one of the most dainty of the articles in a handsome style, that we have chosen to illustrate design and structure common at the time. The lowboy if used as a dressing table should be from 28 to 30 in. high. It should be designed with sufficient knee room, an important consideration if one wishes to sit close to a table. For this reason the apron has been designed with a high opening in the center. The X-type stretcher also makes it possible to sit closer to a table of this

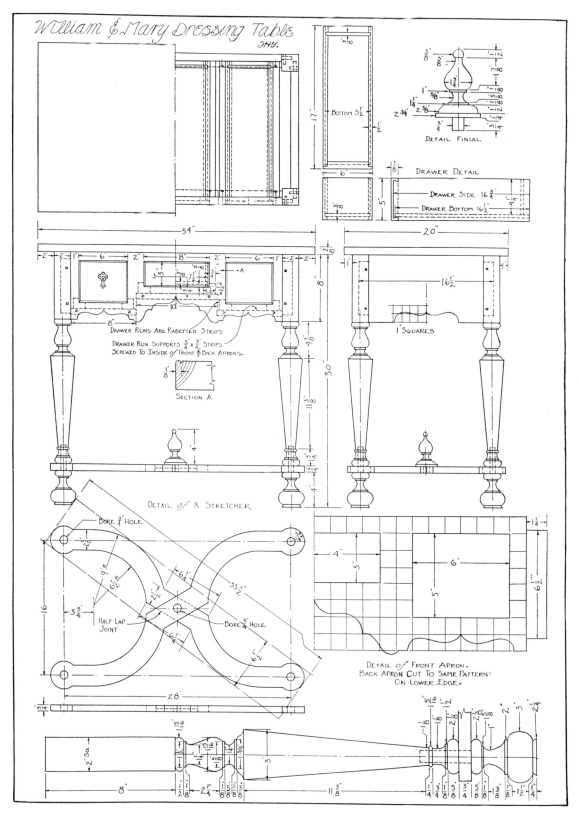

Plate 13. (See Plates 14 and 15.)

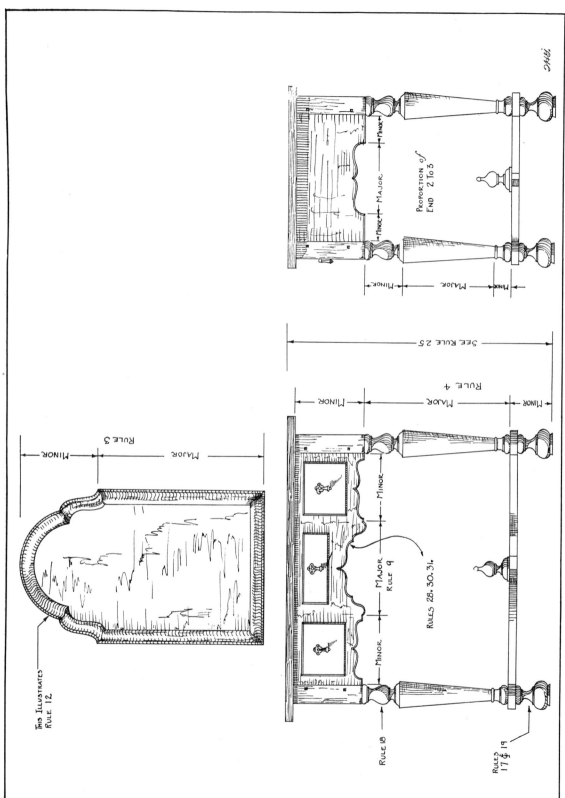

Plate 14. (See Plates 13 and 15.)

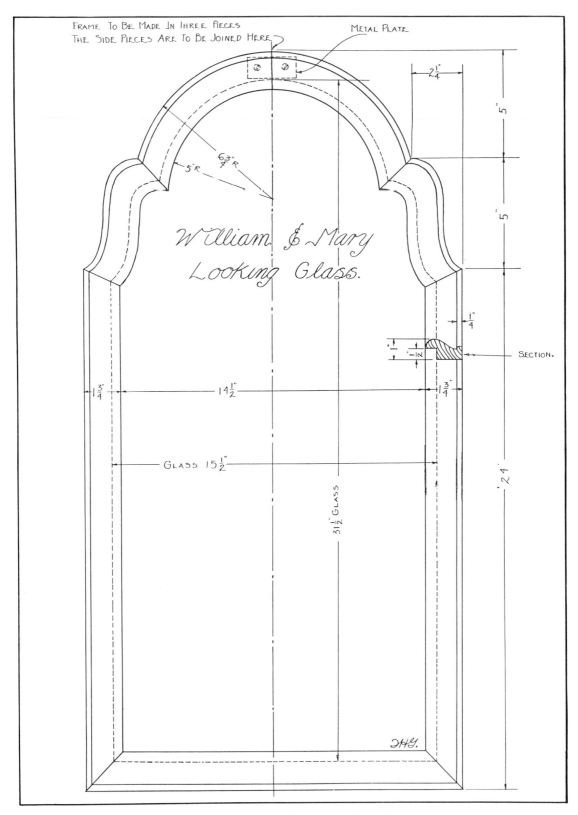

Plate 15. (See Plates 13 and 14.)

kind than would be possible with earlier forms of underbracing. The legs are of the trumpet type. They are mortised and tenoned to the apron on this table. Sometimes the front and end aprons, on tables of this kind, were dovetailed together at the corners. In that case the

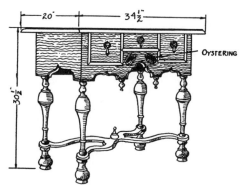

Fig. 125. William and Mary lowboy or dressing table.

leg had a dowel turned on its top, which was glued into a hole bored into a corner block on the inside of the frame. Drawer openings on these tables often had half-round molding applied around them (See Fig. 125). An analysis of the design principles involved in this design are given on Plate 14.

CHESTS OF DRAWERS

The general shape and size of these may be the same as those of the Jacobean style. The construction differed greatly, however. Ends of these chests were seldom framed like Jacobean chests, but were wide solid boards in most cases. Many of the drawer fronts were veneered. Some were painted or inlaid. Panel-like effects were produced on drawer fronts by means of inlaid bands and these panels were decorated by

painting as is shown in Figure 117. The panels usually had semicircular ends, carrying out the arched-hood idea. Bracket feet as well as bun or ball feet were used.

CABINETS

Cabinets of all kinds came into existence. They were used to hold china as well as sundry other objects. The finest ones were decorated with marquetry, a form of inlay consisting of small pieces of wood, laid in very intricate and delicate designs. Some of this decoration was

Fig. 126. William and Mary dressing table and mirror.

very aptly named seaweed marquetry, because the designs were so intricate and covered the surface so completely (See Fig. 117).

Walnut is the proper wood to use for pieces in this style. Maple is a practical substitute, and mahogany is possible. Neither of the latter are, however, as well suited to the spirit of the style as walnut.

QUESTIONS FOR REVIEW

1. What were a few of the radical changes brought about in construction when the William and Mary style superseded the Jacobean style?

2. Was the construction of William and Mary furniture as good as that found in pieces of the preceding style? Give reasons for your answer.

3. Name three important characteristics of the William and Mary style that made the furniture more livable than that of the former styles.

4. What are the characteristics and uses of a William and Mary highboy? Lowboy?

5. Describe chair design as practiced in this style.

6. Describe table design as practiced in this style.

7. What improvements can be noticed in the observance of principles of good design over those practiced during the Jacobean periods?

William and Mary table showing Jacobean influence.

SUGGESTED PROBLEMS

1. Design a rectangular-shaped dressing-table stool to go with the dressing table shown in Plate 14, and Figure 126.

2. Design a small writing desk, similar to the one shown in Figure 122, but make changes in the type of legs, stretchers, and other details.

CHAPTER 8

THE QUEEN ANNE STYLE
1702–1714

HISTORICAL DATA AND GENERAL CHARACTERISTICS

The Queen Anne style, which followed the style of William and Mary, was a great step forward in the production of better furniture. Its most important contributions were the promotion of comfort, and an improvement in gracefulness. The style came into existence soon after Queen Anne came to the throne, though she had little to do personally toward influencing its development. The style was essentially Dutch in character, just as the preceding style had been. One of its important features, the cabriole leg, came from France, but British craftsmen copied the Dutch adaptations of this feature, instead of getting it directly from France; mostly because England and France were not on very good terms at the time. The style lasted a great deal longer than the reign of Queen Anne. It changed very little in form and contour from the time it came into being, about 1703, until Chippendale's style replaced it.

The pieces were quite plain at first, there being a singular lack of ornament. After the death of Queen Anne, in 1714, a more ornate style developed; due in part, no doubt, to the examples set by contemporary French styles.

In this treatment of Queen Anne furniture, the consideration of the style will be limited to the style as it appeared during the original Queen Anne period. After 1714 the designs deteriorated in merit, because of unsuitable ornament. The period between 1714 and 1750 should be termed Early Georgian, though actually it was a grotesquely ornamented Queen Anne style.

The original Queen Anne style, taken as a whole, was somewhat clumsy. The fine proportions found on later styles, developed by the great English designers, had not yet appeared. Curved elements were often clumsy, even though the general tendency of the style was toward a more pleasing form and structure. Among the chief characteristics of the style are: (1) The cabriole leg (See Fig. 127). (2) The prolific use of the cyma curve for structural as well as ornamental elements. (3) A general lack of stretchers and underbracing. (4) Broken pediments, sometimes known as, "bonnet tops," for highboys and tall pieces. (5) Horseshoe-shaped seats and "spooned" backs for chairs. (6) Shells carved on knees of cabriole legs, and on skirts and aprons of other pieces. (7) The use of walnut as the principal and most suitable material for the style. (8) Shaped aprons, similar to those found on William and Mary pieces, except that on Queen Anne pieces, cyma curves largely replaced the arches found on the earlier style. (9) "Fiddle-shaped" backs on chairs. (10) Rectangular structure.

Cabriole legs, in this style, did not attain the perfection of design of the excellent Louis XV cabriole legs. The latter were well balanced, gracefully curved, and the ornament on them was of a highly developed type; while Queen Anne cabriole legs were often straight and stiff, and some of the feet on them came to be known as "pad feet" and "club feet" (See Fig. 127). Despite these drawbacks, the pieces possessed a charm that earlier styles altogether lacked. In designing pieces today, the designer

should try his utmost to correct common faults of early makers. The result will be a style difficult to excel for simplicity and charm.

The cyma, or reverse curve, was exploited to the fullest extent in this style, and it was used on chair backs, cabriole legs, shaped aprons, outlines of openings, and similar places.

One of the most important contributions made by this style was the greater comfort of its chairs. These were designed to fit the curve of the back, or "spooned," as it has been termed, because of a similarity to the curve found on the handle of a tablespoon (See Fig. 129).

The chief ornament, other than the

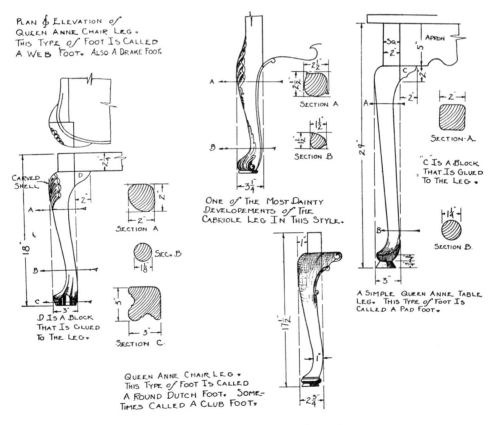

Fig. 127. Queen Anne furniture legs.

cyma curves, were carved sea shells, adapted to many forms. These were used on all kinds of furniture, as we shall see

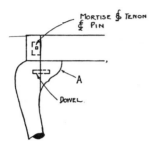

Fig. 128. Method of joining chair leg to seat.

when making a study of individual pieces.

Walnut was the principal wood used during the earlier part of the period, though mahogany was sometimes substituted in its place. By 1750, mahogany had almost completely replaced walnut, but this came later than the time about which we are interested in this chapter. Walnut still is, and should be, the proper wood for pieces in this style. Maple is a possible substitute, it possessing many of the desirable qualities of walnut, except for its color. Many fine Queen Anne pieces, of American origin, built of curly or plain maple, have been cherished for generations in New England homes.

CONSTRUCTION

Since construction is of such vital importance, and since it changed considerably from that of the preceding period, it will be well to give it some attention here. The cabriole leg, for instance, is a member that requires thick stock to make. For the sake of being on the safe

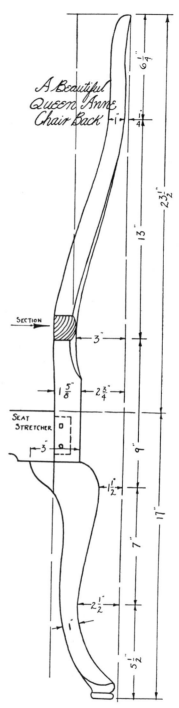

Fig. 129. Queen Anne chair back.

side, so far as sound construction is concerned, and in the interest of greater aesthetic qualities, this type of leg should be made from solid stock only. Thick

FIG. 1
HIGHBOY

FIG. 2
LOWBOY

FIG. 3
SMALL TABLE

FIG 4
SOFA

FIG. 5
HALL TABLE

FIG. 6
SMALL TEA TABLE

Top 40" IN DIAMETER WHEN OPEN.

FIG. 7
LIGHT DROP-LEAF TABLE

FIG. 8
GATE LEG TABLE

FIG. 9
SEAT 18" HIGH
40 TO 46" HIGH
SEAT 24" WIDE 18" DEEP
ARM CHAIR

Top 22 BY 72

FIG. 10
SIDEBOARD

FIG. 11
WRITING DESK

FIG. 12
SIDE CHAIR
WIDTH OF SEAT 21"
DEPTH 17'

THE PROPER WOOD FOR QUEEN ANNE FURNITURE IS WALNUT. MAHOGANY WAS SOMETIMES USED.

FIG. 13
STOOL

Some Representative Pieces of The Queen Anne Period Showing Typical Shapes & Approximate Sizes

Plate 16.

solid stock of the dimensions necessary to make a beautiful cabriole leg is expensive, and sometimes difficult to get; therefore the designer must sometimes hold himself within certain narrow limits when designing pieces in this style. This is not always a good thing, because some of the finer designs require deeply curved cabriole legs to lift them above the commonplace.

When stock from which cabriole legs are to be made is more than three inches thick, it is, in most cases glued. Exceptions to this rule may be found where a

Figure 128. The small block A should be glued and doweled to the leg before it is cut on the band saw. The apron, or chair rail, when it is joined to the leg should be fastened with mortise and tenon, glued and pinned (See also Fig. 130).

In chair backs, chair arms, curved rails, and shaped pieces generally, this factor of stock sizes must be taken into account. Chair rails, table aprons, and other members, where strength is required in the joint, should never be doweled to the legs.

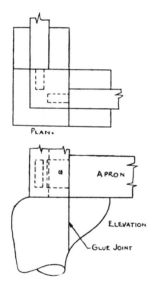

Fig. 130. Method of joining chair leg to seat.

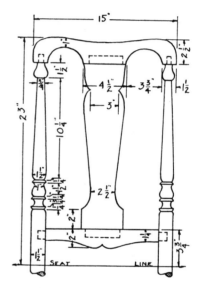

Fig. 131. Country Dutch type, Queen Anne back side chair.

manufacturer has his stock cut to specified dimensions, or where he controls his source of supply. Gluing will not only decrease the value of the piece, but will constitute a danger, because glue joints will open under certain conditions, notwithstanding arguments that glue joints are stronger than the wood itself.

Study the construction of the leg in

In this style, the top rails of the chair backs are always fastened to the tops of the posts. They should be fastened, at all times, with mortise-and-tenon joints. The same rule applies to the fiddle-shaped splat. In country Dutch type chairs, having the turned legs, the splat is usually fastened to a crosspiece, a few inches above the seat, as shown in Fig-

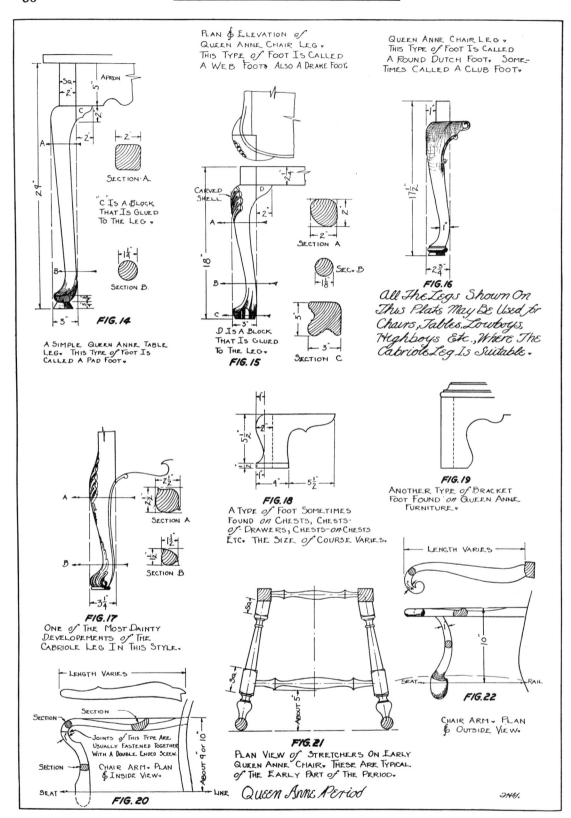

PLAN & ELEVATION of
QUEEN ANNE CHAIR LEG.
THIS TYPE of FOOT IS CALLED
A WEB FOOT. ALSO A DRAKE FOOT.

QUEEN ANNE CHAIR LEG.
THIS TYPE of FOOT IS CALLED
A ROUND DUTCH FOOT. SOME-
TIMES CALLED A CLUB FOOT.

APRON

SECTION A.

"C IS A BLOCK
THAT IS GLUED
TO THE LEG.

SECTION B.

FIG. 14

A SIMPLE QUEEN ANNE TABLE
LEG. THIS TYPE of FOOT IS
CALLED A PAD FOOT.

CARVED
SHELL

SECTION A

SEC. B

D IS A BLOCK
THAT IS GLUED
TO THE LEG.

FIG. 15

SECTION C

FIG. 16

All The Legs Shown On
This Plate May Be Used for
Chairs, Tables, Lowboys,
Highboys Etc., Where The
Cabriole Leg Is Suitable.

SECTION A

SECTION B

FIG. 17

One of The Most Dainty
Developments of The
Cabriole Leg In This Style.

FIG. 18

A TYPE of FOOT SOMETIMES
FOUND on CHESTS, CHESTS-
of-DRAWERS, CHESTS-on-CHESTS
ETC. THE SIZE of COURSE VARIES.

FIG. 19

ANOTHER TYPE of BRACKET
FOOT FOUND on QUEEN ANNE
FURNITURE.

LENGTH VARIES

SECTION

SECTION

JOINTS of THIS TYPE ARE
USUALLY FASTENED TOGETHER
WITH A DOUBLE ENDED SCREW.

SECTION

CHAIR ARM. PLAN
& INSIDE VIEW.

SEAT

FIG. 20

SEAT

RAIL

FIG. 22

CHAIR ARM. PLAN
& OUTSIDE VIEW.

LINE

FIG. 21

PLAN VIEW of STRETCHERS ON EARLY
QUEEN ANNE CHAIR. THESE ARE TYPICAL
of THE EARLY PART of THE PERIOD.

Queen Anne Period

Plate 17.

ure 131. This is usually the case when the seat is to be rush bottomed. It is possible, though unusual, to find a rush-bottomed slip seat on chairs like Figure 132.

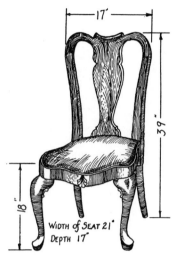

Fig. 132. Side chair.

The rails between drawers on high-boys, lowboys, desks, chests of drawers, and other case furniture, are often dove-

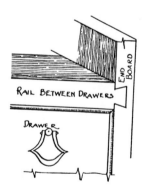

Fig. 133. Detail of construction of rail between drawers.

tailed to the end boards (Fig. 133). When so constructed it is best to build the rest of the frame, which supports the drawer, and then fasten it to the front rail after the rail has been forced into place with clamps. This construction

prevents the danger of the case ever spreading or coming apart. The short stiles, between small drawers, or used as a finish on openings for a single drawer, are also quite often fastened in a similar way (See stiles between drawer and slides, Plate 28; and Fig. 134).

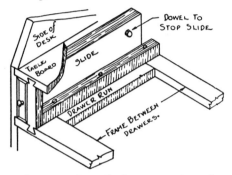

Fig. 134. Detail of construction of desk for slide to support slant lid.

CHAIRS

The chairs of this style are particularly pleasing. Not only are they beautiful, but a sincere effort seems to have been made, in most instances, to make them comfortable. In the better pieces, the backs are formed to fit the natural curve of the spine (See Fig. 129). This requires considerable care on the part of the cabinetmaker and the designer, so that it will be just right. This curvature if carefully kept in mind when working up a chair design, will make furniture that is comfortable as well as beautiful.

In Figures 131 and 135 are shown several typical Queen Anne chair backs. The back in the first one shown in Figure 135 is sometimes known as a fiddle-back, taking its name from the shape of the splat. We wish to point out, how-

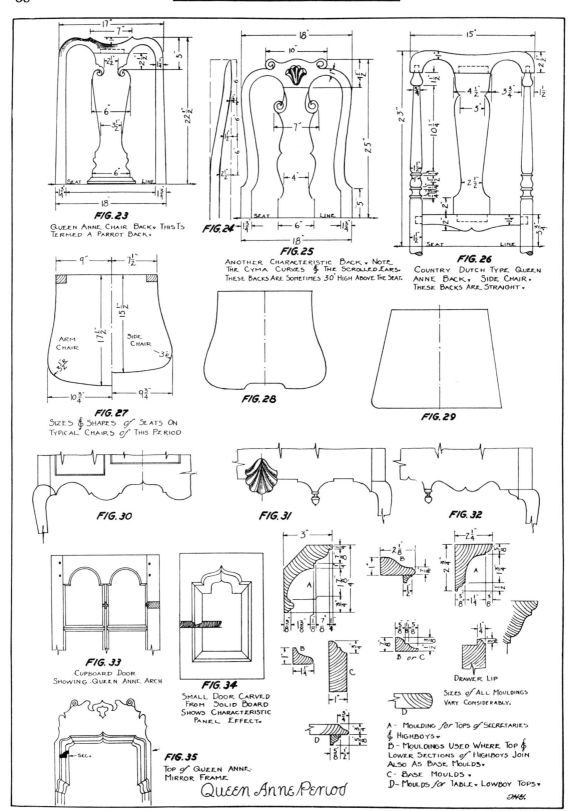

FIG. 23
QUEEN ANNE CHAIR BACK. THIS IS
TERMED A PARROT BACK.

FIG. 24

FIG. 25
ANOTHER CHARACTERISTIC BACK. NOTE
THE CYMA CURVES & THE SCROLLED EARS.
THESE BACKS ARE SOMETIMES 30" HIGH ABOVE THE SEAT.

FIG. 26
COUNTRY DUTCH TYPE QUEEN
ANNE BACK. SIDE CHAIR.
THESE BACKS ARE STRAIGHT.

FIG. 27
SIZES & SHAPES of SEATS ON
TYPICAL CHAIRS of THIS PERIOD

FIG. 28

FIG. 29

FIG. 30

FIG. 31

FIG. 32

FIG. 33
CUPBOARD DOOR
SHOWING QUEEN ANNE ARCH

FIG. 34
SMALL DOOR CARVED
FROM SOLID BOARD
SHOWS CHARACTERISTIC
PANEL EFFECT.

FIG. 35
TOP of QUEEN ANNE
MIRROR FRAME

DRAWER LIP

SIZES of ALL MOULDINGS
VARY CONSIDERABLY.

A - MOULDING for TOPS of SECRETARIES
& HIGHBOYS.
B - MOULDINGS USED WHERE TOP &
LOWER SECTIONS of HIGHBOYS JOIN
ALSO AS BASE MOULDS.
C - BASE MOULDS.
D - MOULDS for TABLE. LOWBOY TOPS.

Queen Anne Period

Plate 18.

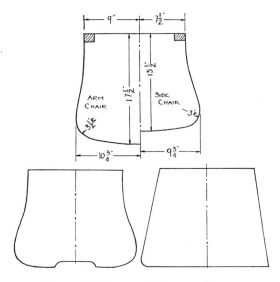

Fig. 136. Sizes and shapes of seats.

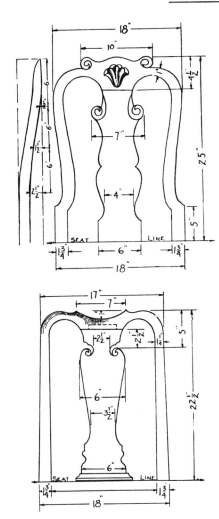

Fig. 135. Details of Queen Anne chair backs.

were usually commodious. The first lay-out in Figure 136, shows seats of both an armchair and a side chair. The dimensions given are representative of the arm- and side-chair seat sizes for other than upholstered wing chairs. Wing chairs were often more than 24 in. deep,

ever, that the shape of a bird's head on each side of the splat is more strikingly apparent than the likeness to a fiddle is in the splat itself. Thus a more appropriate name for this type of back would be, "parrot back." On the best designs these shapes are the result of careful planning by the designer. The backs on these chairs were often quite high, sometimes as much as 46 in. from the floor to the top. Most people desire a somewhat lower back than this.

Figures 136 and 137, show the shapes of several seats. The chairs of this period

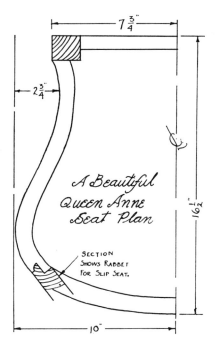

Fig. 137. Plan of Queen Anne seat.

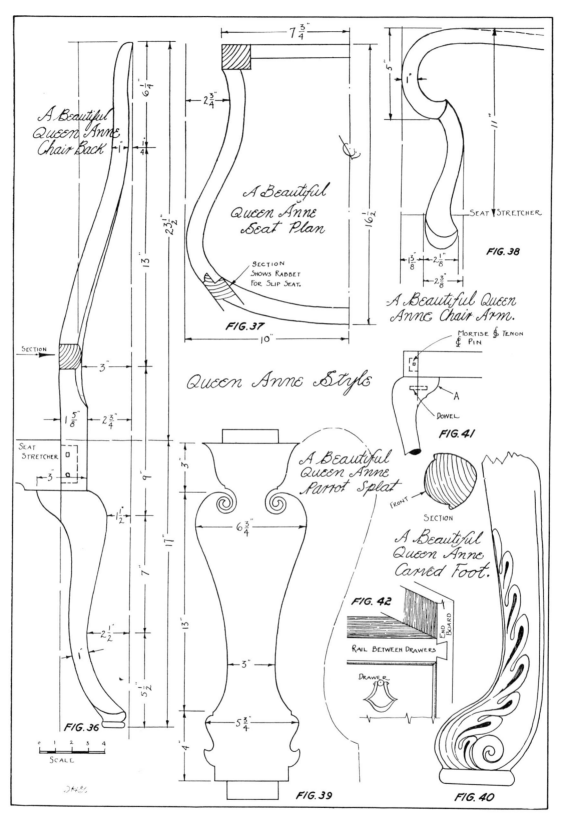

A Beautiful Queen Anne Chair Back

$7\frac{3}{4}$"

$2\frac{3}{4}$"

$6\frac{1}{4}$"

$1\frac{1}{4}$"

$23\frac{1}{2}$"

13"

$16\frac{1}{2}$"

A Beautiful Queen Anne Seat Plan

SECTION SHOWS RABBET FOR SLIP SEAT.

FIG. 37

10"

5"

1"

11"

SEAT STRETCHER

FIG. 38

A Beautiful Queen Anne Chair Arm.

$1\frac{3}{8}$" $2\frac{1}{8}$"

$2\frac{3}{8}$"

SECTION

3"

$1\frac{5}{8}$" $2\frac{3}{4}$"

SEAT STRETCHER

3"

9"

$1\frac{1}{2}$"

17"

7"

$2\frac{1}{2}$"

$5\frac{1}{2}$"

1"

FIG. 36

SCALE

0 1 2 3 4

Queen Anne Style

3"

$6\frac{3}{4}$"

13"

3"

$5\frac{3}{4}$"

4"

FIG. 39

MORTISE & TENON & PIN

A

DOWEL

FIG. 41

A Beautiful Queen Anne Parrot Splat

FRONT

SECTION

A Beautiful Queen Anne Carved Foot.

FIG. 42

END BOARD

RAIL BETWEEN DRAWERS

DRAWER

FIG. 40

Plate 19.

and should be wider than that at the front of the seat. The third layout in Figure 136 shows the shapes of two seats, half of each being shown.

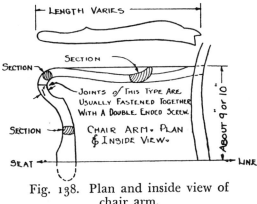

Fig. 138. Plan and inside view of chair arm.

In Figures 138 and 139, are shown two kinds of arms that are commonly identified with the chairs of this period. They are graceful and appropriate. The chairs, except in the early part of the

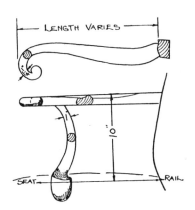

Fig. 139. Plan and outside view of chair arm.

period, rarely had stretchers. When they did they usually took the form of those shown in Figure 140. Sometimes, on the very best chairs, the back legs, from the seat to the floor, are of the cabriole type. These give the chairs, when viewed from the side, a decidedly rakish appearance

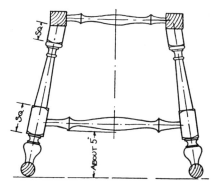

Fig. 140. Plan view of stretchers on early Queen Anne chair.

(See Fig. 129). Upholstering material for chairs of this style may include velvets, tapestry, brocades, needlework tapestry in "petit point"; and for cheaper material, glazed chintz or printed linen may be used.

TABLES

The Queen Anne pieces that are perhaps the most popular today, are the many interesting tables designed in this style. The style is particularly adaptable to small light tables, because of the ab-

Fig. 141. Small tea table.

sence of an elaborate understructure in the form of cross bracing. A number of interesting suggestions for designs of light tables are shown on Plate 16. Figure 141 would make an interesting coffee table. The gallery on top could be made into a removable tray. Well-shaped aprons on these small tables, with an occasional shell carved in the center, make the designing of tables in this style exceedingly interesting, and full of pleasant possibilities.

A hall table, representative of this style, designed by the author, and built in his classes, is shown in Plate 20. The design of the apron is worthy of study, since it is in complete harmony with the rest of the structure, and fulfills the principles of design laid down in Rules 30 and 31. The shape made by the apron and legs at the ends of the table is particularly good.

LOWBOYS

The lowboys of the Queen Anne style were the forerunners of the more handsome Chippendale designs. The almost total lack of carving on Queen Anne lowboys, gives them the great asset of simplicity. The quarter columns, which are found later on Chippendale's lowboys, are absent in Queen Anne pieces if they run true to type. The height of these lowboys varied from 26 to 30 in., and they were seldom more than 36 in. long (See Fig. 142).

HIGHBOYS

Highboys, in the Queen Anne style, should be comparatively light; that is, when compared with those designed in the William and Mary or Chippendale styles. Their width should not exceed 40 in. Because of their slender legs this width is great enough. They should not be too tall. Seven feet should be about the limit. It should be observed that while the lower section of a highboy is similar to a lowboy, they are in nowise the same size. The base of a highboy is always higher and wider than a lowboy. This height varies from 32 to 36 in. If

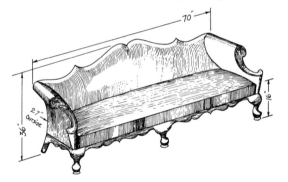

Fig. 143.   Queen Anne sofa.

correctly proportioned, a highboy of the Queen Anne style seems tall and slender and exceedingly graceful.

SOFAS

Figure 143, shows an upholstered sofa with a very beautifully shaped back. The shape of the arms on this piece is typical of the better designs.

Fig. 142.   Queen Anne lowboy.

CABINETS AND CUPBOARDS

Cabinets and cupboards were built in increasing numbers during the Queen Anne period. They may be designed in a variety of ways. The Queen Anne leg

Queen Anne chair.

Fig. 144. Corner cupboard. A fine design with generous use of moldings for decorative effect.

It was during the Queen Anne period that classic design, in some of its forms, became popular, due mostly to the influence of Sir Christopher Wren, an English architect. The classic was not widely exploited in ornament, as was the case later on when the Brothers Adam made their contribution in this field.

and foot may be used for the frame, with a cabinet similar to those found in Figures 60 and 117.

The cupboard shown in Figure 144, offers suggestions for other designs. This example shows some fine paneling, and other details characteristic of the style.

Queen Anne hall table illustrating beauty as a result of simplicity and carefully planned outline.

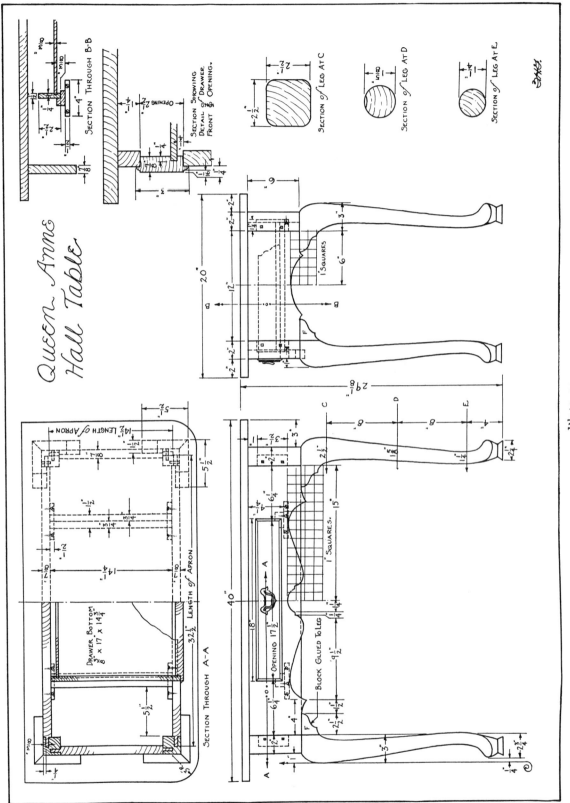

Queen Anne
Hall Table

Plate 20.

Queen Anne settee with drake foot and shaped top.

But important elements such as broken pediments over doors and windows, in the interiors of important buildings; pilasters, classic moldings, urn finials, and similar details, used as early as the William and Mary period, are sufficient indications of the classic influence. These features were adapted by cabinet-makers, especially for highboys, tall cabinets, and cupboards. Some of the pieces designed in this spirit are very handsome indeed.

QUESTIONS FOR REVIEW

1. What peculiarities of the Queen Anne style make it essentially Dutch in character?

2. Name several improvements of design that make this style a more practical one for adaptation to modern conditions than the earlier styles.

3. What are three of the chief distinguishing features of the Queen Anne style?

4. Were the proportions of most original Queen Anne pieces of furniture good? What may be done to improve on original proportions?

5. What other improvements may be made in the design of present-day pieces over original pieces of furniture in the style?

6. What were the chief improvements that may be noted in the chair design of this style over that of the William and Mary style?

7. Was the construction of Queen Anne furniture substantial?

Plate 21.

8. What were the chief forms of ornament used to enrich pieces in the Queen Anne style?

SUGGESTED PROBLEMS

1. Work up a design for a light occasional table in the Queen Anne style.

2. Design a dressing table and mirror.

3. Design a Queen Anne stool or coffee table.

4. Design a Queen Anne side chair using the drake foot.

CHAPTER 9

THE CHIPPENDALE STYLE
1749–1779

HISTORICAL DATA AND GENERAL CHARACTERISTICS

The Chippendale style was the first to be identified by the name of its creator, rather than by the name of the reigning monarch who happened to be on the throne at the time. The eighteenth century is of the greatest importance to the lover of furniture. Few styles that were developed before the eighteenth century are practical for present-day use, as originally conceived; and no really great style has been developed since the close of that century. It was the golden age of furniture, and no style developed during that time is of greater importance than Chippendale's.

Thomas Chippendale is known as a great designer. What he really should be called is an adapter, for it was his ability in adapting and combining important features of other styles successfully, that won for him a distinction enjoyed by few designers. He adapted from French styles, principally from that of Louis XV; and from the Queen Anne style which preceded his own. Some of his motifs were adapted from Gothic sources, and he developed a Chinese Chippendale style, though neither of

these have remained popular, and are seldom copied.

By the foregoing we do not mean to convey the impression that Chippendale had no originality of his own. He was a versatile designer, a master wood carver, and a skilled cabinetmaker. Add to this his ability as a business man and you have a pretty good picture of Chippendale. What we do intend to convey is, that he was not a designer in the same sense of the word that Sheraton was. Despite this fact he developed a style, which for variety and richness has never been surpassed, and gave it something of himself that made it a distinctly British product.

Chippendale had learned his trade in his father's shop, and in 1727 they came to London to open a shop. In 1749 he opened a shop of his own, and four years later moved it to St. Martin's Lane, a more favorable location, which became a gathering place for the fashionable society of London. From this time on his success was assured, and he retained public favor and esteem until the time of his death. One of his greatest contributions, and one which helped him to earn the reputation which he rightfully enjoys, was the publication of his book,

The Gentleman and Cabinet-Maker's Director. His style is exemplified in this book, had a tremendous influence on much of the best mobiliary art from his day to our very own.

Chippendale was continually bringing out new designs to satisfy his discriminating clientele. There was not the tendency for duplication of design at that time, because duplication did not pay. His clients did not want pieces of furniture identical in every respect to those their friends possessed.

Chippendale's early furniture followed, rather closely, the structure of Queen Anne furniture. Later the structure of his furniture changed to the extent that he used straight lines more and curved lines less. This was a concession to the new taste introduced by the Brothers Adam, and it was the only concession he made to the new trends in design. His plainer furniture has stood the test of time best, being more esteemed today than those pieces which he considered his finest. Many of the latter designs were overdecorated with rococo ornament, or other elaborate carving influenced by the Louis XV style, for which Chippendale apparently had a great admiration.

The chief characteristics of the style are: (1) Cabriole legs with ball-and-claw feet. (2) Later in the period, straight legs, either carved or molded on outside faces. (3) Sturdy construction, sometimes a bit ponderous, and not always graceful or well proportioned. (4) No stretchers or underbracing on cabriole-legged pieces, but light, either straight flat, fret sawed, or carved stretchers on straight-legged pieces. (5) Carving, the chief and almost the only form of ornament. (6) A general absence of turning. (7) Carved chair backs that flared outward at the top, most of them similar in shape, and with ladderlike stretchers, or pierced splats joined directly to the seat stretcher. (8) Wide, upholstered seats for chairs. (9) Broken pediments for tall pieces; carved and remarkably rich in design. (10) Richly carved aprons and skirts, on tables, chairs, and cabinet furniture. (11) A Chinese style, having straight-lined construction, and carved with Chinese fretwork, or with members shaped like bamboo. (12) Mahogany, used as the principal and only suitable wood. (13) Pilasters, or quarter columns, used on the corners of case furniture. (14) Serpentine, bowed, or kettle-base construction on some of the richest pieces.

The cabriole leg is one of the chief identification marks of the style, being richly carved with acanthus leaves, or motifs adapted from the rococo. The feet were usually carved ball and claw, but occasionally a dolphin's head, or a richly carved scrolled foot was used. Straight legs were used mostly on his simpler furniture toward the end of the period. These were sometimes almost plain, except for a molding on the outside corner; but others were carved with Chinese fretwork, or a wider molding as in Figure 145.

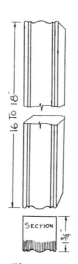

Fig. 145. Straight chair leg.

Carving, in low relief, was the chief form of ornament for the Chippendale style. It was, perhaps, at times, more ornate than good taste would permit today. Inlay was almost entirely absent from Chippendale pieces.

The construction was practically identical with that found on Queen Anne pieces. Lines and contour were somewhat improved by Chippendale, though he never entirely overcame a slight clumsiness. Some of his chair seats, for example, because of their generous width, gave chairs a rather square and somewhat clumsy appearance. Seat rails, or legs, were sometimes a bit too large in scale. Some highboys were extra broad, and aprons on them were occasionally too low, giving the short cab-

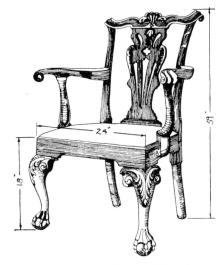

Fig. 146. Armchair with splat showing Gothic motif.

riole legs a bandy-legged aspect (See Figs. 10, 146 and 147).

Another fault for which Chippendale has been criticized, was the indiscriminate manner in which he sometimes mixed his motifs. Gothic, Renaissance,

classical, and oriental motifs were often found on the same piece of furniture (See Fig. 9). Despite these faults, however, he succeeded in producing pieces of merit, which have a charm that will last as long as fine furniture is appreciated. Many of his faults we can afford

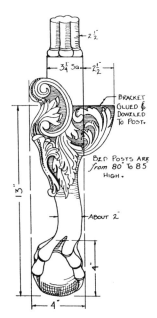

Fig. 147.
Richly carved foot
for four-poster bed.

to overlook, or at least we can avoid them in our own designs.

Chairs

Chippendale's genius is best exhibited in his chairs. These are sometimes too lavishly carved, but others are just as tastefully ornamented. In his early work he favored the cabriole leg and fiddle-shaped splats. In fact, the form of his early chairs followed those of Queen Anne very closely. The ball-and-claw foot, which almost conclusively identifies a piece as belonging to his style, is supposed to have originated in China.

He made use of many other Chinese motifs, such as the fretted, carved, or pierced legs and stretchers; fretted chair backs; and Chinese pagodalike tops for cabinets. He even made chairs in which the legs and stretchers were made to simulate bamboo, although so far as beauty was concerned, we consider these a complete failure, and they have not had continued popularity. For this reason we need pay little further attention to them.

Seats of chairs in the early part of the period were identical to those found on Queen Anne chairs. Later chairs were designed with nearly square seats. Except in the case of armchairs with upholstered backs, or wing chairs, the chairs

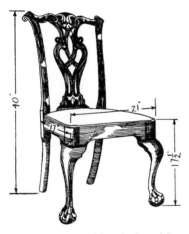

Fig. 148. Side chair with interlaced ribbon splat.

may be made for a slip seat, or the covering may be drawn over the side of the seat frame and tacked with brass-headed upholsterer's nails. The width of the seat, at the back, on these chairs is usually a little less than the depth of the seat. The front corners of the seat may be rounded, as shown in Figure 148. Seat stretchers are nearly always mor-

tised to the legs, and the tops of the front legs come to the top of the seat frame (See Figs. 12 and 148). The seat frame may be mitered at the front corners, however, and the tops of the legs are then fastened to the inside of the stretchers. In some cases the front stretcher may be shaped on the lower edge, into a flat arch as shown in Figure 146, or with cyma curves as shown in Figure 149. In the more ornate chairs

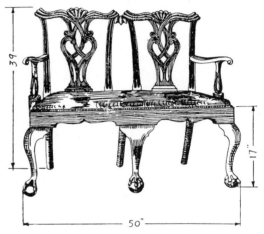

Fig. 149. Double chair settee or love seat.

these front stretchers were sometimes tastefully carved.

The back legs must be cut from a plank that is comparatively wide, and two inches or more thick, in order to give them the shape necessary for beauty and style. A chair leg, such as is shown in Figure 150 can barely be cut from a 2 by 5 in. plank, by placing a pattern for the side of the leg on the face of the plank, although two legs may be cut from a plank only a few inches wider. When the outward flare of the leg at the top is still more pronounced, the plank will have to be thicker. The top rail in Chippendale chair backs invariably caps

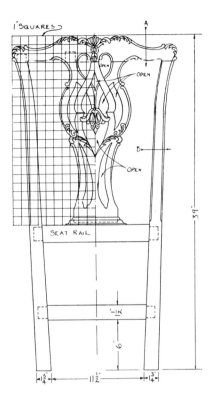

Fig. 150. Detail of interlaced
ribbon chair back.

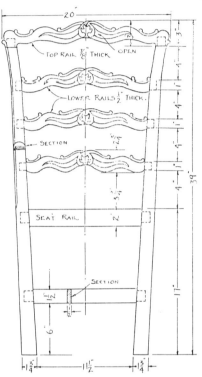

Fig. 151. Detail of back for
ladder-back chair.

in these chair backs are usually cut out before assembling the back.

The lower part of the back legs may be left square, especially on straight-legged chairs, so that stretchers may be

the legs. The back of the top rail should be rounded, and carefully shaped. The same holds true of the back of the legs from the seat to the place where they join the top rail (See Plate 25). Tenons are cut on the tops of the back legs, and fitted into mortises in the top rail (See Figs. 150 and 151). Sometimes, especially on fine chairs, the legs are carved as shown in cross section B, Plate 25.

In case there is a splat, it should be fastened with a tenon to the top rail, and in the same way to the seat rail. The back seat rail is made of mahogany and its top edge is raised and molded where the splat joins the rail, as shown in Figure 150. It is customary for the cabinetmaker to assemble the back and then carve it. The spaces marked "open,"

easily fastened to them. When there are no stretchers the legs may be rounded as shown in Figure 146. The stretchers under the seat are usually about $\frac{1}{2}$ in. thick, and should be joined to the legs with mortise and tenon. The medial stretcher should be joined to the side stretchers with dovetail joints (See Fig.

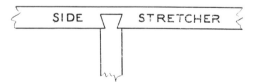

Fig. 152. Method of joining medial
stretcher to side stretchers.

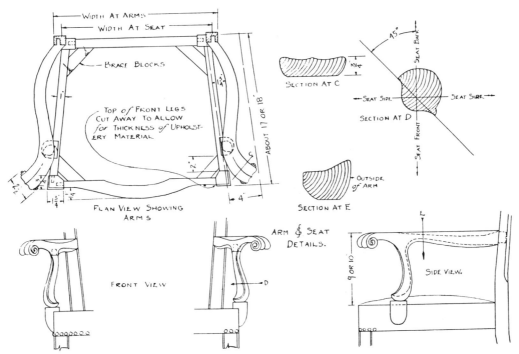

Fig. 153. Arm and seat details.

152). Side stretchers are usually from 4 to 6 in. from the floor, and flush with the outside of the legs. The medial stretcher should be fastened to the side stretchers about 6 to 8 in. from the front of the chair.

The characteristic Chippendale arm for these chairs is the type shown in Figure 153. However, arms like those shown in Figures 138 and 139, may be used, particularly on the earlier models. Arm support may be fastened to the seat stretchers by cutting long dovetails on the arm supports, and fastening them into corresponding slots in the stretchers.

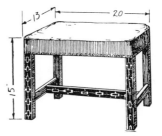

Fig. 155. Stool with Chinese fret legs and stretchers.

In the great armchairs, with upholstered backs, arms, as well as all other members, may be rather plain (See Fig. 154). The legs and arms may be carved with a raised Chinese fret, as in Figure 155; or if straight legs are used they may be molded as shown in Figure 145.

Fig. 154. Armchair with upholstered back.

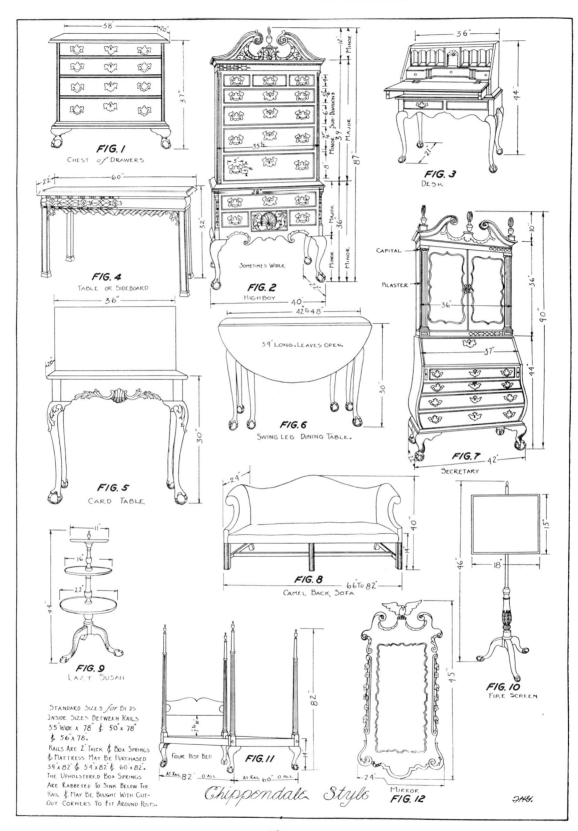

FIG. 1
CHEST of DRAWERS

FIG. 2
HIGHBOY

FIG. 3
DESK

FIG. 4
TABLE OR SIDEBOARD

FIG. 5
CARD TABLE

FIG. 6
SWING LEG DINING TABLE.

FIG. 7
SECRETARY

FIG. 8
CAMEL BACK SOFA

FIG. 9
LAZY SUSAN

FIG. 10
FIRE SCREEN

FIG. 11
FOUR POST BED

FIG. 12
MIRROR

STANDARD SIZES for BEDS
INSIDE SIZES BETWEEN RAILS
35 WIDE X 78 & 50 X 78
& 56 X 78.
RAILS ARE 2 THICK & BOX SPRINGS
& MATTRESS MAY BE PURCHASED
39 X 82 & 54 X 82 & 60 X 82.
THE UPHOLSTERED BOX SPRINGS
ARE RABBETED TO SINK BELOW THE
RAIL & MAY BE BOUGHT WITH CUT-
OUT CORNERS TO FIT AROUND POSTS.

Chippendale Style

Plate 22.

Upholstering materials for chairs in the Chippendale style were chiefly damasks and brocades of exquisite weave. Plain fabrics are also suitable (See Figs. 50, 53, and 54).

CHIPPENDALE FRETWORK BORDERS.

SETTEES

Settees may be made in the form of two or three chairs fastened together (See Figs. 13 and 149). The same things that have been said about chairs apply to settees as well. It may be well to add that the top stretcher in the settee back is usually made in one long piece, and caps the chair legs in the same way as on the chairs.

SOFAS

There were long and short sofas. Two different types are shown (See Figs. 156 and 157). Both types are comfortable and handsome. The construction and

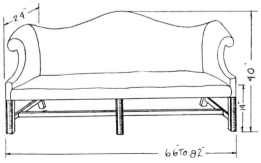

Fig. 156. Camel-back sofa.

ornament on these is essentially the same as on the chairs.

WING CHAIRS

Wing chairs, when correctly built, are wonderfully comfortable. They remain

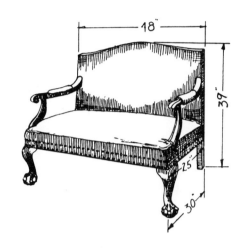

Fig. 157. Upholstered sofa.

very popular pieces of furniture today, and are the correct easy chair of the Chippendale style. The frame, so far as the seat and legs are concerned, differs very little from the ones in the chairs we have described. To design the rest of

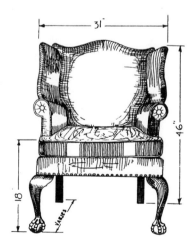

Fig. 158. Barrel-shaped wing chair.

FIG. 13

LADDER BACK SIDE CHAIR
THESE CHAIRS USUALLY
HAVE THE STRAIGHT FRONT
LEG.

FIG. 14

ARM CHAIR WITH SPLAT
SHOWING GOTHIC MOTIF.
NOTICE RICHLY CARVED KNEE.

FIG. 15

SIDE CHAIR WITH INTERLACED
RIBBON SPLAT.

FIG. 16

PLAIN CHIPPENDALE ARM CHAIR
WITH UPHOLSTERED BACK.

FIG. 17

DOUBLE CHAIR SETTEE OR LOVE SEAT.

FIG. 18

STOOL WITH BALL &
CLAW FEET.

The Chairs of
This Period Are
Exceedingly Rich
In Design. The
Variety Is Great &
The Construction
Is of A Sturdy
Character.

EQUAL—SEE RULE 8

FIG. 19

THREE BACK LADDER BACK SETTEE.

CUPIDS
BOW.

FIG. 21

BARREL SHAPED WING CHAIR.

FIG. 20

LOWBOY WITH SUNBURST CARVED
DRAWER.

FIG. 22

UPHOLSTERED SOFA

Chippendale Period

FIG. 23

STOOL WITH CHINESE FRET
LEGS & STRETCHERS.

Plate 23.

the chair, however, some additional information may be necessary.

The back legs should continue as one solid piece of wood to the top of the chair. If the back flares much at the top, a piece may be glued to the side of the leg to produce the shape desired (See Fig. 158). The upper crosspiece is also formed to conform to the shape desired. There should be a horizontal crosspiece between the back legs, several inches above the seat rail, to which the webbing

tacked there (See Fig. 159). Three quarter inches will be just enough to draw the cloth through without leaving an opening afterwards.

For the arms there must be a frame conforming to the shape desired in the finished chair. The front of the arm is usually cut from a glued-up block of softwood. For the chair shown in Figure 158, this is not difficult to make but for an arm like the one shown in Figure 159 this is a more difficult task. A pat-

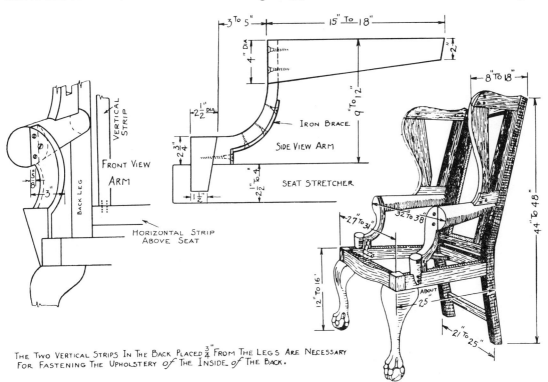

THE TWO VERTICAL STRIPS IN THE BACK PLACED ¾" FROM THE LEGS ARE NECESSARY FOR FASTENING THE UPHOLSTERY *of* THE INSIDE *of* THE BACK.

Fig. 159. Frame and details of a wing chair.

may be fastened when upholstering the chair. There should be two vertical strips about ¾ in. from each leg, fastened to the top rail, and to the crosspiece above the seat. These are placed there to fasten the covering found on the inside of the back, which must be drawn around to the back of the chair and

tern is first of all made for the side of the piece, and after it has been cut out, another pattern is made for the front, and it is cut out. The small vertical rolls on each side of the seat, are turned from blocks of wood, on the lathe. Where a firm round arm is desired, the arm is also turned from a block of softwood, in

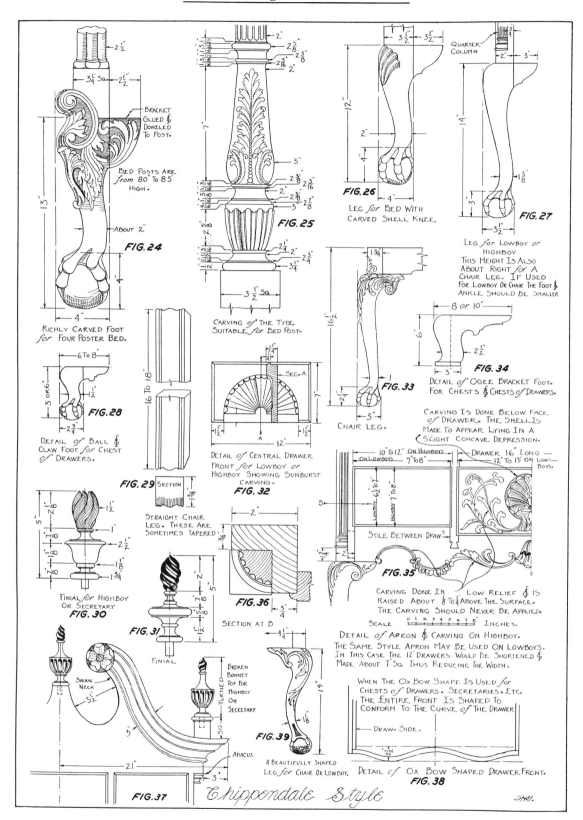

2½"

3¾" SQ. 2½"

BRACKET GLUED & DOWELED TO POST.

BED POSTS ARE *from* 80 TO 85 HIGH.

ABOUT 2"

13"

4"

4"

FIG.24

RICHLY CARVED FOOT *for* FOUR POSTER BED.

2"
2⅝"
2⅜"
2³⁄₁₆"
2"

7"

3"

2⅞" 2⅜"
2" 2⅛"
2⅜" 2⅜"
5"

FIG.25

3½" SQ.

2¼" 2"
2¾"
3¼"

CARVING *of* THE TYPE SUITABLE *for* BED POST.

3½" 3½"

QUARTER COLUMN

2" 3"

12"

2"

4"

FIG.26

LEG *for* BED WITH CARVED SHELL KNEE.

14"

1⅜"

3"

3½"

FIG.27

LEG *for* LOWBOY *or* HIGHBOY
THIS HEIGHT IS ALSO ABOUT RIGHT *for* A CHAIR LEG. IF USED *for* LOWBOY OR CHAIR THE FOOT & ANKLE SHOULD BE SMALLER

6 TO 8"

5 OR 6"
1½"

2¾"

FIG.28

DETAIL *of* BALL & CLAW FOOT *for* CHEST *of* DRAWERS.

16 TO 18"

¾"

SECTION

FIG.29

1¾"

SEC. A

¼"
1¼"

1½"   1½"

A

7"

12"

DETAIL *of* CENTRAL DRAWER FRONT *for* LOWBOY *or* HIGHBOY SHOWING SUNBURST CARVING.

FIG.32

16½"

2¼"
3"

FIG.33

CHAIR LEG.

8 OR 10"

6"

2½"

3"

FIG.34

DETAIL *of* OGEE BRACKET FOOT. *FOR* CHESTS & CHESTS *of* DRAWERS.

CARVING IS DONE BELOW FACE *of* DRAWER. THE SHELL IS MADE TO APPEAR LYING IN A SLIGHT CONCAVE DEPRESSION.

5"
2⅛"
1½"
1"
1"
1⅛"
7"
1⅛"
1¾"

FINIAL *for* HIGHBOY *OR* SECRETARY
FIG.30

2"
1½"
1"
2½"

5"
2"
1⅝"
1½"

FIG.31

FINIAL

2"
¾"

FIG.36

SECTION AT B

4¼"

STRAIGHT CHAIR LEG. THESE ARE SOMETIMES TAPERED.

10" TO 12" ON HIGHBOYS
ON LOWBOYS 7" TO 8"

Drawer 16" Long 12" TO 13" ON LOWBOYS

LOWBOY 6½ TO 7
HIGHBOY 7 TO 8

STILE BETWEEN DRAW

B

2½"

FIG.35

CARVING DONE IN LOW RELIEF & IS RAISED ABOUT ⅛ TO ¼ ABOVE THE SURFACE. THE CARVING SHOULD NEVER BE APPLIED.

SCALE ⌐0 1 2 3 4 5 6 7 8⌐ INCHES.

DETAIL *of* APRON & CARVING ON HIGHBOY.
THE SAME STYLE APRON MAY BE USED ON LOWBOYS. IN THIS CASE THE 12" DRAWERS WOULD BE SHORTENED & MADE ABOUT 7" SQ. THUS REDUCING THE WIDTH.

WHEN THE OX BOW SHAPE IS USED *for* CHESTS *of* DRAWERS, SECRETARIES, ETC. THE ENTIRE FRONT IS SHAPED TO CONFORM TO THE CURVE *of* THE DRAWER.

DRAW. SIDE.

DETAIL *of* OX BOW SHAPED DRAWER FRONT.
FIG.38

SWAN NECK
5½"

BROKEN BONNET TOP FOR HIGHBOY OR SECRETARY

SQ. TURNED

FIG.39

14"

1⅛"

A BEAUTIFULLY SHAPED LEG *for* CHAIR OR LOWBOY.

ABACUS

21"
3"

FIG.37

Chippendale Style

Plate 24.

the form of a roll, as shown in Figure 159. These are then fastened to the back legs, and the shaped pieces at the front of the chair are fastened to them with screws and iron braces. Iron braces should be placed on a wing-chair frame, wherever a joint can be made stronger thereby. Where a soft, padded arm is desired, only a 1 in. strip of wood, about as wide as the arm is to be thick, is used upon which to build the arm.

The wing frames now remain to be designed, and they must be made to the shape desired in the finished wings. A frame for the wing in Figure 158, consists of two pieces, band-sawed to the shape of the front edge, with horizontal crosspieces at the top and bottom. The horizontal webbing is tacked on first, giving the curve of the shaped pieces to the entire surface. These frames are fastened with screws and angle braces to the back legs and arms.

TABLES

Tables were made in great number and variety by Chippendale. The gate-leg table still continued popular, but swing-leg tables (Fig. 6, Plate 22), in many cases took their places. There were card tables, gaming tables, and many occasional tables. It has been said that Chippendale never designed sideboards, but he did design and build sideboard tables which were used for the same purpose.

SWING-LEG TABLES. These tables may have four or six legs. Six is the usual number, and if six are used, the aprons should be mortised and tenoned to four of them. The other two legs are fastened

in a like manner to a short apron that swings on a wooden hingelike arrangement called a finger joint (See Fig. 160). When there are only four legs, two are fastened to alternate corners of the table frame, and at the other two corners the aprons may be held together by corner blocks, which are fastened to the inside

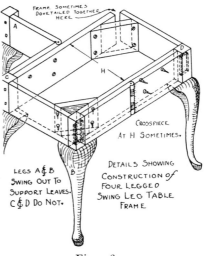

Fig. 160.

(See Fig. 160), or the aprons may be dovetailed together. The two swinging legs, which support the leaves, are hinged in the same way as on the six-leg table. They fit, when closed, flush with the face of the apron. These tables should have the cabriole legs with ball-and-claw feet, since straight legs on this type of table are not very interesting. The tables look best if they have oval tops, with rule joints where the leaves join the middle section. There may be drawers on the ends of the tables.

CARD TABLES. Card tables are light, and are made so that they can be placed against the wall when not in use. They may be made with a double top, half of which folds back and rests on the swing-

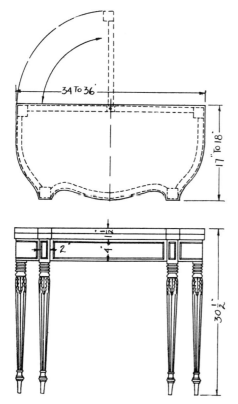

Fig. 161. Sheraton card table.

ing leg when the table is being used to **play cards, as in Figure 161.** When placed against the wall, this extra top

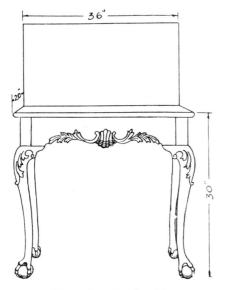

Fig. 162. Card table.

may be raised to a vertical position, and leaned against the wall (See Fig. 162).

Card tables may have cabriole legs or straight legs. It is often customary to tastefully carve the shaped aprons; and

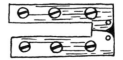

Fig. 163.
Brass hinges.

the knees if cabriole legs are used, since this type of table should be quite rich. The hinges, which should be of the kind that fold up like a jackknife, are fastened to the ends of the tops. They should be made of brass (See Fig. 163).

SIDEBOARD TABLES. A sideboard table is a long, narrow, rather high table, used as a sideboard. Chippendale sideboard tables are often richly veneered, and decorated with carved moldings. The aprons may be carved or fret-sawed, and if straight legs are used there may be brackets where the apron joins the legs

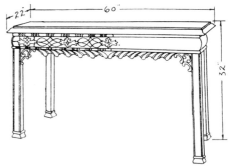

Fig. 164. Table or sideboard.
Chinese type with gadroons carved on lower edge of apron.

(See Fig. 164). Sideboard tables are from 32 to 40 in. high. They seldom have drawers in the Chippendale style.

PIECRUST TABLES. The tops of these range between 15 and 40 in. in diameter. The best tops are made from a single wide board, which should be quite thick. The upper surface of the board is "dished out," leaving a raised, carved, and molded edge, which is also shaped to a pattern greatly resembling a piecrust. This pattern is made of a series of

(A Wallace Nutting Reproduction)
Fig. 165. Chippendale piecrust table. One of the finest gems of a remarkable period.

arcs and cyma curves, and the effect is very rich (See Fig. 165). On English examples, these tops often had galleries made of brass, or of small wooden turned spindles, and a railing surmounting them. American designers never favored this type.

The top on these tables is supported by a crow's nest, consisting of four

turned spindles fastened to two square boards. One of these is a cap, and the other a base, between which the spindles are fastened with dowels. The cap board has dowels cut on two opposite ends. Holes are bored into the cleats, which are fastened with screws and glue, or sometimes with a running dovetail, across the grain, under the top, and into these holes the dowels are fitted. This provides a fulcrum, or hinge, whereby the top may be raised to a vertical position, and the table placed against the wall or in a corner when not in use. The crow's nest is fitted to the shaft of the

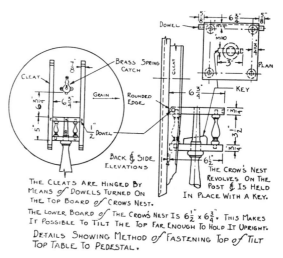

Fig. 166.

pedestal, so that it may be revolved (See detail, Fig. 166).

The feet, or to be more correct, the short legs, are fastened to the base of the shaft with wide dovetails. The dovetails are cut on the legs, and the mortises for the dovetails are cut on the bottom of the shaft (See Fig. 167). There are invariably three of these legs; no more. The ball-and-claw foot is usual, though a less pretentious serpent's-head foot

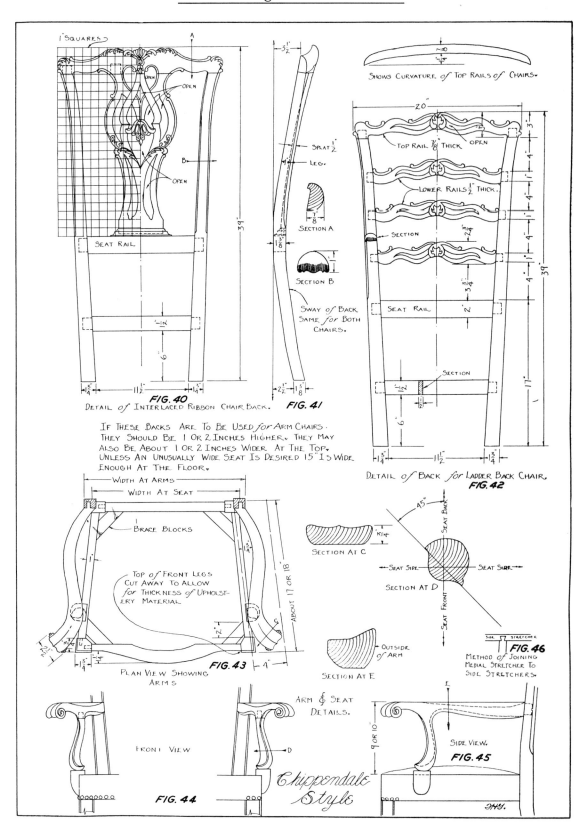

1" SQUARES

OPEN

OPEN

OPEN

SEAT RAIL

FIG. 40
DETAIL of INTERLACED RIBBON CHAIR BACK.

SPLAT 1½"
LEG.
SECTION A
SECTION B
SWAY of BACK SAME for BOTH CHAIRS.
FIG. 41

SHOWS CURVATURE of TOP RAILS of CHAIRS.

TOP RAIL ⅞" THICK   OPEN
LOWER RAILS 1½" THICK.
SECTION
SEAT RAIL
SECTION
DETAIL of BACK for LADDER BACK CHAIR.
FIG. 42

IF THESE BACKS ARE TO BE USED for ARM CHAIRS. THEY SHOULD BE 1 OR 2 INCHES HIGHER. THEY MAY ALSO BE ABOUT 1 OR 2 INCHES WIDER AT THE TOP. UNLESS AN UNUSUALLY WIDE SEAT IS DESIRED 15" IS WIDE ENOUGH AT THE FLOOR.

WIDTH AT ARMS
WIDTH AT SEAT
BRACE BLOCKS
TOP of FRONT LEGS CUT AWAY TO ALLOW for THICKNESS of UPHOLSTERY MATERIAL
ABOUT 17 OR 18
FIG. 43
PLAN VIEW SHOWING ARMS

SECTION AT C
SECTION AT E

ARM & SEAT DETAILS.

SEAT BACK
SEAT SIDE   SEAT SIDE
SECTION AT D
SEAT FRONT
OUTSIDE of ARM

SIDE STRETCHER
FIG. 46
METHOD of JOINING MEDIAL STRETCHER TO SIDE STRETCHERS.

FRONT VIEW
FIG. 44

9 OR 10
SIDE VIEW.
FIG. 45

Chippendale Style

Plate 25.

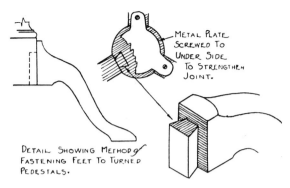

DETAIL SHOWING METHOD OF
FASTENING FEET TO TURNED
PEDESTALS.

Fig. 167.

may be used on simpler tables. The rat's ball-and-claw foot which is smaller, more slender and refined, may be used instead of the usual round foot, for the smaller tables (See Fig. 168).

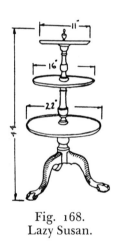

Fig. 168.
Lazy Susan.

DINING TABLES. Dining tables were made in sections. There should be at least three, while tables with as many as seven sections are known. Every alternate section is fastened to a pedestal, with a wide board to fit between. The pedestals are made similar to those found on piecrust tables; that is, they consist of a shaft with short cabriole legs fastened to them, but the pedestal is proportionately heavier. There is this difference, however, in the arrangement

of the legs on the shaft: because, on the two end sections, the pedestals are fastened close to the inside of the boards, the legs must not be angled too much in the direction of the adjacent section, or they will protrude enough to interfere with the legs on that section when there is no board between the sections (See

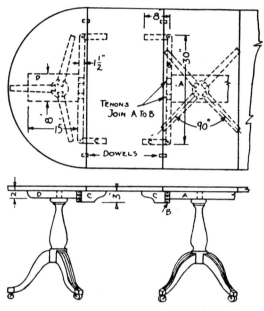

Fig. 169. Detail of Duncan Phyfe dining table in sections.

details, Fig. 169). The middle section has four legs fastened to the pedestal, while the pedestals of the end sections have only three legs. Furthermore, the

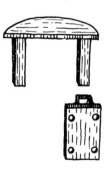

Fig. 170.
Brass keepers.

Plate 26. 2. Clock or highboy finial. 6. **Best** Chippendale type. 11. **Catch for piecrust table.**

legs on the end sections are not spaced equal distances apart.

The sections and boards, when joined together, are held in place by means of brass keepers, which are U-shaped clips, that slide into slots screwed to the undersides of the table boards (See Fig. 170).

LOWBOYS

The lowboys of the Chippendale style are the richest known. Some of the finest examples were made by American cabinetmakers in Philadelphia. The simple ones do not differ much from those found in the Queen Anne style. Their greatest difference lies in the fact that they have ball-and-claw feet, and are, almost without exception, made of mahogany instead of walnut. One other mark of distinction that should be men-

Fig. 172. Lowboy. Chippendale never designed a finer piece of furniture than this which is probably of American manufacture.

passes the beauty of the lowboy. A fine example of one is shown in Figure 172.

The lowboys always have cabriole legs, and in almost every case, ball-and-claw feet. The exception is an occasional one with dolphin feet, or scrolled feet. There should be a beautifully outlined apron on the simple, as well as on the richest, examples. On the rich examples the

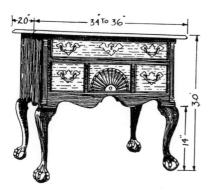

Fig. 171. Lowboy with sunburst carved drawer.

tioned is the use of quarter columns at the front corners (See Fig. 171).

The richest Chippendale lowboys are far superior to the simple ones. For excellence of designs, for beautiful and appropriate ornament, with its harmonious relation to outline and structure, no other piece in this style sur-

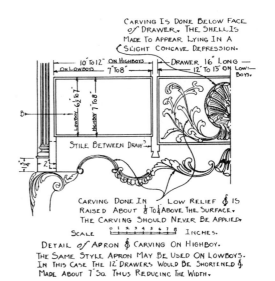

Fig. 173.

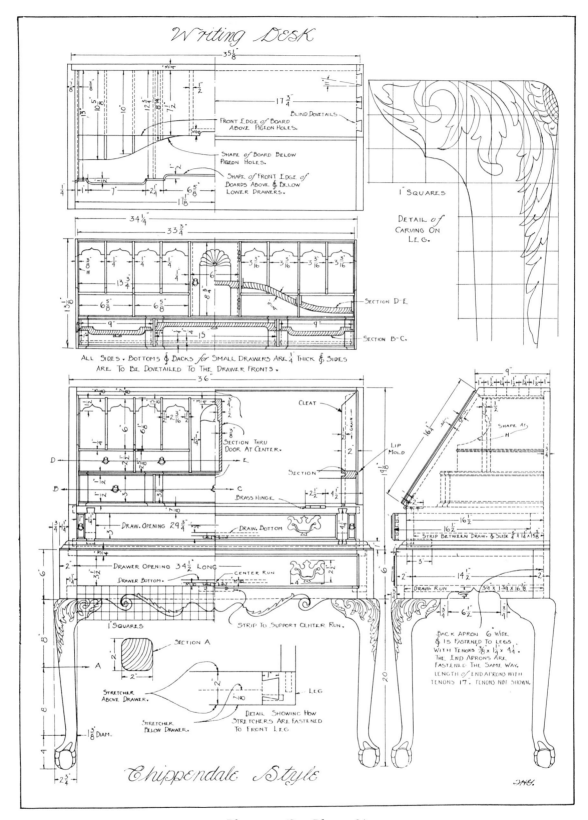

Writing Desk

Chippendale Style

Plate 27. (See Plate 28.)

lower edge of the apron should be tastefully carved. This carving should accentuate the beauty of the curves, and strengthen this outline, thus conforming to rules of design 29 and 31. The ornament should in all cases be carved from the solid board, never applied (See Fig. 173; also Chap. 4).

There are always four drawers on these lowboys — one long and three small drawers below it. The center drawer is usually deeper than the two that flank it. It is also the center of interest of the entire design. A beautifully carved seashell is generally the most important bit of ornament. The point of concentration in Figure 172, is at the flower. This illustrates the part of Rule 39, in which it is stated that on a horizontal panel, interest may be centered on the vertical center line, at a point below the center of the panel (See Chap. 4).

Lowboys designed in the Chippendale style should always have quarter columns. These are sometimes fluted as in Figure 173, and on richer pieces they are sometimes carved as in Figure 172. The quarter columns are set into niches about 1 in. square. These lowboys are never very large. Their length rarely exceeds 36 in., and their height varies from 26 to 30 in.

HIGHBOYS

Closely related to the lowboy, and correspondingly rich in design, are the highboys of the period. The bases of these vary but little in general appearance from the lowboys. They are, in fact, lowboys on a larger scale. Lowboys are

seldom 30 inches high, while highboy bases are seldom that low. These bases are always longer than lowboys. Occasionally a squat highboy base is found.

The upper section, which is a chest of drawers, fits inside a molding fastened to the highboy base. This upper section has a number of long drawers — a deep one below and more shallow ones above. These should be planned

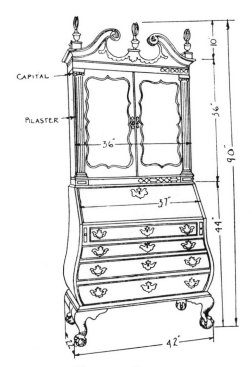

Fig. 174. Secretary.

according to design Rule 5a. At the top of the highboy there may be several smaller drawers. If there are three of these small drawers, the middle one may be a duplicate of the carved drawer in the lower section.

The broken pediment, on a highboy of this type, may be richly ornamented, so long as the scheme is harmonious with the primary mass itself (See Rules 30, 31, and 31a). Sometimes the pediment is

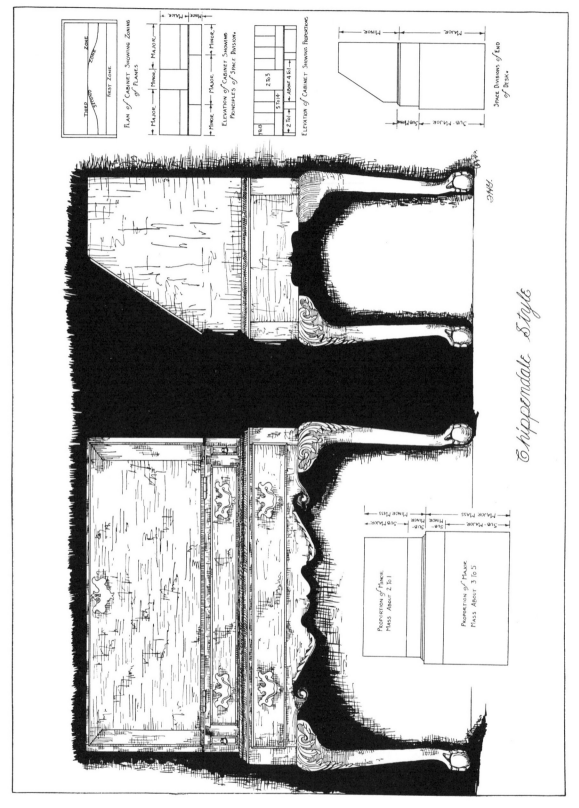

Chippendale Style

Plate 28. (See Plate 27.)

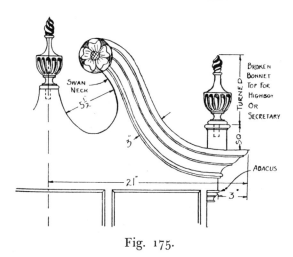

Fig. 175.

carved as in Figure 174, or it may be fretted as in Figure 9. Others are more plain as in the detail, shown in Figure 175. The decoration may even include a carved frieze dividing the pediment from the drawers below it (See Fig. 9). The upper section should have quarter columns (See details of construction in Fig. 176).

CHESTS OF DRAWERS

The chests of drawers that Chippendale designed were finer than any that had been designed previously. They did not, however, excel the beautiful pieces designed by Hepplewhite and Sheraton. Besides straight lines, characteristic of all earlier construction, he introduced the sweeping curve in his frame, as well as in ornament. Thus we find swellfronts, in which the front of the frame is a long, sweeping curve. The ox-bow front, another type, had two convex curves with a concave curve between them (See Fig. 177). The so-called kettle-base was a third type (See Fig. 174).

There can be little doubt that the designs of these latter pieces were inspired

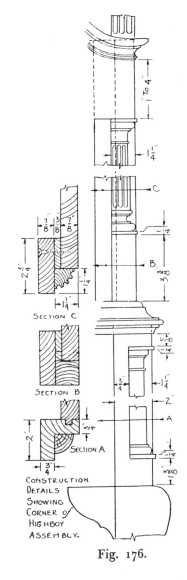

Fig. 176.

by French models. Chippendale usually made them look well. Some of the French designs were apt to be bulged

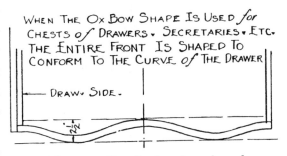

Fig. 177. Detail of ox-bow-shaped drawer front.

rather than bowed, and some of them had a pot-bellied appearance. This undesirable effect should be guarded against when working in the Chippendale style (See Rule 29). The curvalinear structures are almost invariably veneered.

Some of these chests of drawers had ball-and-claw feet. Others had plain or

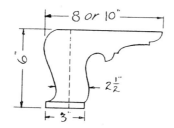

Fig. 178. Detail of ogee bracket foot for chests and chests of drawers.

carved, ogee bracket feet as shown in Figure 178. The carved ones had an acanthus leaf design on the corner of the foot. Quarter columns may be incorporated in the design of a chest of drawers in this style. For suitable drawer pulls see Plate 26.

DESKS

Desks to be used in the home may be of the type shown in Figure 17. A desk similar to this has been selected as a representative piece with which to illustrate the type of design characteristic of the style. From the Chippendale period on, straight-fronted cabinet desks began to be replaced by slant-top desks. The one shown in Plates 27 and 28 is of this kind. The one shown in the frontispiece as well as the one shown in Figure 46 was built from the plans shown in Plate

28. It is a light, graceful, and very interesting piece of furniture.

The cabriole legs are tastefully carved with acanthus leaves. The knees on back legs are sometimes left without carving on desks of this kind, but carving adds so much to the beauty of the piece, and was therefore added on the desks built by the author. On Plate 28 it is possible to compare legs that have this ornament, with others that do not have it. It shows very effectively how much more attractive ornament of this kind can make a modeled surface, giving it emphasis and added elegance. It is a practical illustration of Rules 41 and 42.

The slant front is covered with a lid, which when lowered, forms the writing surface. The lid has cleats, tongued and grooved to each end of it, for added strength and finish. There is a molded lip on three edges of the lid which protrudes ¼ in. and which supports the lid when closed. When let down the lid is supported by two slides, which may be pulled out. These are molded around the edges at the front, but the molding has no protruding lip. The slides are guided by the same runs as the drawer. In order to prevent them from being pulled out too far, small dowels are glued into holes bored in the back ends of the slides.

The top board is fastened to the ends of the desk with large blind dovetails. This prevents the frame from spreading.

The cabinet on the inside of the desk is designed so that it may be made up as a separate unit, and then slipped into place when completed. The space divisions are unusually well planned, and the cabinet is exceedingly handsome. All the vertical partitions between the pigeonholes are shaped to a handsome scotia curve on the front edges, with the exception of the two next to the door. These must be straightedged. The shapes of the horizontal partitions are shown on the plan view, as are also the shapes of the small drawers. Cross-section views show the exact plan of the drawer shapes on the drawing of the cabinet. All drawer sides are dovetailed to the drawer fronts, as they always should be on a fine design of this type.

On Plate 28 are several analyses of the principles of design involved. Since this is the most difficult design problem given in this book, it will be well worth while to study it carefully. Not only are the space divisions interestingly divided, but a new element of design, not before treated, enters into the solution of this problem. Besides the ordinary divisions of space treated under Rules 1 to 11*a,* this one involves the use of a series of receding planes, thus giving additional interest to the problem. In architecture this is known as zoning, and since no better term suggests itself, this will do as well as any. This zoning involves the use of curved as well as straight planes, in the design of the cabinet. No definite rules for zoning of areas is given, since this is a problem the solution of which must rest with the judgment of the designer. It opens up an interesting field for experiment.

SECRETARIES

Secretaries combine the functions of a desk, a chest of drawers, and a book-case. Originally the upper section on secretaries was not used for books, but was divided off in the same manner as the cabinet of a desk — into pigeonholes and small drawers. Later, however, due to the fact that more books found their way into the home, this space was utilized for books. Secretaries in this style should always have a broken pediment.

MIRRORS

The mirror frames of the Chippendale style range from the small, simple looking glasses with sawed-out tops and bottoms, to the ornately carved and gilded rococo pieces. One type is illustrated in Figure 42, but the variety is great. A mirror in this style may be given an architectural treatment by designing it with a pediment. Others may be carved in rococo ornament.

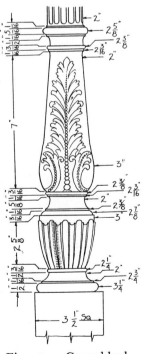

Fig. 179. Carved bed posts.

BEDS

The beds of the Chippendale style became simpler and lighter than any in preceding styles. The finest ones are those sometimes known as field beds. These had tall posts and a tester hung with a canopy. Originally this canopy was used to keep off the drafts or for privacy, but at present its purpose is merely for decoration. Instead of curtains a corded mesh or some other light fabric is used, primarily for the effect, rather than for any practical use. The posts of these beds were designed in varying degrees of richness. Figures 147 and 179 show details of posts and feet. The ball-and-claw design was incorporated into this as well as other designs. It is interesting to note that during this time headposts often were not carved, or at least not as fully as footposts. The draperies were intended to completely hide the headposts, and so it was thought unnecessary to expend money in enriching them. Beds in this style, as in all others, should be designed to provide for box springs.

QUESTIONS FOR REVIEW

1. What was unique about the Chippendale style with reference to its origin when compared to former styles?

2. To what style was the structure of Chippendale's early work similar?

3. Name five characteristics commonly identified with furniture of the Chippendale style.

4. What were a few of the original sources from which Chippendale adapted the motifs for his designs?

5. What criticism may be made regarding the scale of Chippendale furniture?

6. Was the construction of Chippendale furniture sound? Give two reasons to prove your answer.

7. What was the chief form of ornament used by Chippendale to enrich his pieces?

8. Describe the construction of Chippendale's early chairs; late chairs.

9. What may be said concerning his Gothic and Chinese motifs?

10. What factors must be taken into particular account when designing a Chippendale chair back?

11. Did Chippendale use a great deal of underbracing? Would the style, taken as a whole, be considered a heavy or a light style?

12. Name several other pieces made by Chippendale which were similar in construction to his chairs.

13. Describe the construction of a wing-chair frame.

14. Describe the construction of the following types of tables: swing-leg, pie-crust, and dining tables.

15. Name at least two points of superiority of Chippendale lowboys over those of other styles.

16. What is the chief point of difference between a lowboy and a highboy base?

17. Describe the design and construction of a Chippendale chest of drawers.

18. Describe one or more of the following types of construction: kettle-base, ox-bow, serpentine.

19. Describe three kinds of desks designed by Chippendale.

20. Was Chippendale's style influenced in any manner whatever by the new type of design introduced by the Brothers Adam?

21. What may be said regarding Chippendale's mirror frames?

Chippendale wing chair expressing elegance and comfort.

22. Describe a characteristic bed of the Chippendale style.

23. Compare Chippendale design, with special reference to superiority, as exemplified by his furniture, with that of the Queen Anne style; with Sheraton's style.

SUGGESTED PROBLEMS

1. Design a card table in the Chippendale style, having cabriole legs and a carved apron.

2. Design an entire Chippendale living or bedroom suite.

3. Design a Chippendale secretary with an ox-bow front.

4. Design a Chippendale mirror frame rich enough to go with the lowboy shown in Figure 172.

5. Design a magazine rack in the Chippendale style.

6. Design a radio cabinet in the Chippendale style.

CHAPTER 10

THE HEPPLEWHITE STYLE
1770–1790

HISTORICAL DATA AND GENERAL CHARACTERISTICS

George Hepplewhite was the originator of a style that ranks with that of Chippendale — a style so meritorious that it remains to this day a fitting monument to the gentleman cabinetmaker who brought it into being. Little is known of his life, and little need be known, other than that he was one of the four greatest designers of furniture; and the first one to give the world a style having consistent refinements of line, of proportion, and of scale. At the same time he did not lose sight of utility requirements, nor of practical structural qualities.

Hepplewhite conducted a shop in London, and he achieved a reputation of sufficient prominence to gain as his client the Prince of Wales himself. He also executed important commissions for his contemporary designers, the Brothers Adam. It is thought by students of furniture history that he was influenced to a considerable extent by the work of the Brothers Adam, because of the great similarity of the two styles. Be that as it may, his style marks an almost complete revolution of current mobilary art from that developed by Chippendale, and others up to his time.

After his death in 1786, his wife carried on his business, and published several books of designs which had been drawn presumably by himself, or under his direct supervision. These designs were of so worthy a character that they were widely copied by other cabinetmakers, and they form the basis for a style in which utility is charmingly blended with refinement and elegance.

The pieces in the Hepplewhite style are remarkable for their clean-cut, simple outlines, their slender but well-proportioned members, and the good taste of their ornament. It has been said that Hepplewhite was an exponent of curved lines, while Sheraton advocated the straight line on most of his structures. While this may be true to a certain extent, so far as the plan view of Hepplewhite's pieces are concerned; in elevation the tendency was to use straight lines almost exclusively. Hepplewhite did use curved lines on sofa backs, for the feet of some of his cabinets, and on all of his chair backs. Besides this he sometimes imitated Louis XV designs, thus developing an English version of a style that was distinctly French in feeling (See Plate 32). Taken as a whole, however, it is safe to say that Hepplewhite furniture is predominantly straight lined, as is clearly shown by the pieces in Plate 29. His proportions, in most cases, were good.

The chief characteristics of the style are: (1) Straight, slender legs with spade feet, these being tapered; or tapered legs without spade feet. Legs were sometimes turned and reeded, but square tapered legs are typical. (2) Slender, slightly curved, French bracket feet for chests of drawers and cabinets (See Fig. 35). (3) Shield backs, oval backs, or hoop backs for chairs. (4) Seats of chairs shaped somewhat like a shield, swelled at the front, but with a less pronounced swell than that found at the top of the shield back. (5) Chairs well braced beneath the seats with straight rectangular stretchers. (6) Veneered fronts for cabinets, sideboards, and other important pieces of cabinet furniture. (7) Painted ornament predominating, with inlaid and carved ornament in second and third places respectively. Painted ornament was used on all types of pieces. Inlay sometimes took the place of painted ornament, though this form of ornament was more often favored by Sheraton than Hepplewhite. Carving was used mostly on chair backs, where it was extremely delicate and refined in character. (8) There are to be found in this style, a large number of small table designs with oval, or otherwise shaped, tops. (9) Gently outward-swelling fronts for many pieces of cabinet furniture, chair seats, table fronts, sofa seats, etc. (10) Veneered panels, usually rectangular in shape, as shown in Figures 35 and 180. (11) Beautiful moldings, greatly reduced in scale from

those found in former styles. (12) Mahogany used as the principal cabinet wood. Satinwood, and other valuable woods were used mostly for veneering purposes, but occasionally solid. (13)

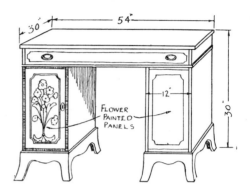

Fig. 180. Flat-top knee-hole desk.

Classic ornament, similar to that used by the Brothers Adam, was greatly favored by Hepplewhite.

CHAIRS

The chairs in this style may be divided into four main groups. These are: the shield backs, Figures 181 and 182, the oval backs, Figure 22, the hoop back (round), and the type popularly known

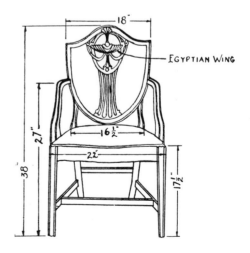

Fig. 181. Shield-back armchair.

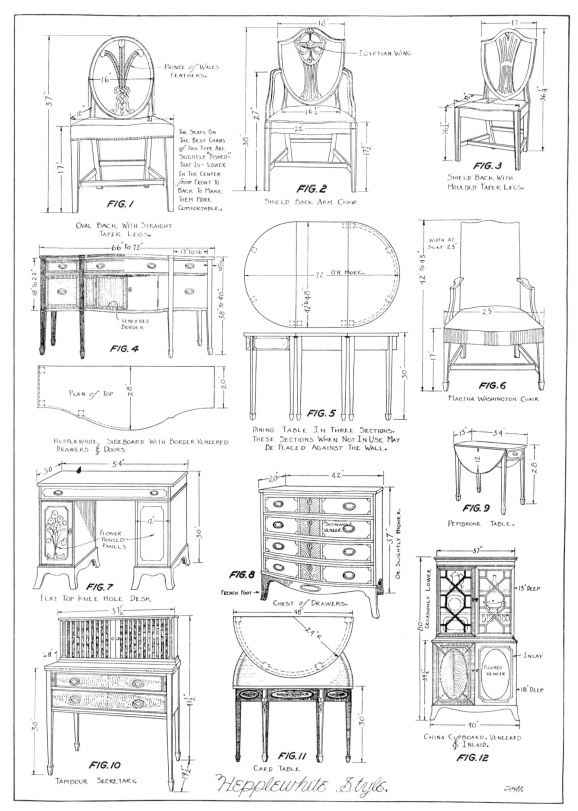

Plate 29.

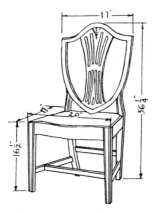

Fig. 182. Shield back with molded taper legs.

upper part of them forming the sides of the shield, as shown in Figure 184. This method of construction is better than that sometimes found, wherein the shield is made as a separate unit, and then fastened to the back legs which end a short distance above the seat. A leg like the one shown in Figure 184, may be made from a plank about 2 in. thick, by laying out the shape for the front of the leg on the edge of the plank. Since the back legs are sometimes more boldly curved, it may be necessary to cut them

to us as the Martha Washington arm-chair, Figure 183. Of these the shield back is the most typical. Figure 67 shows a very beautiful shield-back chair. The shields on these are essentially alike, regardless of the type of ornament with which they are enriched. Some of the backs are straight on the plan view, while the better ones are shaped with a concave curve to make them more comfortable.

Back legs on shield-back chairs should be continued to the top of the chair, the

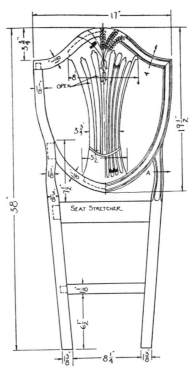

Fig. 184. Detail of wheat-sheaf back.

from a plank that is slightly thicker than 2 in. This is a matter that the designer will have to take into consideration when designing a chair of this type.

The shape and construction of the chair from the seat to the floor is prac-

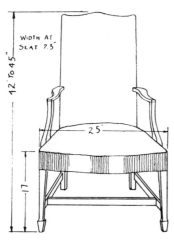

Fig. 183.
Martha Washington chair.

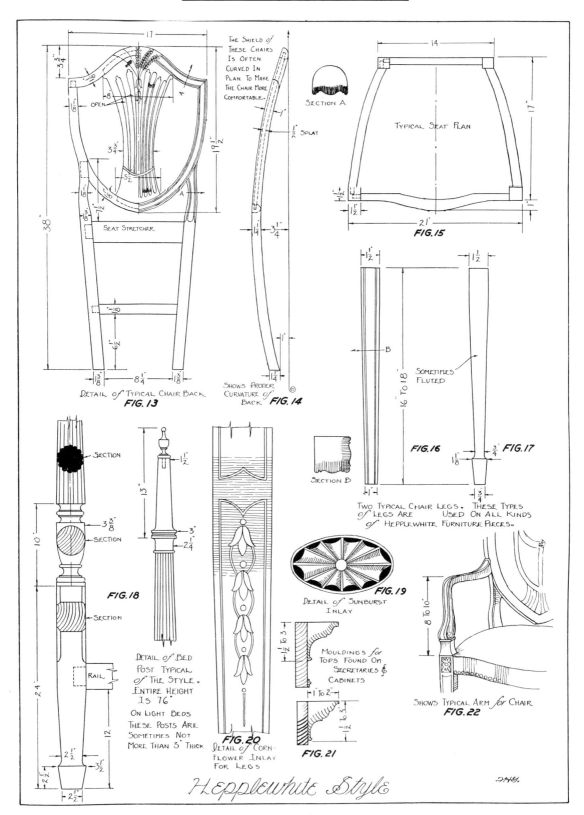

THE SHIELD of THESE CHAIRS IS OFTEN CURVED IN PLAN TO MAKE THE CHAIR MORE COMFORTABLE.

SECTION A

SPLAT

DETAIL of TYPICAL CHAIR BACK
FIG. 13

SHOWS PROPER CURVATURE of BACK **FIG. 14**

TYPICAL SEAT PLAN

FIG. 15

SECTION B

SOMETIMES FLUTED

16 TO 18

FIG. 16   **FIG. 17**

TWO TYPICAL CHAIR LEGS. THESE TYPES of LEGS ARE USED ON ALL KINDS of HEPPLEWHITE FURNITURE PIECES.

SECTION

SECTION

SECTION

RAIL

FIG. 18

DETAIL of BED POST TYPICAL of THE STYLE. ENTIRE HEIGHT IS 76".

ON LIGHT BEDS THESE POSTS ARE SOMETIMES NOT MORE THAN 3" THICK

FIG. 20
DETAIL of CORN-FLOWER INLAY FOR LEGS

DETAIL of SUNBURST INLAY
FIG. 19

MOULDINGS for TOPS FOUND ON SECRETARIES & CABINETS

FIG. 21

SHOWS TYPICAL ARM for CHAIR
FIG. 22

Hepplewhite Style

Plate 30.

tically the same as that found on Chippendale chairs, except that some of the members are often lighter. Occasionally the back legs are brought closer together at the floor than on Chippendale chairs. This is a natural result brought about by the shape of the back. Hepplewhite chairs should always be light and dainty. By making a careful study of the various details on Plate 30, the designer may gain a fairly accurate idea of proportions, style, and construction.

The oval backs differ from the shield backs, in that it is more practical to make the oval separately, and join it to the back legs with tenons above the seat. These backs are, therefore, likely to be weak, making this a less practical design than the shield back. If a very thick plank is available, the legs may be continued to the top of the chair, or nearly so, as on the shield backs; but this method will be very wasteful of stock. When arms are introduced, they help materially to strengthen a chair back of this kind. Hepplewhite chair backs are at the present time often made of laminated stock to insure greater durability. The rules that should be particularly observed when designing chair backs in this style are: 20, 29, 29*a*, 34*a*, 35*a*, 38, and 40.

Three types of splats for Hepplewhite backs are shown, all of which are typical. There are many variations of these and other designs. Some of them have for their ornament, classical urns, swags of flowers, the honeysuckle, carved drapery, etc. Many of these motifs are shown on Plate 41. The Prince of Wales feathers, wheat ears, and painted backs, are often

found. Altogether, chairs in this style offer ample opportunities to the designer for individuality.

The Martha Washington chair is so similar to the Chippendale type shown in Figure 154, that little more need be said regarding it, save that in this style it is a lighter chair.

TABLES

Tables designed in the Hepplewhite style should be distinguished for their tastefulness, simplicity, and clean-cut lines. Dining tables may be made in sections and are usually of the type shown in Figure 185. These sections are held together by means of brass "keepers" shown in Figure 170. The aprons should

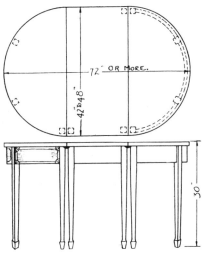

Fig. 185. Dining table in three sections.

be mortised and tenoned to the legs. The veneering is done on a core stock of well-seasoned softwood such as pine or chestnut. Aprons on Hepplewhite tables are nearly always veneered, and often inlaid. The legs may be inlaid as shown in Figure 186. Other designs of inlay may be employed, but variations of the type shown seem to have enjoyed the greatest favor.

Card-table tops were usually semicircular, or semioval in plan (See Fig. 187). Card tables are excellent subjects for decoration with handsome veneers and beautiful inlays. The tops may be painted. These and other card tables of this type, designed in any Georgian style, may be made so that one of the rear legs may be swung back on a short apron to support the top, when the table is being used to play cards. Others

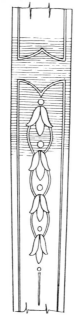

Fig. 186. Detail of cornflower inlay for legs.

have an extra leg at the back for this purpose, there being five legs in all, and the odd one usually found beside the left rear leg when folded. When not in use, the tables form a decorative element if the top is raised to a vertical position and placed against the wall. Hepplewhite also designed card tables with serpentine

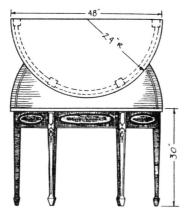

Fig. 187. Card table.

fronts like the one shown in Figure 161. For suggestions to paint or inlay a top of this type see Figure 188.

Another beautiful table commonly designed in the Hepplewhite style is the

Fig. 188. Suggestion for design of inlaid table top.

dainty Pembroke. This is a small, light table, having two drop leaves (See Plate 32). These tables may be designed with oval tops, but serpentine tops are more beautiful. Since the table that has been designed for this style is a Pembroke, a careful study of it will acquaint the student, not only with its merits, but also with many important characteristics of the style (See Plate 31). Pembroke tables are sometimes made even smaller than the example shown. The tables are, as a general rule, made of mahogany, veneered with rare woods of various colors, such as sycamore, rosewood, ebony, tulipwood, curly maple, satinwood, amboyna, and others. Others are painted with leaves, flower motifs, wreaths, and the like. Legs, aprons, and tops may be inlaid or painted.

Attention should be called to several features that are typical of Hepplewhite, and are to be found on this table. The shape of the top is one of these, with its swell at the center and the distinctive corners. Another is the swelled table ends and drawer front, veneered with figured wood. The third is the manner in which the legs are inlaid, this ornament being especially suitable to the style. These features are all to be found in one form or another on various pieces in the style.

The lowboy of former styles was replaced by the dressing table in this style. It assumed forms similar to tables used for the same purpose today. Hepplewhite dressing tables were usually designed with swelled fronts, and as a general rule, with one long drawer and several smaller ones below it. Drawers in these tables often had small compartments for powders and toilet articles. The tables are very light and dainty, and have slender tapered legs. The apron under the long drawer is arched to give knee room, and the smaller drawers are on each side of this arch. Drawer fronts are almost invariably veneered, and sometimes inlaid as well. Mirror frames for Hepplewhite dressing tables were often shaped like a shield, resembling the chair backs in this respect. Some were fastened to the tables, while others were hung above them on the wall.

CHESTS OF DRAWERS

Figure 35 shows a typical chest of drawers designed in the Hepplewhite style. The gently swelled front is veneered, and inlaid with sunbursts and border inlays. The drawer fronts are veneered with figured mahogany in the central portions and with satinwood on the end panels. The legs are the slender French bracket type. These flare out slightly at the floor. With slight variations this is the general method of designing Hepplewhite chests of drawers. Veneered panels on Hepplewhite pieces

Fig. 190. Hepplewhite sideboard table, which is a masterpiece illustrating some of the finest ideals of the style.

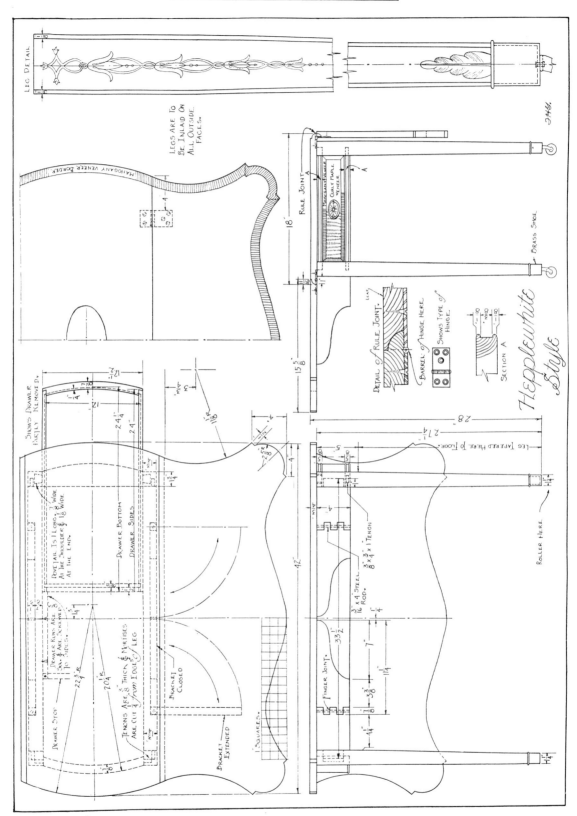

Plate 31. (See Plate 32.)

were usually rectangular, while Sheraton often used ovals instead.

SIDEBOARDS

Sideboards are very important articles in the Hepplewhite style. The pieces made for dining purposes are among the finest in the entire style, and sideboards are among the most important pieces in the style. They may be made in many different designs. A typical sideboard is illustrated in Figure 189, but by comparing it with the one shown in Figure 190, the great variation that is possible

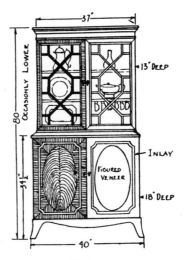

Fig. 191. China cupboard veneered and inlaid.

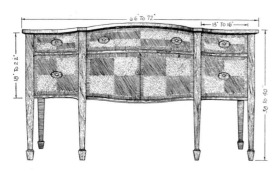

Fig. 189. Hepplewhite sideboard with border veneered drawers and doors.

will at once become evident. The latter is a piece of rare beauty. It is more of a sideboard table than a sideboard, but it has drawers, and therefore should be classed as a sideboard. The proportions, are excellent. Any designer will do well to use it as a mark to shoot at. A design, to surpass it, will have to be a masterpiece indeed.

CHINA CABINETS

China cabinets had come into their own by this time. Figure 191 illustrates a good one. The treatment of the glazed doors is noteworthy. It has been claimed

that on American-made pieces of this kind thirteen panes were used to represent the thirteen original colonies. Whether this be true or not the author does not know, but fifteen and more are often found. The design seems to have been popular with Hepplewhite and Sheraton. Sheraton's cabinets were usually higher, giving the effect of greater

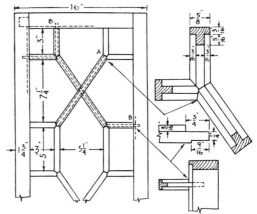

DETAILS OF CONSTRUCTION OF GLAZED DOOR OF THE TYPE USED ON SHERATON & HEPPLEWHITE CABINETS & SECRETARIES.

THE JOINT AT A IS MERELY A CAREFULLY FITTED & GLUED BUTT JOINT. AT B THERE IS THE USUAL MORTISE & TENON. THIS TYPE OF CONSTRUCTION IS SUFFICIENTLY RIGID TO MEET ALL REQUIREMENTS ESPECIALLY AFTER GLAZING.

Fig. 192.

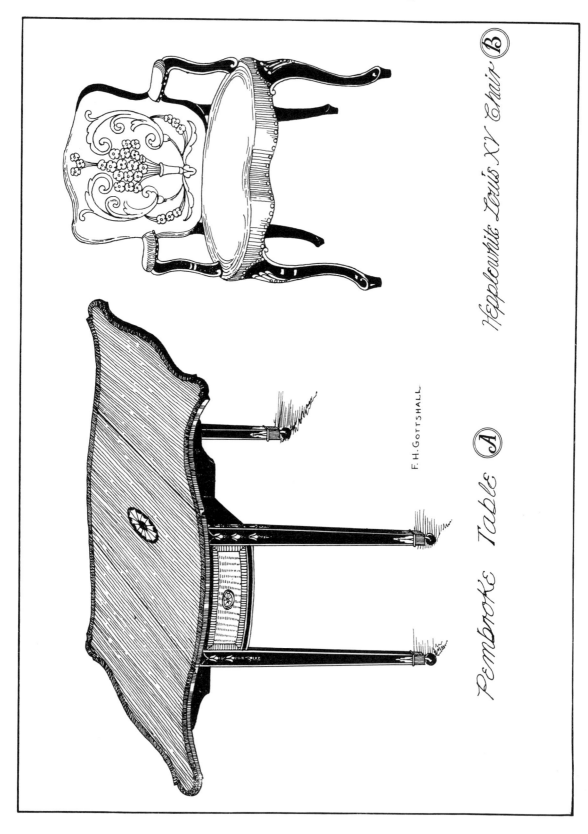

Pembroke Table Ⓐ

Hepplewhite Louis XV Chair Ⓑ

F. H. Gottshall.

Plate 32. (See Plate 31.)

slenderness than Hepplewhite's. The fitting of the pieces into such a door is a matter of interest to the designer. For details of construction see Figure 192. The doors on the lower section of these cabinets are veneered. Special attention is called to the fact that moldings on pieces of this kind are fine in scale, and them to a piece of canvas. They are opened by sliding them back in grooves or tracks, which have been cut into the boards above and below them (See details of construction in Fig. 193). Where the track turns the corner it is curved, so the sticks may turn the corner freely and easily. These secretaries are often beau-

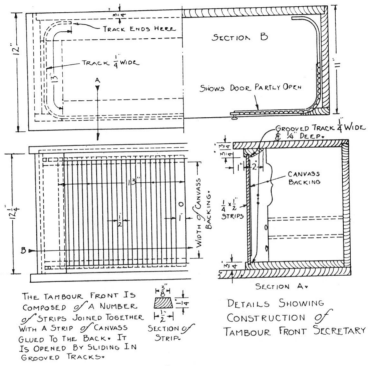

Fig. 193.

not nearly as prominent a feature as on highboys and tall pieces of earlier styles.

Tambour Secretaries

Secretaries built by Hepplewhite were often of the tambour type. They get their name from the sliding panels that close up the desk part of the piece. These are made of a series of narrow strips arranged vertically in a row, and joined together on the inside by gluing

tifully veneered and inlaid. They should have slender tapered legs, with or without spade feet. Sometimes they are designed with a cabinet above the desk, similar to the upper part of the china cabinet. This is used for books.

Beds

Beds are mostly of the high poster type. A good post is shown in Figure 194. Others had spiraled garlands carved on the posts. Little more need be said about them than has been said of Chippendale beds of a similar type. Testers were usually arched on the side and sometimes on all four sides of the bed.

QUESTIONS FOR REVIEW

1. What was Hepplewhite's greatest contribution to the field of furniture design?

2. What general type of construction did Hepplewhite favor for his style?

3. Name at least three distinctive features by which Hepplewhite pieces may be identified.

4. What methods of enrichment did Hepplewhite favor?

5. Name the chief source of ornament for Hepplewhite furniture.

6. Name the important motifs used consistently to enrich Hepplewhite furniture.

7. Describe the construction of a Hepplewhite shield-back chair; oval back.

8. What may be said concerning the scale of Hepplewhite furniture?

9. Describe the construction, the ornament, and uses of a Pembroke table.

10. Describe the construction and ornament of a typical Hepplewhite card table.

11. Were Hepplewhite chests of drawers an improvement over Chippendale pieces of a similar nature? If you think so, enumerate points of superiority.

12. Describe the construction and types of ornament commonly found on Hepplewhite sideboards.

13. What principles of design are in-volved in designing a sideboard of this style?

14. Give a description of a typical Hepplewhite china cabinet. How does one compare with similar pieces in the Sheraton style?

15. Describe the construction of the sliding panels in a tambour secretary.

16. Describe the types of carving found on posts of Hepplewhite four-poster beds.

SUGGESTED PROBLEMS

1. Design a Hepplewhite dressing table, mirror frame, and dressing-table bench. The dressing table may be ve-

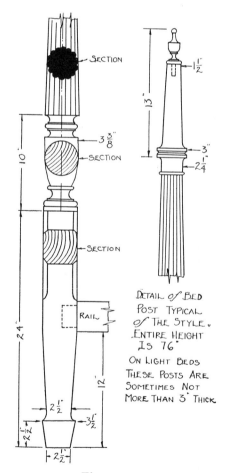

Fig. 194.

neered with satinwood, curly maple, or some similar material; or it may be painted with delicate floral sprays, birds, etc.

2. Design a small Hepplewhite dressing mirror to be placed upon a chest of drawers.

3. Design a Hepplewhite console group, using painted ornament for the design.

CHAPTER 11

THE SHERATON STYLE
1790–1806

HISTORICAL DATA AND GENERAL CHARACTERISTICS

Thomas Sheraton was the last of the great English designers and cabinet-makers. He was born poor, and his life was one of continuous struggle and hardships. Unlike the other three great English designers — Chippendale, Hepplewhite, and Robert Adam — Sheraton was unable to make his vocation pay him more than a bare livelihood. His sensitive, introspective nature probably discouraged friendships, or even contacts, that might have led to more profitable commissions than he enjoyed. Despite this, it is known from his furniture, and from his designs in, *The Cabinet Maker and Upholsterer's Drawing Book,* that he was a designer of exceptional ability. His actual knowledge of the laws governing design and construction, as it pertained to furniture, was superior to that of any of his predecessors or contemporaries, so far as we know. He developed a style, which at its best has been unsurpassed for perfect proportions, simplicity, restraint, and good taste in ornament and structural soundness.

Sheraton's finest work was influenced by the best qualities to be found in the Louis XVI style. To this he turned for inspiration, and his work in this vein was of a high order. Unfortunately for his fame as a designer, he was forced, during the latter part of his career, to cater to the popular demand which clamored for the new French Empire style. With this style he was entirely out of sympathy; too old and broken in spirit to adapt his work to the new forms, and therefore, to give it the best efforts of which he was capable. The results of these later efforts were disappointing, and should not be considered in the same sphere as his earlier efforts. He died in 1806, at the beginning of a period when most of the fine qualities for which his work is famed, were fast disappearing into an obscurity from which they were not, until lately, rescued.

The Sheraton style is noteworthy for its fine cabinets, its well-proportioned and handsome sideboards, and for its excellent small tables. These pieces stand out from among others as the finest examples of their kind, and of the period. His finest chairs were very handsome; and they were sounder structurally than Hepplewhite's chairs. Though there are many points of similarity between the Sheraton and Hepplewhite styles, the points of difference also are great. A few of these will be enumerated for purposes of comparison.

Sheraton preferred rectangular chair backs and turned legs; tapered, and reeded, or occasionally fluted. It is said that he used more underbracing than did Hepplewhite. All of Sheraton's structural elements were essentially straight. His chair backs were rectangular, as we have said; sofa and settee tops were most generally made of straight members; cabinets, and other case furniture, were straight fronted; and table frames were for the most part straight. His cabinets were often comparatively narrow for their height, giving an impression of greater verticality than those of Hepplewhite's. Hepplewhite's panels were mostly rectangular, while Sheraton pieces more often show ovals used as the chief motifs for veneered panel effects (See Plates 33 and 34).

It has been said that Shearer produced the sideboard and that Sheraton perfected it. The superiority of his sideboard lies mostly in the refinement of the proportions. Large masses on fine Sheraton pieces are divided superlatively well. For example, long drawers, which ordinarily are poorly proportioned, were on Sheraton's designs divided into minor masses of great interest by means of varicolored figured veneers. Thus they conformed to design Rules 22 and 23. Ornamental elements were simple, and Sheraton held them consistently in restraint. On fine Sheraton pieces the ornament is nearly always in good taste.

The chief characteristics of the Sheraton style are: (1) Taper turned legs, either reeded or fluted, and with slender, delicately turned feet (See Plates 33, 34, and 35). These legs were used for all

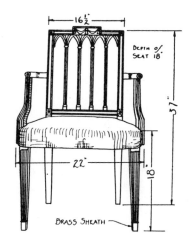

Fig. 195. Armchair with reeded front legs and arm supports.

types of pieces. Legs were sometimes like those found on Hepplewhite pieces, but turned legs are typical. (2) Rectangular chair backs, beautifully proportioned, and with members light, but well constructed. It was usual for these to have a small horizontal panel at the top, slightly raised above the top of the chair (See Figs. 195 and 196). (3) Seats of chairs were most generally of the square type, slightly narrowed toward the back. (4) Handsome tall cabinets, simply but

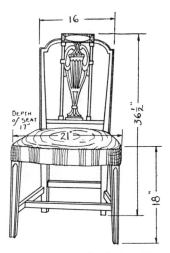

Fig. 196. Side chair with urn motif in back.

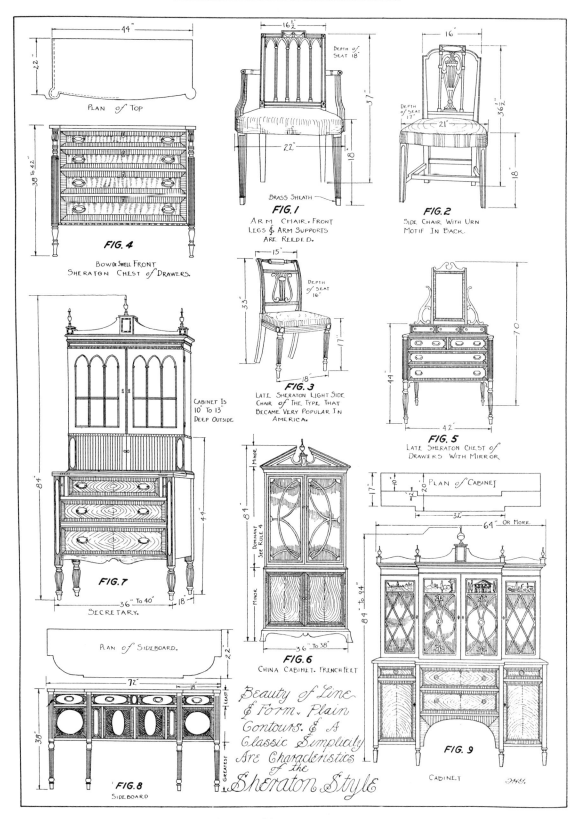

PLAN of TOP

FIG. 4

BOW or SWELL FRONT
SHERATON CHEST of DRAWERS.

BRASS SHEATH
FIG. 1
ARM CHAIR. FRONT
LEGS & ARM SUPPORTS
ARE REEDED.

DEPTH of SEAT 18"

FIG. 2
SIDE CHAIR WITH URN
MOTIF IN BACK.

DEPTH of SEAT 17"

CABINET IS
10" TO 13"
DEEP OUTSIDE

DEPTH
of SEAT
16"

FIG. 3
LATE SHERATON LIGHT SIDE
CHAIR OF THE TYPE THAT
BECAME VERY POPULAR IN
AMERICA.

FIG. 5
LATE SHERATON CHEST of
DRAWERS WITH MIRROR

FIG. 7
SECRETARY.

MINOR

DOMINANT
SEE RULE 4

MINOR

FIG. 6
CHINA CABINET. FRENCH FEET

PLAN of CABINET

CABINET

FIG. 9

PLAN of SIDEBOARD.

GREATEST   LEAST

FIG. 8
SIDEBOARD

*Beauty of Line
& Form. Plain
Contours. & A
Classic Simplicity
Are Characteristics
of the
Sheraton Style*

Plate 33.

beautifully ornamented. (5) Beautiful proportions for major and minor masses. (6) Fancy veneers and inlay, used as the chief forms of ornament, with carving and painting in second and third places respectively. Sheraton claimed that inlay was more enduring than paint. (7)

the principal wood, used mostly as a veneer, forming rich contrasts with rare lighter colored woods. (12) Ornament of classic derivation, and of a dainty type, selected principally from the Louis XVI style. (13) Striped materials frequently used for upholstering (See Fig. 52).

CHAIRS

Sheraton types persist in a large number of present-day chair designs. The seeming slenderness of structural elements on Sheraton chairs is often deceptive. The construction on most of them is superior to that found on Hepplewhite chairs. Even though turned legs

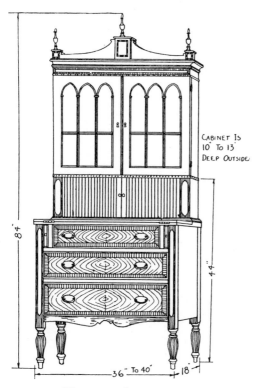

Fig. 197. Secretary.

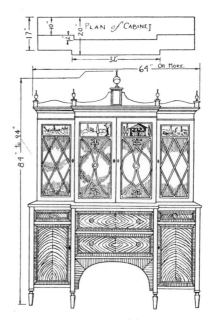

Fig. 198. Cabinet.

Straight lines predominating on structural elements, though occasionally curved fronts were used as on Hepplewhite pieces. (8) Sheraton designed a large number of combination pieces, which could be converted to serve several different purposes, not ordinarily closely associated in a single piece of furniture. (9) The oval was an oft-repeated motif decoratively, on Sheraton pieces. (10) Tops of cabinets often had modified pediments similar to those shown in Figures 197 and 198. (11) Mahogany was

were used at the front of the chair, stretchers were often, though not always, added. The very fact that the chair backs were rectangular, made it possible to make members comparatively light, and still have them sufficiently strong for all ordinary purposes. Vertical splats, which

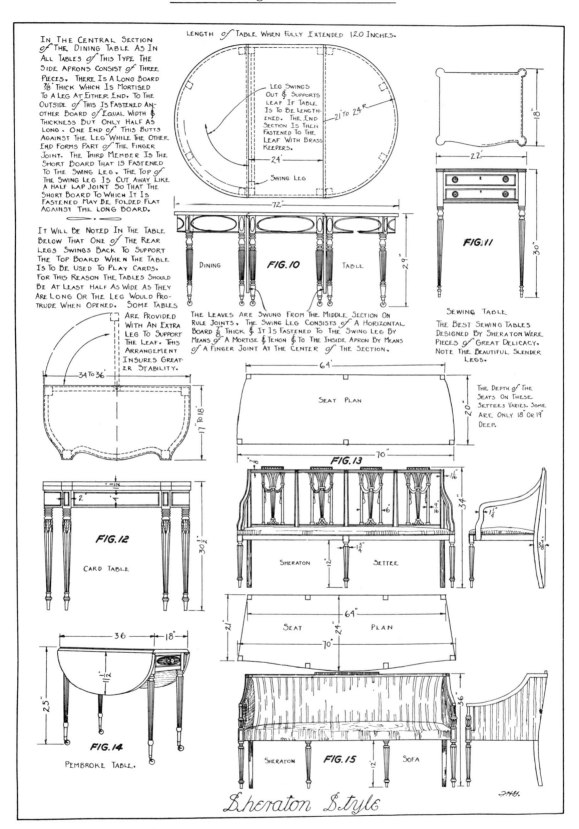

IN THE CENTRAL SECTION OF THE DINING TABLE AS IN ALL TABLES OF THIS TYPE THE SIDE APRONS CONSIST OF THREE PIECES. THERE IS A LONG BOARD 7/8" THICK WHICH IS MORTISED TO A LEG AT EITHER END. TO THE OUTSIDE OF THIS IS FASTENED ANOTHER BOARD OF EQUAL WIDTH & THICKNESS BUT ONLY HALF AS LONG. ONE END OF THIS BUTTS AGAINST THE LEG WHILE THE OTHER END FORMS PART OF THE FINGER JOINT. THE THIRD MEMBER IS THE SHORT BOARD THAT IS FASTENED TO THE SWING LEG. THE TOP OF THE SWING LEG IS CUT AWAY LIKE A HALF LAP JOINT SO THAT THE SHORT BOARD TO WHICH IT IS FASTENED MAY BE FOLDED FLAT AGAINST THE LONG BOARD.

IT WILL BE NOTED IN THE TABLE BELOW THAT ONE OF THE REAR LEGS SWINGS BACK TO SUPPORT THE TOP BOARD WHEN THE TABLE IS TO BE USED TO PLAY CARDS. FOR THIS REASON THE TABLES SHOULD BE AT LEAST HALF AS WIDE AS THEY ARE LONG OR THE LEG WOULD PROTRUDE WHEN OPENED. SOME TABLES ARE PROVIDED WITH AN EXTRA LEG TO SUPPORT THE LEAF. THIS ARRANGEMENT INSURES GREATER STABILITY.

LENGTH OF TABLE WHEN FULLY EXTENDED 120 INCHES.

LEG SWINGS OUT & SUPPORTS LEAF IF TABLE IS TO BE LENGTHENED. THE END SECTION IS THEN FASTENED TO THE LEAF WITH BRASS KEEPERS.

21 TO 24R

24"

SWING LEG

72"

DINING   FIG.10   TABLE

29"

THE LEAVES ARE SWUNG FROM THE MIDDLE SECTION ON RULE JOINTS. THE SWING LEG CONSISTS OF A HORIZONTAL BOARD 7/8" THICK & IT IS FASTENED TO THE SWING LEG BY MEANS OF A MORTISE & TENON & TO THE INSIDE APRON BY MEANS OF A FINGER JOINT AT THE CENTER OF THE SECTION.

FIG.11

22"   18"   30"

SEWING TABLE

THE BEST SEWING TABLES DESIGNED BY SHERATON WERE PIECES OF GREAT DELICACY. NOTE THE BEAUTIFUL SLENDER LEGS.

34 TO 36   17" TO 18"

FIG.12   2"   4"   30 1/2"

CARD TABLE

64"

SEAT PLAN

70"   20"

FIG.13

THE DEPTH OF THE SEATS ON THESE SETTEES VARIES. SOME ARE ONLY 18" OR 19" DEEP.

1/16   9/16   6"   34"

SHERATON   12"   1 3/4"   SETTEE   1 1/4"   3 3/8"

36"   18"

25"   1 1/4"

FIG.14

PEMBROKE TABLE.

64"

21"   SEAT   24"   PLAN

70"

36"

SHERATON   FIG.15   SOFA   12"

Sheraton Style

Plate 34.

were often made up of seemingly delicate pieces of wood, were stronger than the front view disclosed, because of a generous thickness; and they filled a generous third of the chair back. Straight members on vertical splats were mortised and tenoned to horizontal members, and all ordinary stresses were adequately provided for. This was in direct contrast to Hepplewhite chair backs, where the curving of structural elements required heavier members.

On many Sheraton chairs, arms were connected to the back near the tops of the legs, from whence they were brought forward, forming an elongated S, as in Figure 16. Others were brought forward with a single sweep, to join a turned arm support, as in Figure 199. Still others were joined to the backs as shown on the armchair in Figure 195.

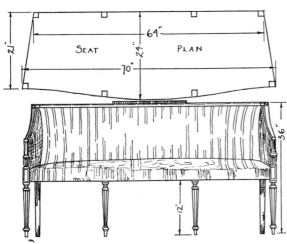

Fig. 199. Sheraton sofa.

On many of Sheraton's chairs, part of the seat stretcher is allowed to show, as in Figure 200. This chair, by the way, is a light side chair of a type that became popular in America during the early

part of the nineteenth century, though it is not in the best Sheraton taste. Compare it with the much finer example of a light side chair (Fig. 73). A more worthy design than the latter is hard to find. The simple restraint of the ornament gives the impression of good taste and careful planning.

The Sheraton armchair in Plate 37 is still another example of the chaste sim-

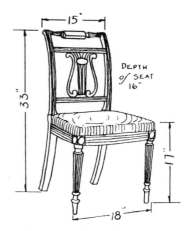

Fig. 200. Late Sheraton light side chair.

plicity and refinement of Sheraton design. This chair, reproduced from an original design, in the author's classes, is exceedingly handsome.

Upholstering materials for chairs included silks, brocades, satins, damasks, velvets, and printed materials. Striped materials, as before mentioned, were very popular. Some of these had fine flowers woven into the stripes. On other materials the figure of the designs were very delicate in scale.

SETTEES AND SOFAS

Settees in the Sheraton style are long seats that have backs similar to those found on chairs. The backs are made up

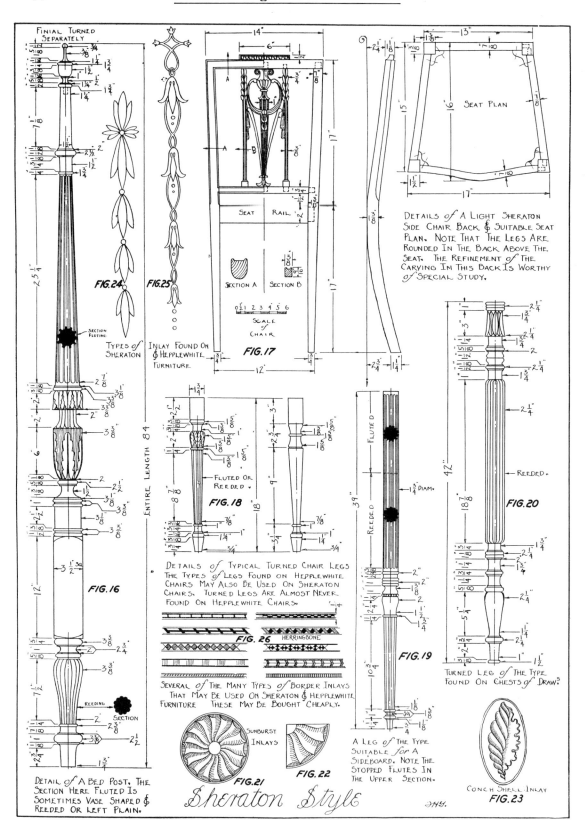

FINIAL TURNED SEPARATELY

FIG. 24

FIG. 25

TYPES of INLAY FOUND ON & HEPPLEWHITE FURNITURE

SECTION FLUTING

TYPES of SHERATON

SECTION A

SECTION B

SEAT   RAIL

SCALE of CHAIR

FIG. 17

SEAT PLAN

DETAILS OF A LIGHT SHERATON SIDE CHAIR BACK & SUITABLE SEAT PLAN. NOTE THAT THE LEGS ARE ROUNDED IN THE BACK ABOVE THE SEAT. THE REFINEMENT of THE CARVING IN THIS BACK IS WORTHY of SPECIAL STUDY.

ENTIRE LENGTH 84

FIG. 16

REEDING

SECTION

DETAIL of A BED POST. THE SECTION HERE FLUTED IS SOMETIMES VASE SHAPED & REEDED OR LEFT PLAIN.

FLUTED OR REEDED

FIG. 18

DETAILS of TYPICAL TURNED CHAIR LEGS THE TYPES of LEGS FOUND ON HEPPLEWHITE CHAIRS MAY ALSO BE USED ON SHERATON CHAIRS. TURNED LEGS ARE ALMOST NEVER FOUND ON HEPPLEWHITE CHAIRS.

FIG. 26   HERRINGBONE

SEVERAL of THE MANY TYPES of BORDER INLAYS THAT MAY BE USED ON SHERATON & HEPPLEWHITE FURNITURE. THESE MAY BE BOUGHT CHEAPLY.

SUNBURST INLAYS

FIG. 21

FIG. 22

Sheraton Style

FLUTED

REEDED

REEDED

FIG. 19

A LEG of THE TYPE SUITABLE for A SIDEBOARD. NOTE THE STOPPED FLUTES IN THE UPPER SECTION.

REEDED

FIG. 20

TURNED LEG OF THE TYPE FOUND ON CHESTS of DRAW.

CONCH SHELL INLAY

FIG. 23

Plate 35.

of two, three, or four sections. They often have six or even eight legs (See Fig. 16). The top rail is made of one long piece of wood which caps the legs. The upholstery material is sometimes drawn down over the seat rail, but more often a part of the rail is left to show. Seats on some of these settees are caned, and so are the backs. In this event it is quite usual for the back legs to be turned above the seat, there being extra, straight, vertical pieces, to which the caning is fastened.

Sofas made in the Sheraton style are simple, excellently proportioned, dignified pieces of furniture. They are usually long, quite low in the back, have clean lines, and are always in good taste. On a few of these the back is slightly arched; and when so treated the rise should be a subtle upward curve from the very ends of the sofa. The wood that shows at the top of the back on these pieces may be veneered with satinwood, curly maple, or other fine woods. Beautiful inlay bands may also be used.

Tables

Dining tables were made similar to the one shown in Figure 201. Sometimes the middle section has a drop leaf on only one side, instead of on both sides as shown. The apron is veneered, and gives the designer the opportunity to use inlays as well. The quarter sunburst, for example, may be used in the corners. Narrow bands of border inlay, as well as long narrow ovals are among the possibilities.

Little more need be said about card

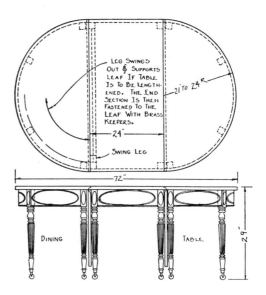

Fig. 201. Dining table.

tables than is contained in the legend above Figure 12, Plate 34. The tops were made in a variety of shapes. It is possible to secure very beautiful effects on these tops by inlaying them.

Some Pembroke tables are made with reeded legs as shown in Figure 202. Sheraton's tables of this type, unlike Hepplewhite's, were sometimes made with crossed stretchers. These tables are fine for light service, or occasional duty as tea or coffee tables. Some are small enough to use at the end of a sofa.

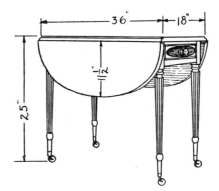

Fig. 202. Pembroke table.

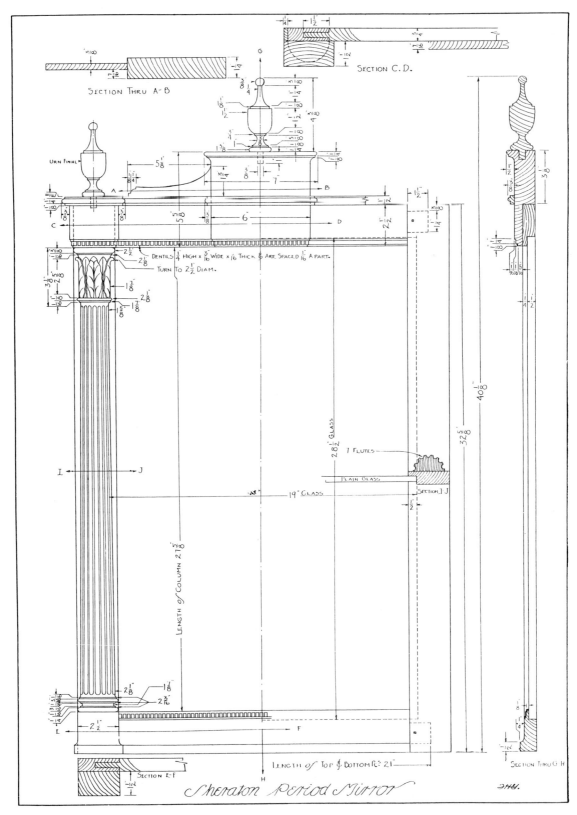

Section Thru A-B

Section C.D.

Urn Finial

Dentils ¼" High x 3/16" Wide x 1/16" Thick & Are Spaced 1/16" Apart.

Turn to 2½" Diam.

Length of Column 27⅝

28½" Glass

7 Flutes

Plain Glass

19" Glass

Section I J

Section E-F

Length of Top & Bottom R. 21"

40⅛"

32⅝

Section Thru G H

Sheraton Period Mirror

Plate 36.

Sheraton's sewing tables are quite famous. He designed many that were very beautiful (See Fig. 203). These may be designed with straight, bowed, or serpentine fronts, the first two types

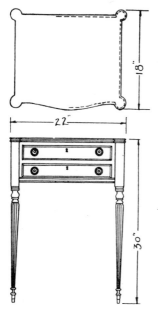

Fig. 203. Sewing table.

being more usual. Other tops were designed in oblong octagon shapes. The turned legs were halved at the tops and fastened to the splayed corners of the box containing the drawers. The legs should be very slender, almost needle-like. A diameter of a half of an inch at the floor is not unusual. A silk bag was often suspended beneath the lower drawer, which was so arranged that it could be swung out, or was fastened to the lower drawer which had a hole cut into the bottom, or had no bottom at all. The drawers may be divided into compartments for spools of thread, etc., if so desired. Drawer fronts may be veneered

and inlaid. Table tops for these should not be more than about ⅝ in. thick.

CHESTS OF DRAWERS

Two types of chests of drawers are shown in Figures 6 and 204. The earliest, as well as the best type, is the one shown in Figure 204. The fronts

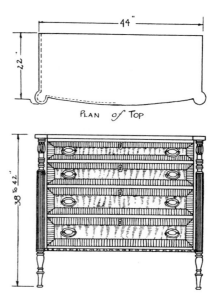

Fig. 204. Chest of drawers.

were straight or very gently bowed like the one illustrated. These pieces should always be handsomely veneered and inlaid. The corners of the case are sometimes splayed, and the turned legs flattened at the back, so they may be fastened to the chest.

Figure 6 shows a later type Sheraton chest of drawers. This type marked the beginning of the present-day bureau, or dresser, which is often so ugly. Several refinements on the piece shown are worthy of being pointed out, however. The brackets supporting the mirror are beautifully formed, and graceful.

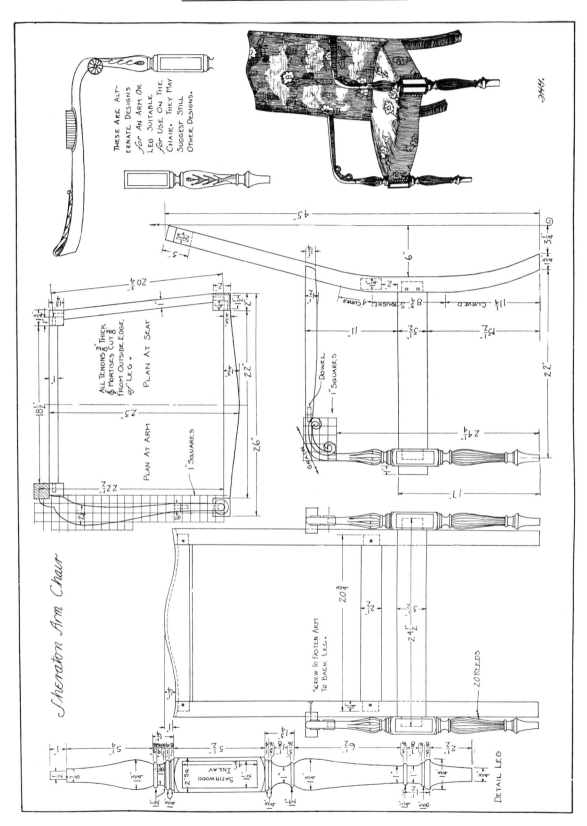

These are alternate designs for an arm or leg suitable for use on the chair. They may suggest still other designs.

Sheraton Arm Chair

Plate 37.

Frame for a chair of Sheraton design
of delicate but beautiful proportions.

SIDEBOARDS

It has been said that Sheraton's sideboards were the finest, and the best proportioned sideboards ever made. It is
claimed that Thomas Shearer, a contemporary craftsman, made the first sideboards of this type, but that Sheraton
perfected them. Since the sideboard is
rather a large piece of furniture, and
one that presents a number of difficulties of construction, it requires careful
planning. It is long, but the structural
elements must not be too large or the
proportions will suffer. Sheraton had
these details very nicely worked out, so
that neither beauty nor strength were
sacrificed.

If the proportions on a sideboard of
this type are carefully planned the
masses should be so broken up into component parts that each will be beautiful
in itself, and yet be completely related
to the whole. On long narrow drawers,
for example, which ordinarily are poorly
proportioned because they break Rule
22, a treatment similar to the one given
the drawer at the top of the central section of the sideboard (Fig. 5), is very
effective. On this drawer the major mass
is broken up into a number of interesting subdivisions which are very
attractive.

Both Sheraton and Hepplewhite used
the principles given under Rules 3 and
9, for the major divisions on their sideboards. These principles are very effective for the design of a piece of furniture of this kind. The other rules involved may be easily determined by an
examination of the drawing. Except for
the few peculiarities of form and orna-

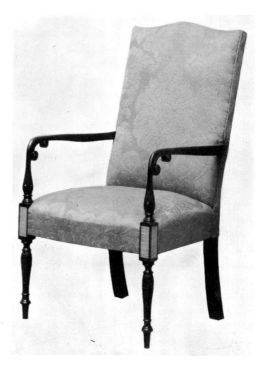

Finished chair of Sheraton design.

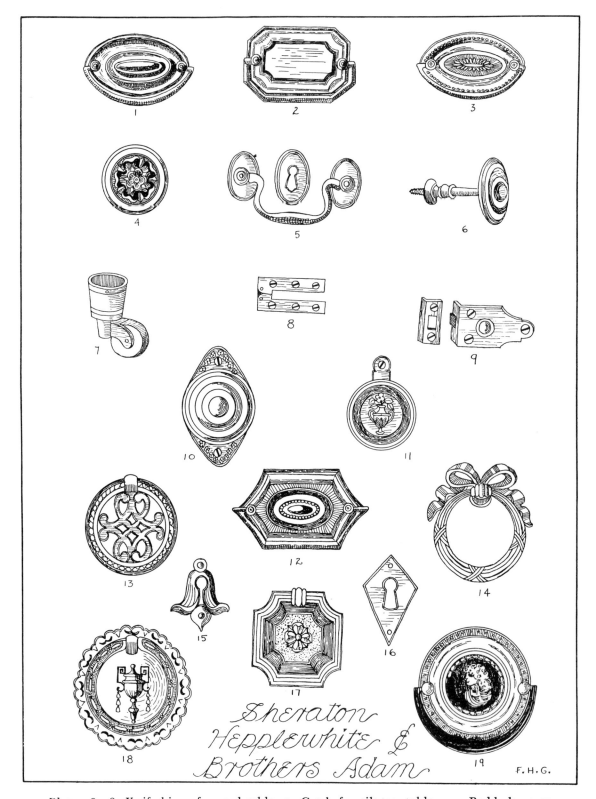

Plate 38. 8. Knife hinge for card table. 9. Catch for tilt-top table. 10. Bed-bolt cover.

ment already mentioned, many of the sideboards designed by Sheraton and Hepplewhite are very similar.

CABINETS AND SECRETARIES

Figures 197 and 198 show two pieces of this type. Many of Sheraton's cabinets and secretaries are almost identical to those designed by Hepplewhite. Sheraton pieces were nearly always straight fronted, however; had turned and tapered legs, either reeded or fluted; and were often more inclined to verticality, or at least produced that impression because of the emphasis placed upon vertical lines. Sheraton also used a unique type of modified pediment, shown in Figures 197 and 198. Both of these ex-

Sheraton wing chair.

A handsomely designed mirror of Classic inspiration.

amples shown are simple and attractive. Bookcases with glazed doors became a common adjunct of secretaries and tall cabinets from Sheraton's time on.

On a piece like that shown in Figure 198, it is quite probable that the upper drawer would have been designed by Sheraton to contain the cabinet of a desk — pigeonholes, small drawers, and all. Drawers of this type had a front that could be lowered with quadrants supporting it when in that position, thus forming a part of the writing surface of the desk. At other times, pieces of this type were used as china cabinets.

Figure 197 is a tambour secretary with a bookcase above. Sheraton delighted in handsome cabinets of this type. Figure 4 shows a very attractive Classic design.

1. What may be said regarding Sheraton's relative importance when compared with other great designers of the eighteenth century?

2. What style was the chief source of Sheraton's inspiration?

3. Describe the general structure of Sheraton pieces.

4. What is the general impression one gets when looking at typical Sheraton cabinets?

5. Name several distinctive features found on Sheraton furniture by which it may be identified.

6. What important motif was consistently used by Sheraton to enrich his pieces?

7. Describe a typical Sheraton chair; its construction, ornament, and scale.

8. Enumerate several reasons why Sheraton deserves the distinction of being called the greatest furniture designer who ever lived.

9. Describe the construction of a typical Sheraton dining table.

10. It has been said that Sheraton designed the most perfect sideboards ever built. If this is so, what were some of the points of their superiority?

11. What may be said regarding Sheraton's inventive ability, especially as it is evidenced in unique mechanical contrivances occurring in his designs?

12. How do the scale and proportions of Sheraton pieces compare with the same factors on contemporary styles?

13. Why is it not fair to consider Sheraton's late work as a basis upon

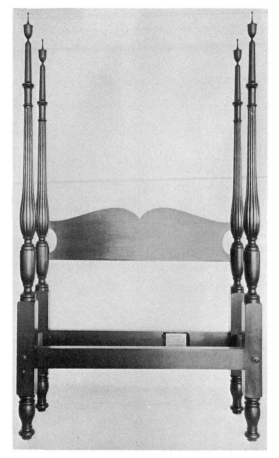

(A Wallace Nutting Reproduction)

A simple, clean-cut, beautiful
Sheraton bedstead.

which to form a judgment of the value of his contribution to the field of furniture design?

SUGGESTED PROBLEMS

1. Design a Sheraton sideboard, or an entire dining-room suite.

2. Design a Sheraton side chair.

3. Design a Sheraton double settee.

4. Design a doll house, and furnish it with miniature furniture of Sheraton design.

5. Design a nest of tables in the Sheraton style.

CHAPTER 12

THE BROTHERS ADAM STYLE
1762–1792

HISTORICAL DATA AND GENERAL CHARACTERISTICS

With the style of the Brothers Adam we complete our picture of the individualistic styles, developed during the golden age of furniture. These four great styles — the Chippendale, Hepplewhite, Sheraton, and the Brothers Adam — stand forth as models, exemplifying the finest ideals to be found in all furniture design since the days of their creation. With one exception, that of Duncan Phyfe's, these four styles are the only ones to be identified with the names of the designers who produced them. All of them are readily adaptable to modern needs; fulfilling present-day requirements as adequately as they did those of a hundred and fifty years ago.

The Brothers Adam were architects, and not furniture designers in the strict sense of the term. There were four brothers, but Robert and James were the two who designed furniture, and with whose work we are concerned. Robert Adam was born in Scotland; was educated at the University of Edinburgh, and pursued his studies of architecture in Italy. It was during his stay in Italy that he came into direct contact with Classic architecture, which influenced all his subsequent work. At the age of forty he was appointed architect to the king, by George III. James Adam, a younger brother, succeeded Robert to this honor. It was during this period, from 1762 to 1792, that the four brothers embarked upon the building ventures which brought them fame and also considerable wealth. Many fine homes and public buildings remain standing today in London, as tributes to their genius.

The work of the Brothers Adam in the field of furniture design was in the nature of that done by our present-day interior decorators. They looked upon furniture as upon other architectural details — considering it an important unit necessary for the proper fulfillment of a commission, and therefore worthy of the same careful planning they would have given to a fireplace or a doorway. Their furniture designs reflect this attitude, for many of them are extremely formal architectural structures when compared with the more livable styles of the three great designers whose work has just been studied. Many of their original designs were impractical, and were modified by the cabinetmakers who built the pieces. Among these was Hepplewhite, whose work was considerably influenced by contact with the Brothers Adam style; and Chippendale, who, adapter though he was, never allowed it to greatly influence his style.

The principal contributions made by the Brothers Adam to the field of furniture design were: (1) The simplification of structure by the substitution of straight lines for curved elements. (2) The introduction and adaptation of classical ornament, of a fine type, to furniture design. (3) The bringing about of a closer relation between mobiliary art and its proper architectural setting. They observed design Rule 45 more closely than any other designer of furniture. For the above three things they were directly responsible.

The chief characteristics of the Brothers Adam style are: (1) Rectilinear construction on cabinets, tables, and frequently on chairs (See Figs. 65, 205, and

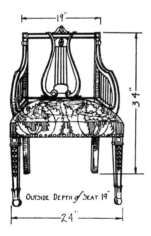

Fig. 205. Lyre-back armchair.

206). Cabinets had straight tops, straight fronts, and were rectangular throughout, in most cases. (2) Their furniture had square, tapered, slender legs, with or without spade feet, similar to those found on Hepplewhite furniture. The feet were sometimes cubical as in Fig-

ure 74. Other types of fect were rather fanciful as in Figures 72 and 205. (3) Chair backs were often rectangular as on Plate 42. Others were similar to the ones shown on Plate 40. (4) Underbracing was generally absent from Brothers Adam furniture. This fact helped to

Fig. 206. Bookcase.

give the furniture a light, clean-cut appearance. (5) The furniture was very formal in character; due to the straight clean lines, and to the arrangement and character of the ornament. (6) Classical ornament of a refined, delicate character, comprising Greek urns, the lyre, egg-and-dart moldings, and other typical motifs as shown on Plate 41 were used. These were conventionalized motifs, and were employed for carving in low relief, inlaying, and painting. (7) Oval-fronted commodes and console tables were typical; these pieces often being veneered. Veneers, on Brothers Adam furniture, were used for the figured effects to be obtained from the fancy woods more than for sound structural qualities or any other reason. (8) Mahogany was the chief cabinetwood, though cheaper woods were extensively used when the entire surface was to be painted or gilded, as was often the case. (9) Moldings were delicate and fine in scale. (10) Proportions were generally

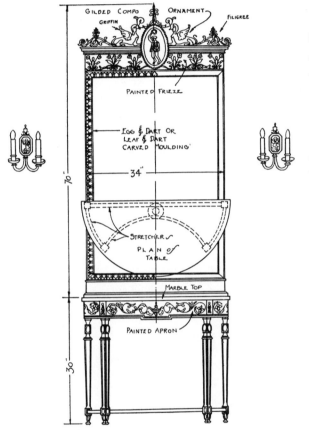

Fig. 207. Carved, gilt and painted mirror and console table.

good. (11) Pieces were often designed to be placed in definitely predetermined positions. Many of these were, therefore, quite grand and imposing pieces, such as Figure 207. (12) Hand-painted panels, or miniature oil paintings of great artistic merit, often done by famous artists, were used on fine cabinets in the

manner shown in Figure 74. (13) A kind of filigree work, made up of a plaster composition, built upon a network of wires was often used to ornament important places on cabinets or mirrors, as shown on the top of Figure 207. (14) Upholstering materials consisted of fine brocades, silk materials, damasks, etc. These were usually fine in scale as to figure. (15) Rare woods for inlay consisted of harewood, tulipwood, holly, ebony, thuja, emboyna, rosewood, satinwood, and others.

CHAIRS

Chairs designed in this style may be oval backed (Fig. 208), wheel (round) backed, shield backed, or the back may

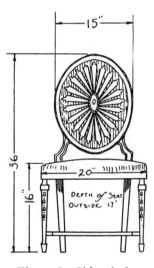

Fig. 208. Side chair.

be rectangular (Fig. 205). The oval and shield backs are similar to those found in the Hepplewhite style, and therefore need no further discussion here.

A chair that has very excellent qualities of line and proportion, has been designed, and may be studied in detail from the drawing on Plate 42. This

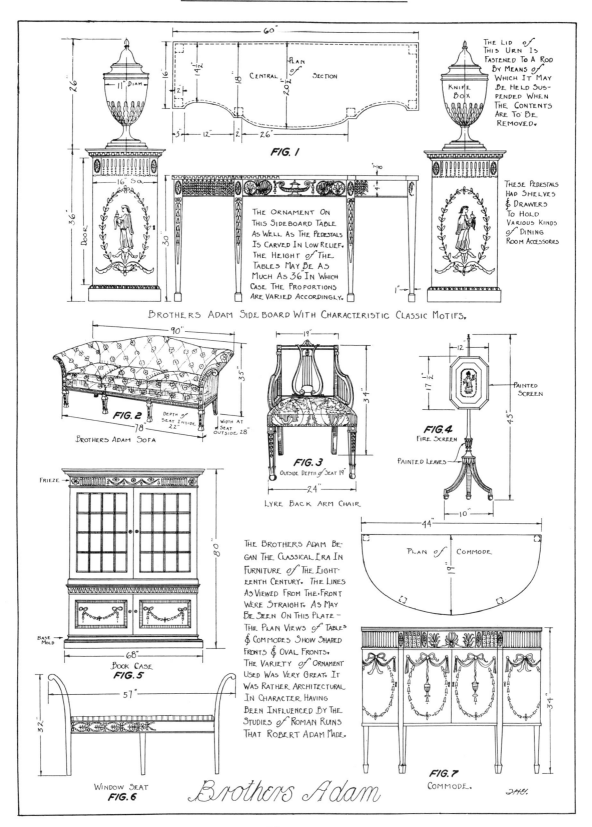

FIG. 1

THE LID of THIS URN IS FASTENED TO A ROD BY MEANS of WHICH IT MAY BE HELD SUSPENDED WHEN THE CONTENTS ARE TO BE REMOVED.

KNIFE BOX

THESE PEDESTALS HAD SHELVES & DRAWERS TO HOLD VARIOUS KINDS of DINING ROOM ACCESSORIES

THE ORNAMENT ON THIS SIDEBOARD TABLE AS WELL AS THE PEDESTALS IS CARVED IN LOW RELIEF. THE HEIGHT of THE TABLES MAY BE AS MUCH AS 36 IN WHICH CASE THE PROPORTIONS ARE VARIED ACCORDINGLY.

BROTHERS ADAM SIDEBOARD WITH CHARACTERISTIC CLASSIC MOTIFS.

FIG. 2
BROTHERS ADAM SOFA
DEPTH of SEAT INSIDE 22"
WIDTH AT SEAT OUTSIDE 28"

FIG. 3
OUTSIDE DEPTH of SEAT 19"
LYRE BACK ARM CHAIR

FIG. 4
FIRE SCREEN
PAINTED SCREEN
PAINTED LEAVES

FRIEZE
BASE MOLD
BOOK CASE
FIG. 5

THE BROTHERS ADAM BEGAN THE CLASSICAL ERA IN FURNITURE of THE EIGHTEENTH CENTURY. THE LINES AS VIEWED FROM THE FRONT WERE STRAIGHT AS MAY BE SEEN ON THIS PLATE THE PLAN VIEWS of TABLES & COMMODES SHOW SHAPED FRONTS & OVAL FRONTS. THE VARIETY of ORNAMENT USED WAS VERY GREAT. IT WAS RATHER ARCHITECTURAL IN CHARACTER HAVING BEEN INFLUENCED BY THE STUDIES of ROMAN RUINS THAT ROBERT ADAM MADE.

PLAN of COMMODE

FIG. 7
COMMODE.

WINDOW SEAT
FIG. 6

Brothers Adam

Plate 39.

chair has been built in the author's classes, and it is in every way a beautiful, authentic Brothers Adam design.

The chair back is low and square. The whole effect is one of lightness; and the simplicity, and careful distribution of masses, give it dignity and grace. The fretted splat, against which the back rests, is curved to insure comfort. The splat, in a chair of this kind, should be set at the proper angle, so that the bottom edge will not cause discomfort to the person seated in the chair. The bars and disks in this splat are sawed and carved from a solid board, the wood having been cut away to give the latticed effect. This gives a lacylike appearance, though strength is not sacrificed thereby, since the bars are 5/8 in. deep, and sufficiently strong to support all normal strains.

The chairs of this type all have a square-backed effect. This would ordinarily be poorly proportioned, and therefore open to criticism for being contrary to Rule 21. This natural consequence is relieved by the interesting manner in which minor masses are treated. Major and minor centers of interest, cleverly arranged, make this design exceedingly effective and attractive.

The arms require a piece of mahogany three inches thick by five inches wide. They are graceful and neat in appearance, but somewhat wasteful of material. These are mortised and tenoned to the back legs near the top, and when the joint has been properly dressed, impart the feeling of being continuous to the very top of the chair. They thoroughly brace the chair at a place where this is necessary.

The turned arm supports, and the top rail, are reeded. The central part of the top rail is shaped, so that a cross section of it looks much like the shape of an egg (See Section A-B, Plate 42). The straight tapering legs, and other rectilinear elements give the chair a clean-cut aspect, which is an outstanding trait of all furniture of Brothers Adam design.

SIDEBOARDS

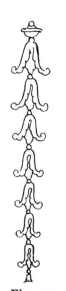

Fig. 209. Bell-shaped flower pendant.

Strictly speaking the pieces of furniture designed for this purpose were not sideboards. They were long tables flanked by pedestals. The pedestals were square cupboards, supporting knife urns. The tables are designed with square tapering legs. These may be inlaid, but are often carved in low relief with bell-shaped flowers of the type shown in Figure 209. The apron of the table is often carved in a manner similar to the one shown in Figure 210. Practically all ornament used was adapted from architectural forms found in the ruins of excavated Roman cities, many of which Robert Adam carefully measured, made drawings of, and later adapted to his furniture designs. Typical examples of this ornament may be found on Plate 41.

The pedestals are made to open in front, the whole front usually being a

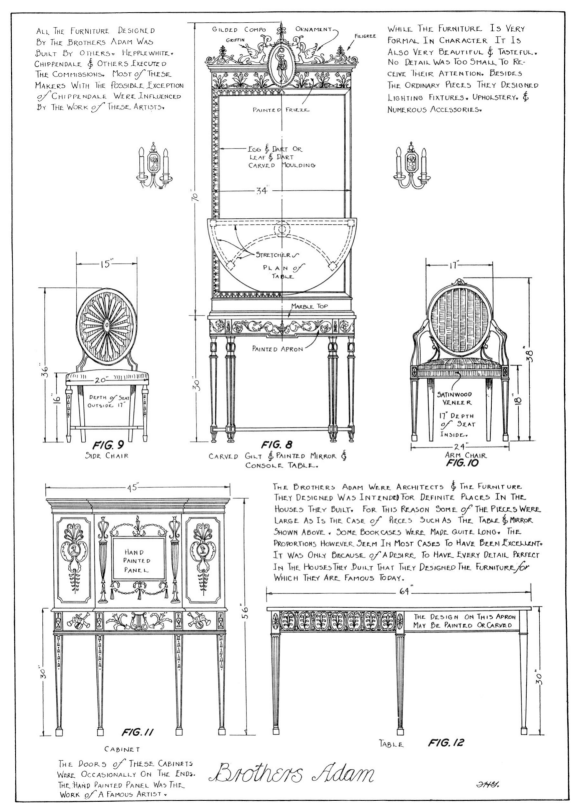

ALL THE FURNITURE DESIGNED BY THE BROTHERS ADAM WAS BUILT BY OTHERS. HEPPLEWHITE, CHIPPENDALE & OTHERS EXECUTED THE COMMISSIONS. MOST OF THESE MAKERS WITH THE POSSIBLE EXCEPTION OF CHIPPENDALE WERE INFLUENCED BY THE WORK OF THESE ARTISTS.

WHILE THE FURNITURE IS VERY FORMAL IN CHARACTER IT IS ALSO VERY BEAUTIFUL & TASTEFUL. NO DETAIL WAS TOO SMALL TO RECEIVE THEIR ATTENTION. BESIDES THE ORDINARY PIECES THEY DESIGNED LIGHTING FIXTURES. UPHOLSTERY, & NUMEROUS ACCESSORIES.

GILDED COMPO ORNAMENT
GRIFFIN
FILIGREE
PAINTED FRIEZE
EGG & DART OR LEAF & DART CARVED MOULDING
34"
70"
STRETCHER
PLAN OF TABLE
MARBLE TOP
30"
PAINTED APRON

FIG. 8
CARVED GILT & PAINTED MIRROR & CONSOLE TABLE.

15"
36"
16"
20"
DEPTH OF SEAT OUTSIDE 17"

FIG. 9
SIDE CHAIR

17"
38"
18"
SATINWOOD VENEER
17" DEPTH OF SEAT INSIDE.
24"

ARM CHAIR
FIG. 10

THE BROTHERS ADAM WERE ARCHITECTS & THE FURNITURE THEY DESIGNED WAS INTENDED FOR DEFINITE PLACES IN THE HOUSES THEY BUILT. FOR THIS REASON SOME OF THE PIECES WERE LARGE AS IS THE CASE OF PIECES SUCH AS THE TABLE & MIRROR SHOWN ABOVE. SOME BOOKCASES WERE MADE QUITE LONG. THE PROPORTIONS HOWEVER SEEM IN MOST CASES TO HAVE BEEN EXCELLENT. IT WAS ONLY BECAUSE OF A DESIRE TO HAVE EVERY DETAIL PERFECT IN THE HOUSES THEY BUILT THAT THEY DESIGNED THE FURNITURE FOR WHICH THEY ARE FAMOUS TODAY.

45"
HAND PAINTED PANEL
56"
30"

FIG. 11
CABINET
THE DOORS OF THESE CABINETS WERE OCCASIONALLY ON THE ENDS. THE HAND PAINTED PANEL WAS THE WORK OF A FAMOUS ARTIST.

64"
THE DESIGN ON THIS APRON MAY BE PAINTED OR CARVED
30"

TABLE   FIG. 12

Brothers Adam

Plate 40.

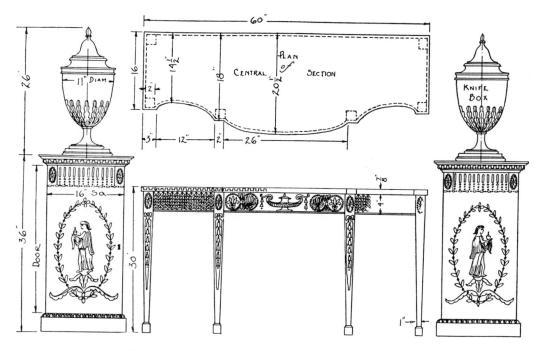

Fig. 210. Brothers Adam sideboard with characteristic Classic motifs.

door. The inside may be divided into compartments, with shelves and drawers to hold the things usually relegated to the drawers of a sideboard.

The lids of the knife urns are fastened to a rod or stem, which holds them up when the lids have been raised. This is accomplished by means of a small catch or trigger spring, which may be released to lower the lids.

SOFAS

Figure 25, shows a fine example of an Adam sofa. Except for several minor unique features it might be of Hepplewhite origin. It has the square tapered legs, and characteristic Adam ornament.

FIRE SCREEN

Figure 211 shows a very fine type of fire screen of Adam inspiration. The

painted screen on these is always longer than it is wide; but whether it is rectangular, oval, or some other shape, does not particularly matter. Screens of this type offer opportunities for fine designs in needlework, painting, or other forms of ornament. They were used to shade the eyes from the glare of artificial light,

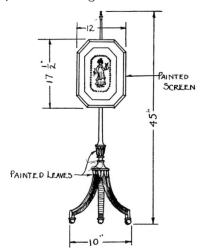

Fig. 211. Fire screen.

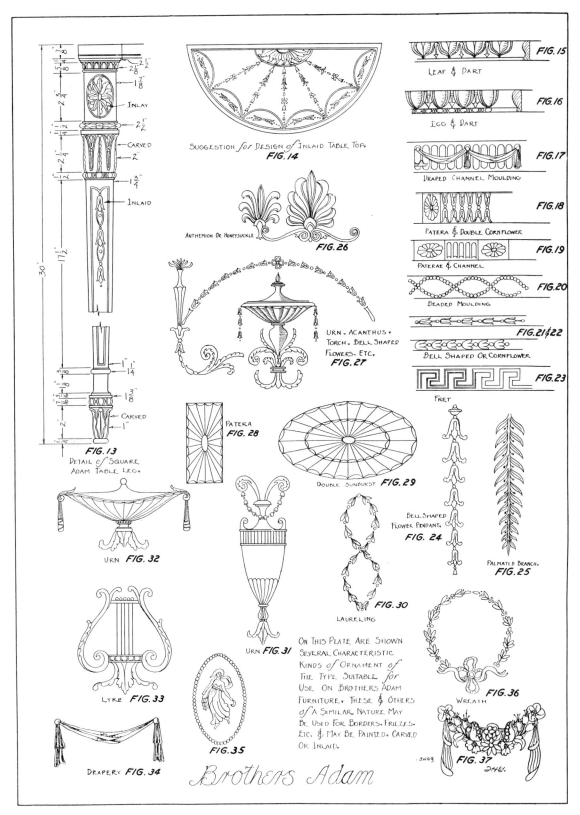

INLAY

CARVED 2"

INLAID

30"

CARVED 1"

FIG. 13
DETAIL of SQUARE
ADAM TABLE LEG.

SUGGESTION *for* DESIGN *of* INLAID TABLE TOP.
FIG. 14

ANTHEMION OR HONEYSUCKLE
FIG. 26

URN - ACANTHUS -
TORCH - BELL SHAPED
FLOWERS - ETC.
FIG. 27

PATERA
FIG. 28

DOUBLE SUNBURST FIG. 29

LAURELING FIG. 30

URN FIG. 31

URN FIG. 32

LYRE FIG. 33

DRAPERY FIG. 34

FIG. 35

LEAF & DART FIG. 15

EGG & DART FIG. 16

DRAPED CHANNEL MOULDING FIG. 17

PATERA & DOUBLE CORNFLOWER FIG. 18

PATERAE & CHANNEL FIG. 19

BEADED MOULDING FIG. 20

FIG. 21 & 22
BELL SHAPED OR CORNFLOWER

FRET FIG. 23

BELL SHAPED
FLOWER PENDANT.
FIG. 24

PALMATED BRANCH.
FIG. 25

FIG. 36
WREATH

SWAG FIG. 37

ON THIS PLATE ARE SHOWN
SEVERAL CHARACTERISTIC
KINDS *of* ORNAMENT *of*
THE TYPE SUITABLE *for*
USE ON BROTHERS ADAM
FURNITURE. THESE & OTHERS
of A SIMILAR NATURE MAY
BE USED FOR BORDERS. FRIEZES.
ETC. & MAY BE PAINTED. CARVED
OR INLAID.

Brothers Adam

Plate 41.

Frame for Brothers Adam armchair
of fine proportions and lacy aspect.

or from the sun shining through a window.

Bookcases

The bookcase shown in Figure 206, is a good example, showing the architectural character of the furniture designed in this style. Some pieces of this type were built especially to fill an entire wall space in a pretentious private or public library. Some of these bookcases were often quite elaborate. The central section (for such pieces were often built in several sections) was usually brought forward, being deeper than the sections on each side of it. It often had a pediment instead of being perfectly flat-topped like the one shown. The end sections, however, receded from it, and were flat-topped. There was thus a close analogy to a building with wings, having a clas-

sical façade. Design Rule 9 should be followed in designing a large important bookcase of this type; that is, the central section should be the widest with two smaller ones of equal size on each side. The pediment, on Brothers Adam bookcases, when there was one, was nearly always triangular; sometimes with a break in the center. If there was a break, it was usually ornamented with a carved bust, or even an eagle. Typical ornament of classical derivation was found on most bookcases of this style, particularly carved moldings, such as the egg-and-dart. Doors were glazed; sometimes as shown in Figure 4, and again as shown in Figure 191.

Window Seats

The piece of furniture shown in Figure 26, is known as a window seat. These articles of furniture were commonly placed before a window, hence the name.

Finished Brothers Adam armchair.

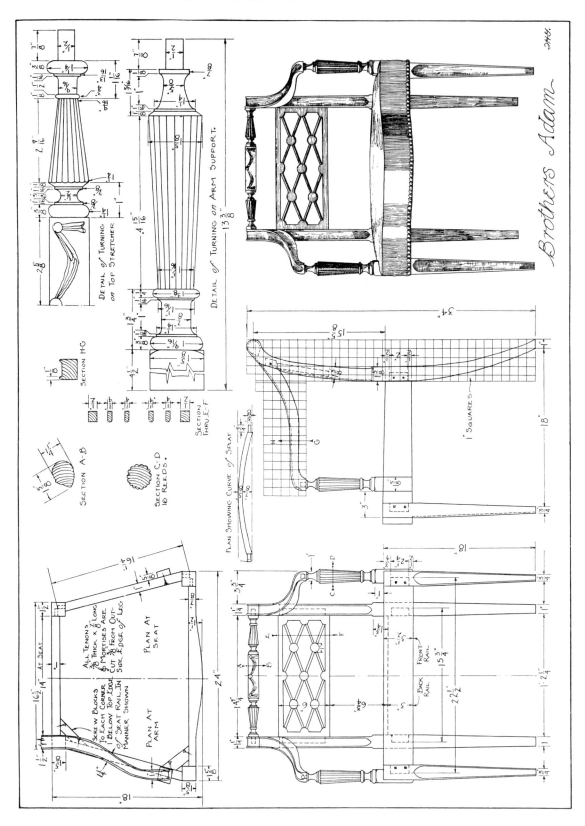

Brothers Adam

Plate 42.

They are quite appropriate before a fine Adam or McIntyre fireplace.

The ends may be designed like a chair back. The one shown would look well if the ends were copied directly from the chair back in the design on Plate 42. The seat rail on each side of the window seats may be decorated with suitable ornament of classical design.

COMMODES

Every style of furniture possesses one piece of furniture that is distinctly more characteristic of that style than of any other. In the Brothers Adam style this piece of furniture is the commode, or console cabinet. These are intended for a hallway, or a fine drawing or living room. They always properly belong in a formal scheme of furnishing. Very often two of them are placed on each side of a doorway leading into an important room. They should have mirrors hung above them.

In plan the commodes may be semicircular, or semielliptical. They usually have four square or turned, tapered legs. Sometimes these are very short, the cabinet reaching almost to the floor. Others have slender, French bracket feet, of the type used by Hepplewhite (See Fig. 35). Some commodes have drawers at the ends, such drawers being three cornered. The tops and fronts of these pieces were often beautifully painted or veneered.

CONSOLE TABLE AND MIRROR

Figure 207 shows a piece of furniture often associated with the type of design for which the Brothers Adam were famous. The mirror is very high, showing that it was intended for a large pretentious room. These pieces are particularly appropriate when placed between two windows in a finely furnished room of a large house. The one shown has a painted apron and a painted frieze. Carving in low relief, or inlay, may be employed. Gold leaf was often applied to the carving on such pieces, and indeed to the whole piece in some cases. Filigree work, such as that used at the top of the mirror, cannot well be made of wood. It is built up of compo, molded on a network of wires. This form of ornament came into much favor for the decoration of mirrors, and sometimes other pieces of furniture, at about this time. Marble was also sometimes used for the tops of tables on pieces of this nature, and it added a note to the already rich effect.

CABINETS

Beautiful cabinets were built during this period, of which the one shown in Figure 74 is a good example. Decorative motifs of this type might denote it as a piece used to hold sheet music, or for modern homes it would be a fine radio cabinet. Other modifications in the design could be made, to make it into a bookcase, a china cabinet, a trophy cabinet, a desk, or a piece having some similar purpose. Finely decorated panels, and hand-painted oil paintings, decorated cabinets such as this in the Brothers Adam style.

TABLES

Long rectangular tables of the type shown in Figure 65 were typical of the style. Longer ones had more legs. The apron of the one shown is decorated with a type of ornament often found on tables of this kind. It is known as the anthemion, or honeysuckle, motif.

Questions for Review

1. Why is it incorrect to call the Brothers Adam, cabinetmakers?

2. What was the nature of the work done by the Brothers Adam in the field of furniture design?

3. Name several unique characteristics of Brothers Adam design by which it may be identified.

4. What was the greatest contribution made to the field of furniture design by the Brothers Adam?

5. What may be said regarding the structural qualities of Brothers Adam designs?

6. Describe a typical Brothers Adam armchair design.

7. Why has the Brothers Adam style never caught the popular fancy to the same extent as have the Chippendale, Hepplewhite, and Sheraton styles?

8. What is unique about Brothers Adam sideboards?

9. Describe a typical Brothers Adam bookcase.

10. What was, perhaps, the most typical piece of furniture of the Brothers Adam style?

11. To what type of architectural setting is the Brothers Adam style particularly well suited?

Suggested Problems

1. Design a Brothers Adam commode.

2. Design a Brothers Adam console group for a small Georgian home.

3. Design a Brothers Adam sofa.

4. Design a radio cabinet using this style as the basis for the design.

CHAPTER 13

THE FRENCH STYLES
Louis XIV — 1643–1715
Louis XV — 1715–1774
Louis XVI — 1774–1793

HISTORICAL DATA AND GENERAL CHARACTERISTICS

The three most important styles of French furniture are the Louis XIV, Louis XV, and Louis XVI. A comparison of the dates at which these styles occurred, with those during which the great English styles flourished, will reveal the fact that they were contemporaneous. The Louis XIV and the Jacobean styles were being developed at about the same time. The last two great styles, the Louis XVI and Sheraton's, were also contemporaneous.

During the reign of Louis XIV, France attained first rank among the nations of Europe. The consequent influences exerted by so powerful a nation made themselves felt in the field of art as well as in politics in most neighboring countries.

Louis XIV, early in his reign, became a patron of the arts; and because of various advantages and inducements offered, artists, designers, and craftsmen, from other countries came to France in great numbers. Some of the best of these were employed in the royal workshop, set up in the Louvre by Jean Baptiste Colbert, one of the king's ministers. Colbert, was also architect to the king, and he chose as an assistant whom he placed in direct charge of the workshop, a clever artist and designer, by the name of Charles LeBrun. LeBrun designed tapestry, furniture, painted pictures, did engraving, and modeled for sculpture. This placing of the work under a competent head, and quartering the workmen in a single place, was probably responsible for the good results obtained.

During the latter part of the reign, Colbert died, and soon thereafter LeBrun was replaced by artists of inferior ability, who instituted the rococo and naturalistic ornament, which became the chief motifs of the Louis XV style. When this had occurred, straight lines and balanced arrangement of elements gave way to curved lines and occult balance, and a mixture of motifs that was, in many cases, bewildering.

Because of the unusually long reigns of both Louis XIV and Louis XV, the styles bearing their names were carried to pinnacles of development never reached by English styles, which were of shorter duration. An important factor aiding this remarkable development was the large sums of money expended upon things with which to satisfy the desire for personal luxury and aggrandizement. Ideals of this kind, carried to the limits of excess, are not conducive to the development of good taste. Individual art objects, ornament, or even pieces of furniture, were beautiful; but the ensemble, though very rich, was showy, and resulted in confusion. It is, therefore, fortunate that we owe our heritage of furniture traditions mostly to England, whose designers, though they adapted freely from French styles, nevertheless discarded many of their superficialities, with the result that their efforts produced a more satisfactory product.

Despite conditions that existed, these two French styles are important to the furniture designer of today for several reasons. He owes a great deal to the styles for the high degree of excellence to which many phases of his craft were developed. New materials were invented, new processes were employed, and old ones were greatly improved. There were new decorative processes, a larger range of color tones, new fabrics — in short every resource was fully exploited in order to build richer pieces than had ever been produced before. Another reason why the styles are of great significance to the designer is because they are essentially feminine in character; and they therefore furnish him with patterns that are uniquely suited to the more delicate and refined amenities of living. This is true of all three French styles. They appeal particularly to women, because they were created to satisfy the creature comforts,

and the vanities of an effeminate court. Fine silks, laces, and delicate perfumes were of as much concern to the men of this sophisticated age as they were to the members of the opposite sex. It is, therefore, not strange that much finer, more elaborate materials and trimmings were used on furniture.

The designer of furniture will seldom wish to reproduce French pieces exactly as they were originally. The Louis XIV period was one given over to magnificent pageantry and show; and this was reflected in the furniture, much of which was heavy and formal, though its trappings were rich (See Fig. 63). During the latter part of the period some of this heaviness disappeared, and we have a finer type of furniture, as typified by the long bench on Plate 46. The Louis XV period was given over to excesses of every description, and the furniture

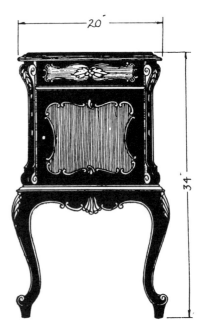

Fig. 215. Louis XV
cabinet.

proved no exception. Ornament, trimmings, and valuable materials were exploited to the fullest extent, so that finally they entirely obscured and destroyed logical structure. Good taste was in the discard; not always, it is true, but in most cases. Individual elements of great beauty and refinement were developed, such as the Louis XV cabriole leg (See Fig. 215). This leg, in its finest form, is slender, with subtle, perfectly balanced, well-supported curves.

The profligacy of the reign of Louis XV paved the way for the French Revolution, which followed soon after its conclusion, bringing to a close the great French furniture styles. This did not occur, however, until a new style, the Louis XVI, had come upon the scene, which was in many respects as simple. and as charming as the former one had been sophisticated and frivolous. Its development marked a new era in decorative art. The style as a whole is rather flaccid, and many of its elements are, "pretty," rather than beautiful and expressive of character. Nevertheless, it is a source of much that is commendable and refined. Louis XIV and Louis XV had imposed heavy taxes, and spent money with so lavish a hand, that the resources of the people were almost exhausted. Money for a program of spending, such as had been carried on during the former two periods, was not available. All of this influenced a return to a less sumptuous style of interior decoration and furniture design.

In order to design pieces of furniture in the French styles, it will be more important for the designer to be able to interpret the spirit of each style accurately, and to choose the proper elements and combine them intelligently, than it will be for him to copy them as they were originally produced. We know that Chippendale was successful in doing this with the Louis XIV and Louis XV styles. Hepplewhite did excellent work in the Louis XV style. Sheraton's style has the character which the Louis XVI style often lacks, though he used it as a model. The same methods should be followed at present in the interpretation of the styles, if full value and satisfaction is to be derived from the pieces.

CHIEF CHARACTERISTICS OF THE STYLES

The chief characteristics of the Louis XIV style are:

1. A somewhat heavy formality. Pieces were imposing, and individual members on them, especially at the beginning of the period, were quite heavy, and often cumbersome. Toward the end of the period, a slight reduction in scale resulted in considerable improvement.

2. The design elements were balanced bisymmetrically.

3. Straight and curved lines were used, but straight lines and rectilinear structure predominated. The construction was solid and substantial in all respects.

4. There was a tendency toward a great profusion of ornament, gorgeous in itself, but a bit too generously employed.

5. There was an evolution in the types of legs used on Louis XIV furniture, the legs going through several

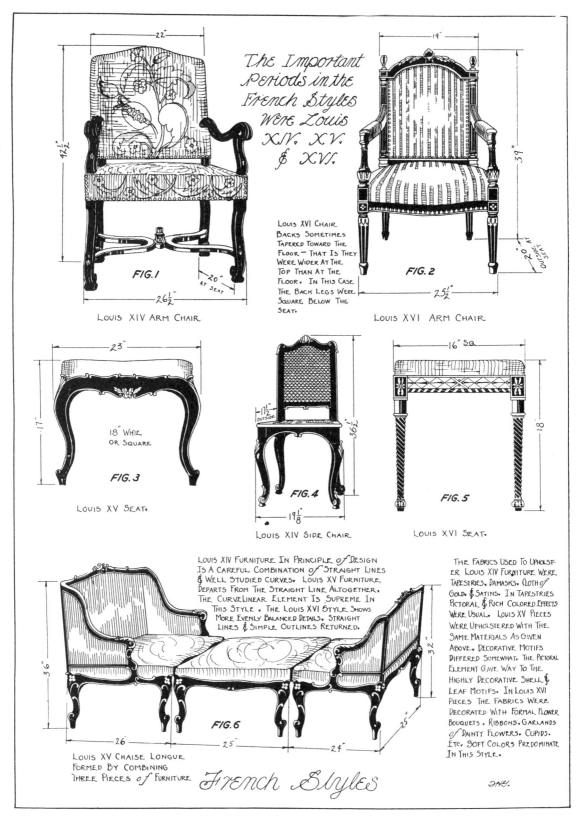

The Important Periods in the French Styles were Louis XIV. XV. & XVI.

LOUIS XVI CHAIR BACKS SOMETIMES TAPERED TOWARD THE FLOOR — THAT IS THEY WERE WIDER AT THE TOP THAN AT THE FLOOR. IN THIS CASE THE BACK LEGS WERE SQUARE BELOW THE SEAT.

FIG. 1

LOUIS XIV ARM CHAIR

FIG. 2

LOUIS XVI ARM CHAIR

FIG. 3

LOUIS XV SEAT.

18" WIDE OR SQUARE

FIG. 4

LOUIS XIV SIDE CHAIR

FIG. 5

LOUIS XVI SEAT.

LOUIS XIV FURNITURE IN PRINCIPLE OF DESIGN IS A CAREFUL COMBINATION OF STRAIGHT LINES & WELL STUDIED CURVES. LOUIS XV FURNITURE DEPARTS FROM THE STRAIGHT LINE ALTOGETHER. THE CURVELINEAR ELEMENT IS SUPREME IN THIS STYLE. THE LOUIS XVI STYLE SHOWS MORE EVENLY BALANCED DETAILS, STRAIGHT LINES & SIMPLE OUTLINES RETURNED.

THE FABRICS USED TO UPHOLSTER LOUIS XIV FURNITURE WERE TAPESTRIES, DAMASKS, CLOTH OF GOLD & SATINS. IN TAPESTRIES PICTORAL & RICH COLORED EFFECTS WERE USUAL. LOUIS XV PIECES WERE UPHOLSTERED WITH THE SAME MATERIALS AS GIVEN ABOVE. DECORATIVE MOTIFS DIFFERED SOMEWHAT. THE PICTORAL ELEMENT GAVE WAY TO THE HIGHLY DECORATIVE SHELL & LEAF MOTIFS. IN LOUIS XVI PIECES THE FABRICS WERE DECORATED WITH FORMAL FLOWER BOUQUETS, RIBBONS, GARLANDS OF DAINTY FLOWERS, CUPIDS, ETC. SOFT COLORS PREDOMINATE IN THIS STYLE.

FIG. 6

LOUIS XV CHAISE LONGUE FORMED BY COMBINING THREE PIECES OF FURNITURE

French Styles

Plate 43.

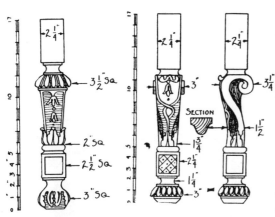

Fig. 216.
Louis XIV square
leg for chairs, day
beds, etc.

Fig. 217.
Louis XIV chair leg.

one is used on the chair, Figure 220, and on the long bench, Plate 46. Table legs, and legs used on cabinet furniture in general, were similar to the ones found on chairs.

6. Underbracing was used in most

stages of development, four of which we show. The first was a square type of leg, like Figure 216. The second one, shown in Figure 217, shows tendencies in the direction of the cabriole type, making

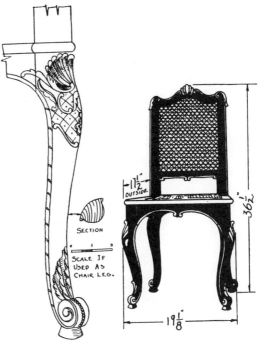

Fig. 219.
Louis XIV chair
or table leg.

Fig. 220. Louis XIV
side chair.

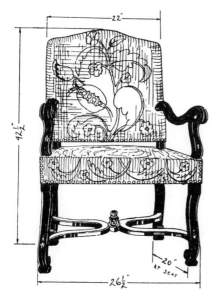

Fig. 218. Louis XIV armchair.

use of the Flemish scroll. The third type, shown in Figure 218, is a modified cabriole leg; while the fourth, and best leg is the one shown in Figure 219. This

cases on all types of pieces; and consisted, in many cases, of crossed stretchers similar to those found on William and Mary furniture.

7. Upholstering materials were very rich. Materials, especially fine tapestry and velours, were turned out expressly for individual pieces, so that the pattern was worked out with a thought to its final disposition. The motifs were, on the whole, quite large in scale.

8. The principal woods used were oak, walnut, and some of the fruit

CROWN MOLD

SOFFIT

DETAIL MOULDINGS

STRETCHER DETAIL

22"

76" OR HIGHER

44"

X STRETCHER

FIG. 7

LOUIS XIV CABINET.

THE FURNITURE OF THE LOUIS XIV STYLE WAS VERY RICH & GRAND. OFTEN IT WAS EVEN POMPOUS BEING AN EXPRESSION OF THE WEALTH & ARTISTIC ABILITY EXPENDED IN ITS CREATION.

20"

34"

FIG. 8

LOUIS XV CABINET.

LOUIS XV FURNITURE IN ITS SIMPLER FORMS IS OFTEN VERY DELIGHTFUL. WHERE THE ROCOCO DECORATION WAS GIVEN FULL EXPRESSION IT DEGENERATED IN MANY CASES INTO A BEWILDERING & DISQUIETING MASS OF DECORATIVE DETAIL.

60"

3"

HEADBOARD & FOOT BOARD UPHOLSTERED.

54"

38"

LENGTH ABOUT 82"

FIG. 9

LOUIS XVI BED

LOUIS XVI FURNITURE WAS SIMPLE & OFTEN VERY CHARMING. THOUGH IT WAS PLAIN WHEN COMPARED TO THE TWO PRECEEDING STYLES IT DID NOT LACK ELEGANCE.

34"

PLAN OF TOP & STRETCHER

72"

31"

FIG. 10

LOUIS XVI TABLE

French Styles

Plate 44.

woods, such as pear and lime. Later in the period more valuable woods were used.

9. The principal method of decoration was carving. Many pieces were gilded in their entirety, while others were parcel gilt; that is, parts of the surface were covered with gold leaf, while other parts of the design were painted with another color. At the end of the period, inlay and painting came into great favor, as did also lacquering. Plain surfaces and panels were often filled with diaper work, which consists in the main of lightly incised lines crossing each other as shown at the top of the leg, Figure 219.

10. Rococo ornament; that is, rock and shell ornament, came into popular favor toward the close of the period, but is not as typical of this style as of the Louis XV style.

11. The principal colors used at the beginning of the period were mostly those found on the dark side of the value scale, such as crimson, dark green, and dark blue. These in combination with gold leaf, often formed striking combinations. At the end of the period colors were considerably brightened.

The chief characteristics of the Louis XV style are:

1. A lighter, more graceful structure than that found on Louis XIV furniture. There was a reduction in scale, an improvement in proportions, more subtlety and grace.

2. Curved elements and structure were used to a greater extent in this style than ever before, or since. In the finest interpretation of the style, individual

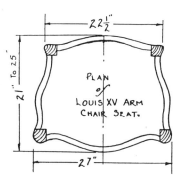

Fig. 221. Louis XV armchair seat.

pieces and elements attained the highest type of development ever achieved in any style. But as the style progressed through its final stages it degenerated, because all forms of ornament were carried to excess. On many pieces, straight lines were entirely absent, as shown in Figures 20, 221, and 226. Pieces were bowed and bulged.

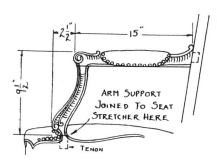

Fig. 222. Louis XV chair arm.

3. Structure was often entirely obscured and weakened by ornament and decorative detail, with a consequent loss of character and usefulness.

4. The principle of occult balance, of ornament (See Chap. 4) and even of structural elements, became one of the principal features, distinguishing this style from all others.

5. Cabriole legs of the finest type ever

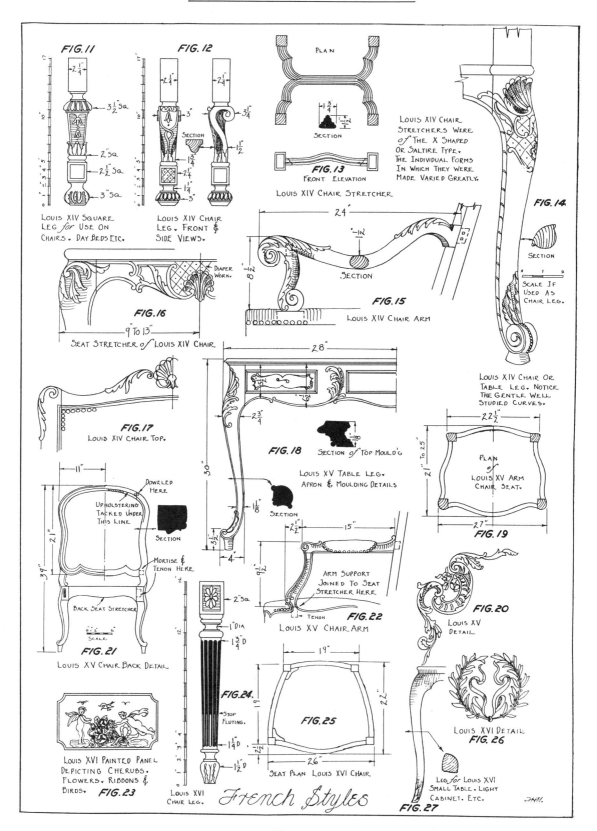

FIG.11

LOUIS XIV SQUARE LEG for USE ON CHAIRS. DAY BEDS ETC.

FIG.12

LOUIS XIV CHAIR LEG. FRONT & SIDE VIEWS.

SECTION

PLAN

SECTION

FIG.13
FRONT ELEVATION
LOUIS XIV CHAIR STRETCHER

LOUIS XIV CHAIR STRETCHERS WERE OF THE X SHAPED OR SALTIRE TYPE. THE INDIVIDUAL FORMS IN WHICH THEY WERE MADE VARIED GREATLY.

FIG.14

SECTION

SCALE IF USED AS CHAIR LEG.

DIAPER WORK.

FIG.16
SEAT STRETCHER OF LOUIS XIV CHAIR

24"

SECTION

FIG.15
LOUIS XIV CHAIR ARM

LOUIS XIV CHAIR OR TABLE LEG. NOTICE THE GENTLE WELL STUDIED CURVES.

FIG.17
LOUIS XIV CHAIR TOP.

FIG.18

SECTION

LOUIS XV TABLE LEG. APRON & MOULDING DETAILS

SECTION of TOP MOULD'G

PLAN of LOUIS XV ARM CHAIR SEAT.

FIG.19

DOWELED HERE

UPHOLSTERING TACKED UNDER THIS LINE

SECTION

MORTISE & TENON HERE

BACK SEAT STRETCHER

SCALE

FIG.21
LOUIS XV CHAIR BACK DETAIL

ARM SUPPORT JOINED TO SEAT STRETCHER HERE

TENON

FIG.22
LOUIS XV CHAIR ARM

FIG.20
LOUIS XV DETAIL

FIG.24

STOP FLUTING.

LOUIS XVI PAINTED PANEL DEPICTING CHERUBS. FLOWERS. RIBBONS & BIRDS. FIG.23

FIG.25

SEAT PLAN LOUIS XVI CHAIR

LOUIS XVI CHAIR LEG.

LOUIS XVI DETAIL
FIG. 26

LEG FOR LOUIS XVI SMALL TABLE. LIGHT CABINET. ETC.
FIG.27

French Styles

Plate 45.

designed were used almost exclusively on Louis XV furniture.

6. Underbracing was almost entirely absent from Louis XV furniture, making for a lighter, more graceful style.

7. Every conceivable type of ornament known was employed to decorate furniture, especially in naturalistic and rococo motifs. Carving; inlay; Boulle work, a type of ornament in which the inlaying material consisted of tortoise shell and metal; pictorial art of an advanced type in painting and marquetry; veneering in valuable woods; painting and lacquering; and work in precious and semiprecious metals, were among those employed.

8. Upholstering materials included tapestry, fine brocades, velours, silks, damasks, and printed materials. Some of the motifs were very elaborate.

9. Colors were brighter, and the variety of hues was greater than in any previous style.

10. All kinds of cabinet woods were employed, with walnut and mahogany easily leading the field. Cheaper woods were employed where the pieces were to be painted or gilded.

The chief characteristics of the Louis XVI style are:

1. Structure changed radically from curved and bowed, to straight and rectilinear forms.

2. Legs were mostly straight, many of them turned and fluted, reeded, or spiral turned (See Plates 43, 44, and 45).

3. A naïve classicism developed in furniture design; not the pure classicism employed by the Brothers Adam, but a dainty, playful, idealistic type.

4. Elements were generally fine in scale and proportion.

5. Ornament was of a quiet, simple nature, quite different from the sensuous, overdone forms, found on the Louis XV style. Pastoral scenes, love birds, nymphs, cherubs, and similar idealistic motifs were constantly used.

6. Bisymmetric balance again became the rule.

7. Colors were light and dainty, tending toward pastel tints, especially in fabrics. Hues were less mixed than during the former style. Striped materials became quite popular. Neutral colors played an important part in the color schemes.

8. A great deal of the furniture of this style was painted, perhaps more of it than in any other style.

9. The style is pre-eminently feminine in all of its aspects. There were many small dainty tables, cabinets, lounging chairs, and the like.

10. The wood used was the same as was used during the former style, though mahogany was favored above all others.

11. Upholstering materials included brocades, and other materials mentioned as characteristic of the Louis XV style. The scale of the motifs was perhaps finer, and they expressed more idealistic tendencies than during the former style.

CHAIRS, STOOLS, BENCHES, DAYBEDS

All of these pieces of furniture are similar in construction, contour, and decorative elements, each in its respective period. Thus when chairs are discussed, what is said about them also holds true, in a large measure, of the

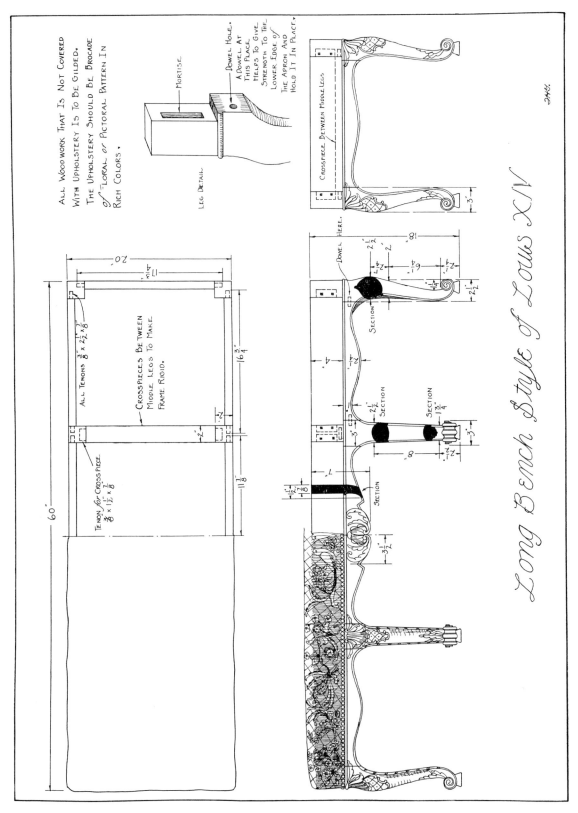

All Woodwork That Is Not Covered With Upholstery Is To Be Gilded. The Upholstery Should Be Brocade of Floral or Pictorial Pattern In Rich Colors.

Mortise.

Dowel Hole. A Dowel At This Place Helps To Give Strength To The Lower Edge of The Apron And Hold It In Place.

Leg Detail.

Crosspiece Between Middle Legs.

Crosspieces Between Middle Legs To Make Frame Rigid.

All Tenons $\frac{3}{8}$ x 2$\frac{1}{2}$ x $\frac{7}{8}$

Tenon for Cross Piece $\frac{3}{8}$ x 1$\frac{1}{2}$ x $\frac{1}{8}$

Dowel Here.

Section

Long Bench Style of Louis XIV

Plate 46.

Fig. 223. Louis XIV chair. An expression of grandeur now seldom found. Upholstered in tapestry.

other pieces, insofar as types of legs, arrangement of stretchers and legs, and decorative details are concerned.

Figures 216, 217, and 219 show typical chair legs of the first period. Figure 216 shows the square leg, which is found on the heavy chairs of the early part of the Louis XIV period. This type of leg may be adapted for use on tables, cabinets, and other pieces of furniture (See Fig. 63). On very rich pieces, the center of the leg was sometimes hollowed out, leaving the corners of the leg as a supporting framework. This framework was draped with carved festoons, or swags of flowers and fruit, all carved from the originally solid wood. Chair legs, of the type shown in Figures 218 and 223 came a little later, and are similar to those found on Charles II, and other late Jacobean armchairs. The evolution from the early types to the finer types of the latter part of the period has been pointed out, and there is no need of repeating here. It should be pointed out that the curves used in the leg, Figure 219, are very well executed, as they commonly were on chairs during the latter part of the period.

Stretchers were common throughout most of the period, and they were usually of the saltire, or X-type. Later, when cabriole legs came into common use stretchers were sometimes dispensed with, but even on chairs using the leg (Fig. 219), stretchers were still found.

Chair arms are quite heavy on most chairs of the Louis XIV style. They are

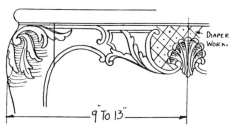

Fig. 224. Seat stretcher of Louis XIV chair.

curved, shaped, and flare outward toward the front. Many of them are highly decorated with carving (See Fig. 223).

Front stretchers, under the seats of chairs made during the latter part of the period, are shaped and carved. Such a

Fig. 225. Louis XIV chair top.

Louis XIV
& Louis XV
Louis XVI

Plate 47. 1, 2, 3, 4, and 5 may be used on Louis XIV and on Louis XV pieces. 5 is a particularly good example of the most ornate rococo ornament of Louis XV style. It illustrates the principle of occult balance. 6, 7, 8, 9, and 10 are Louis XVI patterns.

treatment is shown in Figure 224. On such chairs it is in keeping with the scheme to treat the top of the chair in a similar manner (See Fig. 225). Chairs of this type were often caned (Fig. 220), but more often they were upholstered. As we have pointed out earlier in the chapter, the figure of the materials used for upholstery was quite large in scale (See Fig. 53).

Chair backs of the Louis XIV style should be designed with considerable rake. They may lean back as much as six or seven inches, on a tall chair.

Stools, benches, and chaise longues became popular pieces of furniture during the period, and continued as important pieces throughout the three periods.

LOUIS XV CHAIRS. On Plate 45 are shown typical details of a Louis XV chair. The structural elements are serpentine in character, with hardly a straight line in the entire structure. Some of the more simple designs are quite beautiful. A chair of this type is shown in Figure 226. Had it not been for the impossible forms, and amounts of ornament, on most pieces of this kind, the style would probably be unsurpassed for grace and elegance. As it was, it may be truthfully said that the style, in merit,

Fig. 226. One of the better Louis XV chairs, delicate, graceful, and rich. It is upholstered in tapestry.

ranged from the pinnacles of craftsmanship to the depths of banality.

Chair arms, in the Louis XV style, are rather short. The chair backs, in some cases, are very wide, especially on pieces which were to be used in combination as the one shown in Figure 227. It should be noted that moldings on the Louis XV style are not as refined as they are on English styles of furniture. They have a tendency to bulge unexpectedly,

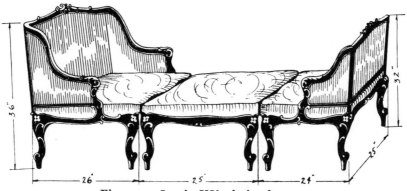

Fig. 227. Louis XV chaise longue.

and are often undercut, so that a cross section shows lopping tendencies. It is an indication that the desire of designers to create something new, often led them astray from the simple and more beautiful forms.

Louis XVI Chairs. The revival of simpler classical forms and ideals brought about a more possible form of construction. Straight lines were again supreme in structure, and a more dignified product resulted. The classical motifs are not of the finest type. They are of a reduced scale, and ot a fanciful character that makes them at times seem childish. The style as a whole, however, was quiet and dainty. Particularly is this true of the colors used which were mostly of light values, tending toward pastel tints, and usually applied on backgrounds of large neutral areas. Chairs were painted pearl gray, light ivory, silver, and other neutral colors. Fabrics were fine in the scale of motifs, and in perfect accord with the spirit of the style. Figure 66 shows a chair that is in excellent taste. Figure 228, shows still another type with a rectangular back.

Striped coverings for these chairs, and other pieces in the style, became very popular, so much so that they were made the subject of jests by wits of the day.

The seat plan on Louis XVI chairs is similar to that found on Hepplewhite chairs. The turnings and their methods of decoration were the inspiration for Sheraton.

Sofas in the Louis XVI style are often straight backed. Legs and arms on these pieces are similar to those found on the chairs.

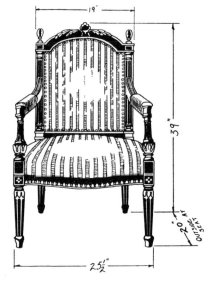

Fig. 228. Louis XVI armchair.

TABLES

The tables of the Louis XIV style are often very rich. Many of them were extremely ornate with carving and gilding The earliest tables in the style had square legs, as before mentioned. The aprons were often overloaded with decoration, and even the bracing on console tables was carved to represent garlands of flowers, and horns of plenty. Rams' heads, and other animal and human forms, were carved on legs and other places.

Original Louis XIV pieces are often of rather generous proportions, and should be scaled down for present-day adaptations. The bench design on Plate 46, should be an inspiration for table design. Long rectangular tables were the rule in all styles at this early date. Stretchers were similar to those found on chairs. The fact is that in all periods, chair design sounds the keynote for the design of all other pieces of a style.

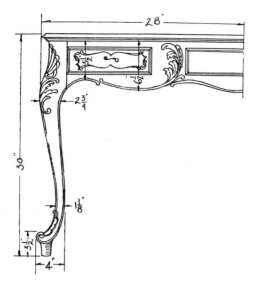

Fig. 229. Louis XV table leg, apron,
and molding details.

Therefore a study of chair design is of
the utmost importance to every designer,
and must be his starting point in gain-
ing a clear picture of the entire style. If
a designer is familiar with chair design
he has the key to the entire style.

As shown in Figure 229, the compara-
tively simple treatment of a table in the
Louis XV style may be very pleasing.
Dainty pieces of this style may be used

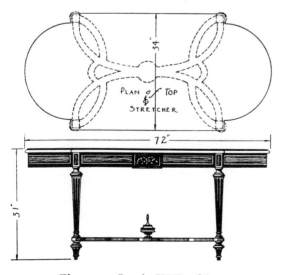

Fig. 230. Louis XVI table.

successfully with a scheme of decoration
in which one of the later English styles
is used principally. The Louis XV table
shown in Figure 41 is a piece of greater
elaboration. The piece is shown principally for its value as an indicator of
design tendencies throughout the period.
It still is not one of the extreme examples of pieces in the style.

Figure 230 shows a Louis XVI table.
The legs and other details show the distinct changes brought about by designers of this period, from the designs
of the former period.

DESKS, BUREAUS, AND WRITING FURNITURE

Desks in the Louis XIV style may be
designed as flat-topped desks, with typical legs of the square type in an arrangement similar to that shown on the
lower part of Figure 63. Others may be
of an Oriental cabinet type, more like
the one shown in Figure 60, but with
Louis XIV legs and ornament. Chinese
motifs were popular during this time in
France, and lacquered furniture was
greatly prized. Instead of doors there
was often a drop lid to form the writing
surface. Later ones had the cabriole legs
of the type shown in Figure 219.

Desks in the Louis XV style assumed
a different form. Many of these were
low slant-front desks, or roll-topped, or
cylinder-fall desks. These latter were
quite different from the roll-topped
desk of today, however. They were
dainty in proportion in many cases,
but the frames were curved and
bowed, and had cabriole legs. Many
of these were quite loaded with orna-

ment, while others were covered with Boulle work in intricate patterns. The carved ones had female figures, satyrs, or satyr masks, on the knees of legs; clocks in ornate cases at the top; and rococo ornament carved on skirts and other places.

Louis XVI desks may be designed as mere writing tables with turned and fluted legs. Small dainty ladies' desks

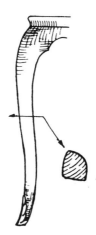

Fig. 231. Leg for Louis XVI small table, light cabinet, etc.

may be designed, using legs like those shown in Figure 231. Small writing desks and writing tables may be designed in rare wood such as rosewood or satinwood. Some designers used the tambour front on desks of this style. Others had delicately painted panels on small drawer or door fronts.

BEDS

Beds of the Louis XIV period were often merely a raised dais with a curtained canopy of rich damask or velvets. Others had heavy posts, ornately carved,

and rich canopies. The chaise-longue design (Fig. 227), will offer suggestions for beds to be designed in the Louis XV style. Figure 232, shows a Louis XVI bed design. Head and foot boards in this

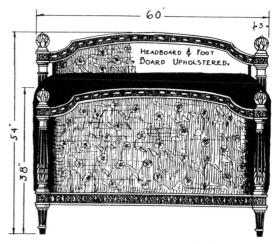

Fig. 232. Louis XVI bed.

and the preceding period were sometimes upholstered as shown. Others were richly veneered or otherwise decorated in keeping with the taste in vogue at the time.

CABINETS

A tall cabinet typical of the Louis XIV style is shown in Figure 63. Cabinets in this style almost invariably have a flat top with well-defined cornices and moldings. Legs may be of the square type, or of the cabriole type, depending upon the period to be represented. Inlay, or painted decoration, on drawers or panels may be richly colored, and backgrounds may be gilded. Cabinets of strong architectural feeling are to be found in the Louis XIV style. Many of these are supported by columns derived from the classic orders of architecture. They may even have triangular shaped pediments. Drawer fronts and door panels were carved with hunting scenes, or battle scenes, in deep relief. The columns sometimes rested on a shelf close to the floor, which was in turn supported by carved or turned feet. The upper section consisted of doors or drawers, often flanked by pilasters, or half columns.

Cabinets in the succeeding two periods became smaller and daintier, and were designed, in many cases, especially for the boudoir. Pieces of the type shown in Figure 215 were now designed in ever-increasing numbers. Callers were entertained in the boudoir, and it was always comfortably and adequately furnished in well-appointed homes. Mens' apartments took on a feminine touch, being furnished with reclining couches; soft lounging chairs, richly upholstered; tea tables; card tables; etc.

OTHER PIECES

Besides the pieces discussed there were armoires, chests of drawers, wardrobe cabinets, clocks, mirrors, in great profusion, especially during the last two periods. These latter were, in many cases, unusually rich, especially during the Louis XV period.

QUESTIONS FOR REVIEW

1. What are the three most important styles of French furniture?

2. What factors were directly responsible for the remarkable degrees of development to which these styles were carried?

3. Name several reasons why French styles are of great importance to the furniture designer.

4. To whom does French furniture particularly appeal?

5. Name several distinctive characteristics of the Louis XIV style.

6. Name several distinctive characteristics of the Louis XV style.

7. Name several distinctive characteristics of the Louis XVI style.

8. Compare the construction, scale, and contour of the Louis XIV style with that of Louis XV. Make a similar comparison between the Louis XV and the Louis XVI styles.

9. What unique principle of design was commonly practiced in the design of Louis XV furniture?

10. Describe the types of ornament commonly found in the Louis XIV style; Louis XV; Louis XVI.

11. What may be said concerning molding of the Louis XV style?

12. What may be said regarding the use of color on each of the three styles?

13. Describe the evolution of chair design during the Louis XIV period.

14. What are some of the precautions that should be observed in adapting French designs to present-day schemes of furnishing?

15. What significant lesson may be learned from the fact that Chippendale, Hepplewhite, and Sheraton successfully adapted French motifs and used them to produce their greatest masterpieces?

16. Describe table design in each of the three styles.

17. What does the term *bureau* signify in speaking of French furniture?

18. Describe the evolution of bed design during the three periods.

SUGGESTED PROBLEMS

1. Design a cabinet for the display of valuable china or bric-a-brac in the Louis XIV style.

2. Design a Louis XV hall table; a Louis XV chaise longue.

3. Design a Louis XVI mirror frame.

4. Design a light Louis XVI ladies' writing desk.

CHAPTER 14

THE FURNITURE OF THE SPANISH RENAISSANCE
1500–1650

HISTORICAL BACKGROUND AND GENERAL CHARACTERISTICS

The most important style produced in Spain was that of the sixteenth and early seventeenth centuries, when the furniture, which today is easily recognized by its distinctive features, came into existence. The style is the result of a mixture of influences, chief among which are Moorish and Gothic art and architecture. The mark of Italian and other southern European art influences is also indelibly stamped upon the style.

The most important contribution to the development of a Spanish style was made by the Moors, who were Arabs and Mohammedans. The Moors invaded and conquered Spain, making it their home for over seven hundred years. They were finally driven from the peninsula in 1492, the very year that Columbus discovered America. Among these Moors were architects and artisans of exceptional skill, and the contributions they made to Spanish art were of inestimable value. Among these contributions were the Moorish arch, spiral turning, and the excellent ironwork, so typical of Spanish furniture. Suggestions of all of these influences are found on the design of the Spanish vargueno on Plate 50 (See also Fig. 235).

At this early date the influence of the church was very great, with the result that Gothic structural forms and decorative motifs are more strongly in evidence in the Spanish than in any other important furniture style used today. Italy contributed a great deal to the Spanish style.

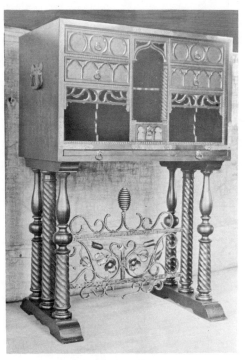

Fig. 235. Spanish vargueno. The possibilities for ornament of unusual character on Spanish furniture are unlimited.

183

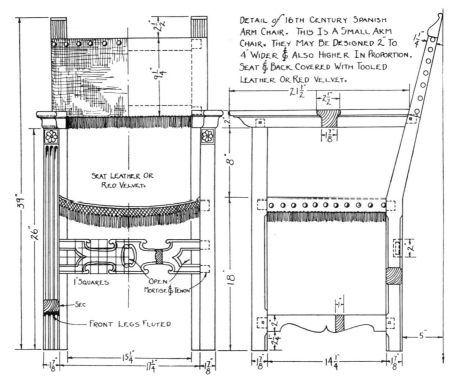

Fig. 236. Detail of sixteenth-century Spanish armchair.

Charles V, who ascended the throne about 1500, was emperor of Italy, the Netherlands, and a large part of central Europe. He imported workmen from Italy, a country rich in artistic experience; and they were responsible for much of the dignity and the simple directness of pieces such as the chair shown in Figure 236. The Flemish scroll was adapted from the Netherlands, and it became an important motif on many Spanish pieces. An example is Figure 237, where it is used on the Spanish foot, and on the apron of the table.

The Spaniards themselves contributed the rich colors which they loved — vivid reds and rich blues — and the virile forms commonly found on their turnings.

All of these influences became fused into a distinctive and an exceedingly in-teresting style. A great deal of the ornament found its way to other countries,

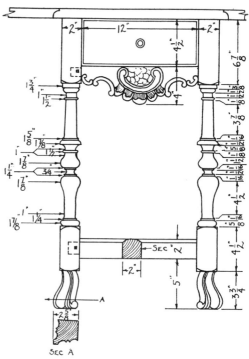

Fig. 237.   End of Spanish gate-leg table.

where it was adapted to the furniture of later periods. The Spanish foot, for example, was highly prized for banister-back chairs in England and America during the Jacobean period. The shell, a favored form of Spanish ornament, was highly prized as a decorative element on several later styles.

Spanish furniture has a peculiar charm, all its own, but it belongs, and shows up to the greatest advantage, in a setting of the type for which it was originally designed. Northern architecture and Spanish furniture have no affinity for each other, and should not be used together. We can imagine few exceptions to this rule. In the New England home of a retired sea captain, who has spent his days sailing the Spanish Main, a Spanish vargueno, or an iron-bound chest might be appropriate, if surrounded by a collection of other appropriate objects. There will be few other cases where Spanish furniture can be appropriately used in a northern home. But in Florida, southern California, or New Mexico, no other style would, perhaps, be so appropriate, especially if the architecture is of the adobe type. The furniture belongs to plain rough-textured walls, in a setting of palms and pine trees, under a tropical sky.

The chief characteristics of the Spanish style are:

1. A rectangular, straightforward, substantial structure. Straight, well-braced structural elements are used throughout.

2. Walnut was the chief wood used for fine cabinetwork, and is the proper wood for pieces of the style. Oak and other woods, of course, were used, especially in the rural districts.

3. Turning, of a virile, deeply cut sort, was a popular medium, expressing the love of form which is apparent in so many Spanish pieces. Turning was employed on table and chair legs, and for underframing on case furniture. Rows of turned spindles formed into grilles, or arcades, were used for ornament on various pieces (See Fig. 238).

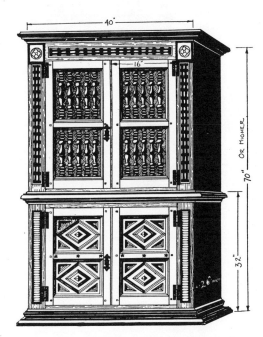

Fig. 238. Cupboard of the sixteenth-century Renaissance period.

4. Wrought-iron work of excellent design, skillfully executed, distinguishes Spanish furniture from all other important styles (See Plate 51).

5. Wood carving, deep cut and well executed, is typical on many pieces. The shell, a religious symbol of the period, and the Flemish scroll, were greatly favored motifs for carving.

6. Tooled leather was used for uphol-

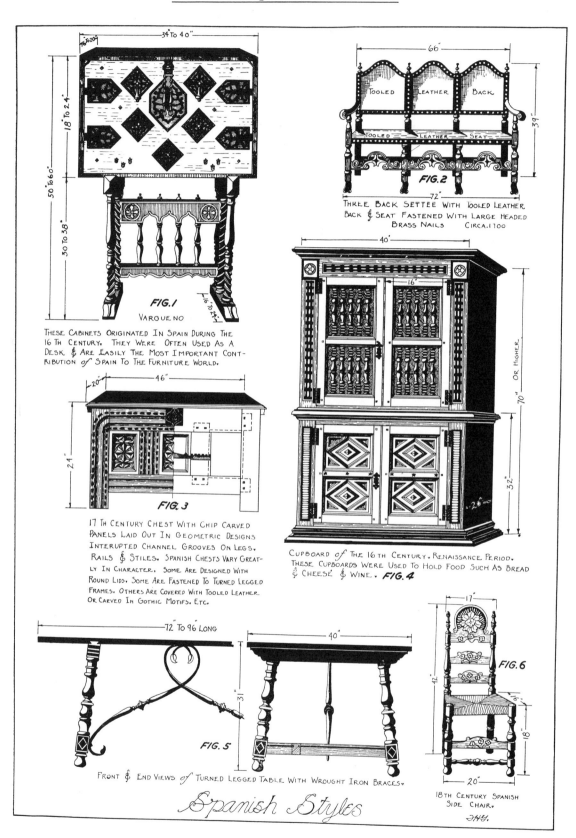

FIG. I
VARGUENO

THESE CABINETS ORIGINATED IN SPAIN DURING THE
16 TH CENTURY. THEY WERE OFTEN USED AS A
DESK & ARE EASILY THE MOST IMPORTANT CONT-
RIBUTION OF SPAIN TO THE FURNITURE WORLD.

FIG. 2
THREE BACK SETTEE WITH TOOLED LEATHER
BACK & SEAT FASTENED WITH LARGE HEADED
BRASS NAILS   CIRCA.1700

FIG. 3
17 TH CENTURY CHEST WITH CHIP CARVED
PANELS LAID OUT IN GEOMETRIC DESIGNS
INTERUPTED CHANNEL GROOVES ON LEGS.
RAILS & STILES. SPANISH CHESTS VARY GREAT-
LY IN CHARACTER. SOME ARE DESIGNED WITH
ROUND LIDS. SOME ARE FASTENED TO TURNED LEGGED
FRAMES. OTHERS ARE COVERED WITH TOOLED LEATHER
OR CARVED IN GOTHIC MOTIFS. ETC.

CUPBOARD OF THE 16 TH CENTURY. RENAISSANCE PERIOD.
THESE CUPBOARDS WERE USED TO HOLD FOOD SUCH AS BREAD
& CHEESE & WINE. FIG. 4

FIG. 5
FRONT & END VIEWS OF TURNED LEGGED TABLE WITH WROUGHT IRON BRACES.

FIG. 6
18TH CENTURY SPANISH
SIDE CHAIR.

Spanish Styles

Plate 48.

stering, on chairs, settees; and as a covering for chests, table tops, and the like. Quite often the leather was colored. Sometimes designs were formed upon a leather-covered surface with gilt nail heads, or nail heads formed to the design of a rose, a shell, or some such form (See Fig. 239).

Fig. 239.
Decorated
nail heads.

7. Surfaces were decorated with inlays of ivory, bone, silver, tortoise shell, and mother of pearl, in unique and intricate patterns.

8. The Spanish loved rich colors against severe backgrounds. There are handsome pieces on which red, blue, and old gold are used to form attractive color schemes. Red velvets were often used as a background under perforated iron ornaments, or behind open grilles of carved Gothic tracery. Warm spectrum colors such as yellow and orange were also greatly favored.

9. Applied ornament such as split spindles, bosses, lozenges, etc., was commonly used.

10. Animal feet, such as the ball and claw, hoof foot, lion's foot, etc., were employed. Other forms were the Spanish foot, and turned-pear or ball feet.

11. Velvets, velours, and tapestries were used for upholstering, in addition to the leather which has already been mentioned.

CHAIRS

Two types of chairs are shown on Plates 48 and 49. The one shown in Figure 240 is a type developed in the rural

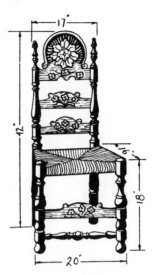

Fig. 240. Eighteenth-century Spanish side chair.

districts of Spain. It may be carved and painted. Some are only painted, sometimes with flowers in pictorial fashion on the large upper splat. The shell motif on the top of this one could be carved, then painted or gilded. The seat is bottomed with rushes. It is a comfortable, attractive chair.

The chair shown in Figure 236, is simple in line, but it has merits that are worthy of special mention. It belongs to a class of furniture that is only too rare. It has an honest, lasting construction. It is a piece upon which beautiful proportions may easily be worked out. A tooled-leather back, colored if so desired, a handsomely carved stretcher, together with other forms of decoration suggested by the drawing, will offer ample oppor-

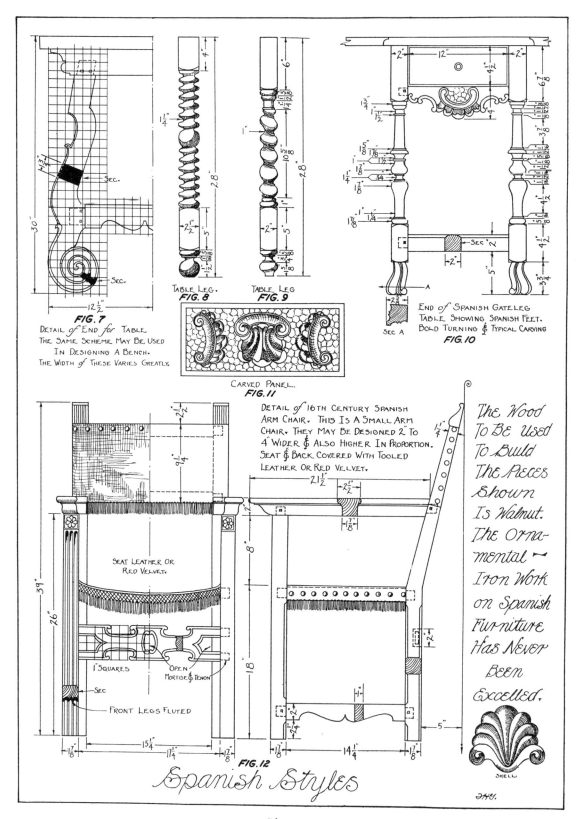

TABLE LEG.
FIG. 8

TABLE LEG.
FIG. 9

FIG. 7
DETAIL of END for TABLE
THE SAME SCHEME MAY BE USED
IN DESIGNING A BENCH.
THE WIDTH of THESE VARIES GREATLY.

CARVED PANEL.
FIG. 11

END of SPANISH GATELEG
TABLE SHOWING SPANISH FEET.
BOLD TURNING & TYPICAL CARVING
FIG. 10

SEC A

DETAIL of 16TH CENTURY SPANISH
ARM CHAIR. THIS IS A SMALL ARM
CHAIR. THEY MAY BE DESIGNED 2" TO
4" WIDER & ALSO HIGHER IN PROPORTION.
SEAT & BACK COVERED WITH TOOLED
LEATHER OR RED VELVET.

SEAT LEATHER OR
RED VELVET.

1" SQUARES

OPEN
MORTISE & TENON

SEC.

FRONT LEGS FLUTED

*The Wood
To Be Used
To Build
The Pieces
Shown
Is Walnut.
The Orna-
mental ~
Iron Work
on Spanish
Furniture
Has Never
Been
Excelled.*

SHELL

FIG. 12

Spanish Styles

Plate 49.

tunities for enrichment. Artists and designers have acclaimed this as the most perfect type of chair ever developed. The claim has a great deal of justification, as a careful analysis will reveal. It is, of course, adapted from Italian forms. Its lines being straight, it conforms to the lines of a room. It has great dignity, and is exceedingly comfortable; attributes that should belong to every chair, but which strangely enough are often lacking. Wood for these chairs should be walnut. Two fine chairs of this period are shown in Figure 241.

Still another type of chair often found is one similar to the settee shown in Figure 242. This settee is quite handsome.

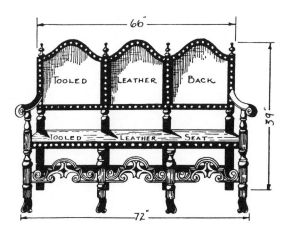

Fig. 242. Three-back settee with tooled leather.

Pieces of this type were usually upholstered in tooled leather. The finials at the top were of brass.

Fig. 241. Spanish side chairs. Examples of exquisite tooled leather work, typical of the finest Spanish traditions. The feet have probably been worn away a great deal.

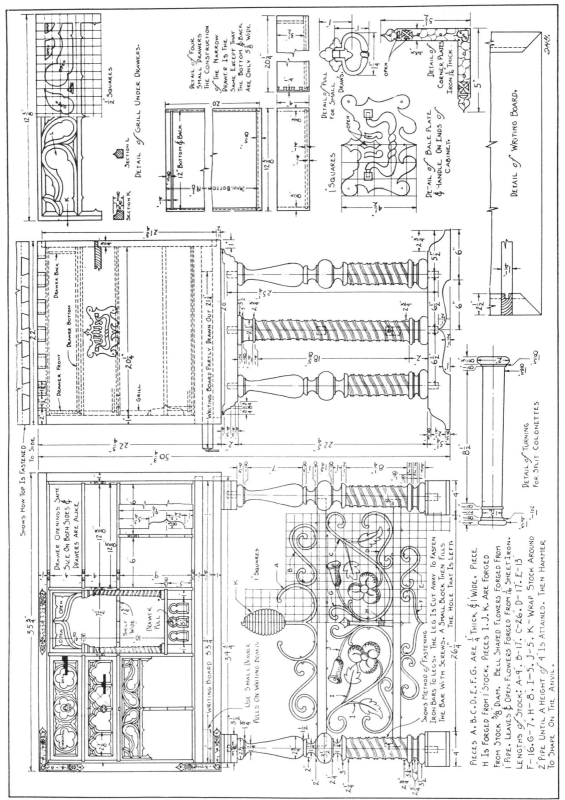

Plate 50.

Fig. 243. Spanish sofa with scrolled legs and feet. Excellent example of Spanish design.

SOFAS

A fine sofa in the Spanish style is shown in Figure 243. These have the familiar scrolled legs and feet, with iron bracing. The lines, and evident comfort of the piece, are attractive features.

TABLES

Most of the tables in the Spanish styles are of the trestle type. One kind may be designed with turned legs, often splayed, and braced with the iron crossed bars (See Fig. 244). The other type has sawed-out legs of the type shown in Figure 245, and may have scrolled feet as shown. Long refectory tables are also to be found. These, while they are similar to the Jacobean refectory tables in form and structure, differ in the types of ornament employed, and in the style of turning (See Fig. 246). In some cases these turnings are quite heavy. Grape-vine carving (Fig. 247), is in excellent taste for aprons on such tables. Long benches designed in the same spirit usually accompany the tables.

Figure 237 shows an interesting treat-

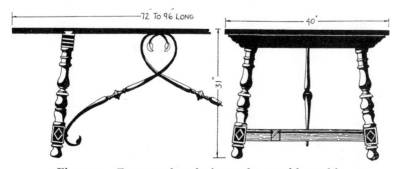

Fig. 244. Front and end views of turned-leg table.

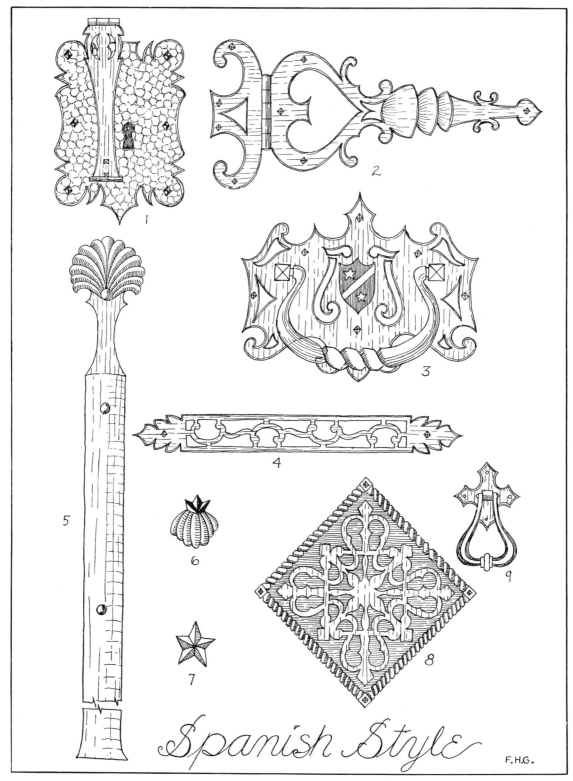

Spanish Style

F.H.G.

Plate 51. 1. Chest lock. 2. Chest hinge or cabinet hinge. 3. Handle for vargueno or chest. 4. Perforated plate used on varguenos and chests. 4 and 8 are usually tacked on crimson velvet. 5. Metal strip used as binding iron on outside of chests and coffers. 6 and 7. Decorated nail heads. 8. Perforated mount for vargueno. 9. Drawer pull.

ment for a typically Spanish gate-leg table. It has Spanish feet, a fine type of turning, and beautiful carving.

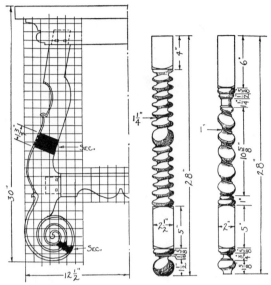

Fig. 245. Detail of end for table.   Fig. 246. Table legs.

Fig. 247. Apron with grapevine carving.

CHESTS

Chests were among the most important pieces in early Spanish households. Many of these were supported on frames, either turned or sawed out, similar to the tables. In fact, chests and coffers were frequently placed upon tables. Many of these had round tops, much like an old-fashioned trunk of the kind with which many of us are still familiar. These were often covered with tooled leather, bound with strap iron. Others were painted in rich colors, or were carved, and decorated with metal mounts and decorative locks and hasps.

Still other chests were of the type shown in Figure 40. This has panels decorated with chip carving, done with a sloyd knife.

CUPBOARDS

The Spanish style has a place for many kinds of cupboards and cabinets. These were used to hold food, clothing, and armor. The cupboard shown in Figure 238, is a typical design. It should offer many suggestions to the designer. For example, a hanging cupboard may be designed with grilled doors of turned spindles, or of wrought iron. The bottom of such a cupboard could be worked with a scroll-sawed apron or skirt, carved with an appropriate design. Bold moldings are used on Spanish pieces. The type of paneling also suggests many interesting possibilities.

VARGUENOS

The Spanish vargueno, or desk is the most important piece of furniture this style produced, as well as one of the most interesting pieces of furniture to be found in any style. The possibilities for interesting solutions of problems relating to them are almost endless. The author has designed and built two, one of which is shown on Plate 50, and in Figure 235. Sometimes, instead of being carved, the small drawer fronts are inlaid with bone, ivory, ebony, or other materials. Beautifully painted drawer fronts are known with handsome religious pictures, ably executed. The backgrounds of the carvings on the varguenos built by the author were painted with rich, imported bronze paints in

Spanish table with decorative nail heads.

colors of blue, vermilion, green, and old gold.

Stretchers for these pieces may be of wrought iron, or an arcade of turned spindles, as shown in Figure 76. Lions' heads and feet may be carved on the ends of heavy timbers such as the feet or crosspieces supporting the box. Most of the varguenos have a lid to be let down, which forms the writing surface. The outside of this is exquisitely decorated with metal mounts as shown in Figure 76. The one shown on Plate 50 has a thick board which may be drawn out to form the writing surface. Thus the decorated cabinet will always be open to view.

Questions for Review

1. Describe the mixture of influences that was responsible for the furniture of the types developed during the Spanish Renaissance.

2. In what type of architectural setting is Spanish furniture suitable?

3. Name three important characteristics of construction found in Spanish furniture.

4. Enumerate several unique ornamental features used to enrich Spanish furniture.

5. What may be said about the importance of Spanish Renaissance chair design?

6. What is the proper wood to use in building Spanish furniture?

7. Describe a typical Spanish Renaissance table; its construction and ornament especially.

8. Describe the construction and ornament of Spanish chests and coffers.

9. What may be said about the scientific use of principles of good design on Spanish furniture in general?

10. Describe the construction, types

of ornament, and use of a typical Spanish Renaissance cupboard.

11. What colors found greatest favor with designers of the Spanish Renaissance?

12. What is the most important piece of furniture developed in this style, and what is it used for?

13. What two materials, not commonly associated with furniture of other styles, were used to good advantage in this style?

Suggested Problems

1. Design a Spanish coffer, to be used as a receptacle for important correspondence.

2. Design a Spanish Renaissance armchair.

3. Design a Spanish vargueno.

4. Design a long bench or stool with grapevine carving

5. Design a table lamp, using iron, wood, or both materials.

CHAPTER 15

THE STYLE OF DUNCAN PHYFE
1790–1830

HISTORICAL DATA AND GENERAL CHARACTERISTICS

Duncan Phyfe ranks as the greatest American cabinetmaker. He is sometimes spoken of as the American Sheraton. He is the only American to whom we can attribute a style of furniture. Only one other man in America is doing work that is comparable to that of Duncan Phyfe's. That man is Wallace Nutting of Framingham, Massachusetts, whose furniture will one day be heralded as the equal of any that has ever been done by the great cabinetmakers of the eighteenth century.

Duncan Phyfe's best work was directly influenced by the work of Sheraton and Hepplewhite, and some of his designs are so similar to Sheraton's that they may be classed as reproductions. This is particularly true of tables and sewing stands.

Duncan Phyfe was born in Scotland, and came to America with his parents about 1784. He worked at the cabinetmaker's trade in Albany until about 1790 when he came to New York, and located on Broad Street. Five years later he removed to 35 Partition Street, later renamed Fulton Street, where he had a shop for the remainder of his life. Soon after opening this shop Phyfe's business began to thrive, due to the superior merit of his work, and to the patronage of some of the wealthiest and most influential people of the city, among whom were the family of John Jacob Astor.

His early work, following very closely the work of the great English cabinetmakers, was his best. The strong influence exerted by the French styles and fashions, then being imported directly from Paris in great numbers, led him to adapt their motifs to his own work. He greatly reduced the scale, improved the proportion, and discarded much of the impossible ornament found on the French Directoire and Empire furniture, with the result that his style was a great improvement on the original style. All of Phyfe's best furniture shows a fine feeling for beautiful proportions, for consistent scale, and for conservatism and good taste in the use of ornament. Only his best furniture will be considered in this short chapter.

A study of Plate 52, will show a consistent use of certain important elements by which his style is distinguished from others we have studied. Among these are the pedestal type of base for tables; the consistent use of reeding on legs, columns, and the edges of table tops; the use of distinctive veneers; the repeated use of distinctive features such as the lyre, and brass animal feet, and a few unique types of curved legs. Particularly do we find evidence that the decorative details employed by Phyfe, on his best work, were limited in number, but the variety of ways in which they were employed was great. For example, the use of the lyre as a structural element for supporting a table top is unusual, and shows no mean inventive ability (See Fig. 250).

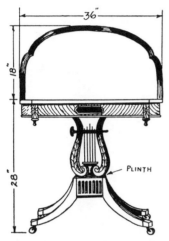

Fig. 250. Lyre-base card table.

fort and livableness in Phyfe's furniture; a feeling so often found lacking in the Brothers Adam designs.

The chief characteristics of the style are:

1. Strikingly fine proportions, especially in his early work. Note the subtle relationships of length to width of the masses in Figures 251 and 252.

2. Clean and simple lines. The outline structure is remarkably clean cut. Curves were generously employed on structural elements, but the rules of good design were given due considera-

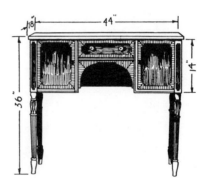

Fig. 251. Small veneered sideboard.

The proportions on his furniture give ample evidence of careful planning. Supporting members, such as legs, pedestal bases, and columns, are light and graceful, but are evidently of sufficient strength to support the load required of them, and at the same time are harmonious in scale with the rest of the mass. The curved elements, such as chair legs and table legs on pedestal tables, are carefully designed, giving ample evidence of their adequacy as supporting members. These curved members, and the excellent scale, give the personal touch responsible for the feeling of com-

tion, especially Rules 13, 14, 15, 16, 29, and 30. Mechanical curves were not employed; freehand curves taking their place, as they should in all good design. Curves on horizontal elements were in some cases so subtle as to almost escape detection.

3. Restraint in the use of ornament. Duncan Phyfe employed a few distinctive motifs so often that they became a characteristic feature of his style. These motifs, though not great in number, were ingeniously employed. The lyre, for example, was used effectively on a great many pieces (See Plate 52).

Fig. 252. Three-back settee. A clean looking piece of excellent design.

4. Materials of the finest quality were constantly employed on all good work. Figured mahogany veneers, of superior quality and figure, were used. Where solid wood was employed, it was in most cases high-grade Cuban mahogany, which is unexceled for hardness, fine texture, and good working qualities. It is said that Phyfe caused extra fine trees in the forests of Cuba to be earmarked for him, to insure fine quality lumber.

5. Structural soundness, but at the

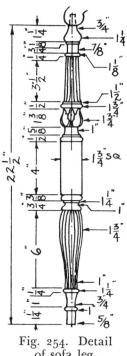

Fig. 254. Detail of sofa leg.

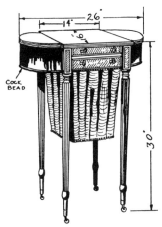

Fig. 253. Sewing table.

same time a proper economy in the use of materials. There is nothing superfluous; no undue waste of materials in Phyfe's work. Neither is there weakness from too great a skimping of materials.

6. Supporting structural elements

consisted of turned legs of the most delicate refinement (See Figs. 253 and 254); of pedestal bases with curved legs, these taking the form of reverse curves, or one-direction freehand curves of genuinely adequate strength. Curved chair legs consist of well-balanced supporting curves, refined in grace and proportion, but of sufficient strength to perform their function.

7. Brass mounts were used quite extensively, but almost invariably good taste was evidenced in their selection and use. French Empire furniture was often loaded down with applied brass ornaments against a background of red mahogany. Duncan Phyfe limited its use almost entirely to brass feet, and drawer pulls.

8. The ornament which was most often employed included the following:

Fig. 255. Duncan Phyfe armchair.

The acanthus leaf was typical, though it differed in most cases from that usually found in other styles of furniture. The Phyfe acanthus is very much simplified, and in many cases is quite similar to a holly leaf. The water leaf was also employed for carving on posts and turn-

Fig. 256. Duncan Phyfe table.

14"
32"
16"
Depth of Seat
At Center Line 16"
17"
FIG. 1

DUNCAN PHYFE SIDE CHAIR
REEDED HORSESHOE SHAPED
SEAT.

2½"
16"
6½"
32"
12½"
Depth of Seat
17"
16"
17"
19"
FIG. 2

SIDE CHAIR WITH LYRE BACK.

Depth of Seat At
Center Line 18"
16"
16"
32" to 34"
19"
FIG. 3

DUNCAN PHYFE ARM CHAIR.

66"
46"
22"
28"
16"
34"
54"
FIG. 4

TWO BACK SETTEE WITH LYRE ENDS. THESE MAY BE MADE
WITH THREE BACKS & ARE SOMETIMES CANED. THEY
SOMETIMES HAVE ANIMAL FEET.

30"
28"
FIG. 5

CONSOLE TABLE. VENEERED APRON.

14" 26"
6"
COCK
BEAD
30"
FIG. 6

SEWING TABLE. THE SILK BAG
IS FASTENED TO THE LOWER DRAWER
WHICH HAS NO BOTTOM. THE
SEMI-CIRCULAR ENDS ARE BOXES &
THE LIDS HAVE INVISIBLE HINGES.

*Though Duncan
Phyfe Adapted
Freely From The
Work of Sheraton,
Heppelwhite & Others
He Developed A
Distinct Style.*

12" 36" 24"
29"
FIG. 7

LIBRARY TABLE WITH LYRE ENDS.

18" 44"
36"
14"
FIG. 8

SMALL VENEERED SIDEBOARD.

36"
18"
28"
PLINTH
FIG. 9

LYRE BASE CARD TABLE.

120"
48"
30"
FIG. 10

DINING TABLE. THESE MAY BE MADE IN TWO, THREE OR
FIVE SECTIONS. WIDE BOARDS MAY ALSO BE ADDED
BETWEEN EACH SECTION TO LENGTHEN THE TABLES.

THE PRINCIPLE PIECES OF FURNITURE MADE
BY PHYFE WERE CHAIRS, TABLES, SOFAS
& SETTEES. HE ALSO MADE SIDEBOARDS,
BEDSTEADS, MIRRORS, WASHSTANDS, WRITING
DESKS, ETC. SOME OF HIS FAVORITE
MOTIFS WERE THE LYRE, THE ACANTHUS
LEAF, TURNED & REEDED LEGS, TURNED
PEDESTALS SUPPORTED ON CURVED LEGS,
& ANIMAL FEET OF BRASS. THE PRINCIPAL
WOOD USED WAS MAHOGANY, OFTEN
VENEERED.

Duncan Phyfe Style

Plate 52.

ings. For panels on chair backs, etc., various forms of ornament were employed, these being mostly of classical derivation, such as the thunderbolt (Fig. 255), ribbands, oak leaf and acorn, etc. Reeding was a favorite means of decorating turned columns, legs, and edges of table tops. It is more characteristic of this style than of any other. Animal feet, such as the dog's foot, lion's foot, eagle's claw, and others, mostly in brass, but occasionally carved, were typical. Other carved motifs included the egg-and-dart molding, leaf-and-dart molding, rosettes, cornucopias, whorle fluting, laurel leaves, Prince of Wales feathers, wheat ears, etc. The lyre was a favorite decoration, as well as a structural feature on Duncan Phyfe pieces.

Tastefully colored inlaid bands and borders were used on table aprons, and around drawer fronts. These used with

Fig. 257. Table with fine lacy effect of figured veneer on apron and tasteful ornament on turnings.

veneers of striking figure, resulted in distinctive pieces of furniture. All of the foregoing forms of ornament are depicted in the drawings on Plates 52, 53, and 55, and in Figures 252, 256, and 257.

9. The furniture was almost invariably dyed a rich red color.

CHAIRS

Chairs, sofas, and tables were the chief pieces of furniture made by Duncan Phyfe. He also made beds, and other articles, but the above-mentioned ones are the most numerous.

There are several distinct types of chairs. One of these has a horseshoe-shaped seat, and straight-turned, reeded front legs. These are either turned clear to the floor, or have brass animal feet. The back legs on many of these chairs have beautifully formed curves of a type that would result if a piece of spring steel were held by both ends and bent (See Fig. 24). The backs on these chairs have various motifs, but the lyre and crossed bar are common (See Plates 52 and 53). The horseshoe-shaped seat is usually made with a slip seat when it is upholstered. Other chairs are caned.

Another type of chair is one on which the Directoire influences predominate. Figures 255 and 258 are examples of this type. Some of these have the back leg formed in a compound curve (Fig. 258). The front legs are in the form of reverse curves, carved on the front with either reeding or acanthus leaves. These leaf motifs in some cases go all the way to the floor. The legs are slightly tapered

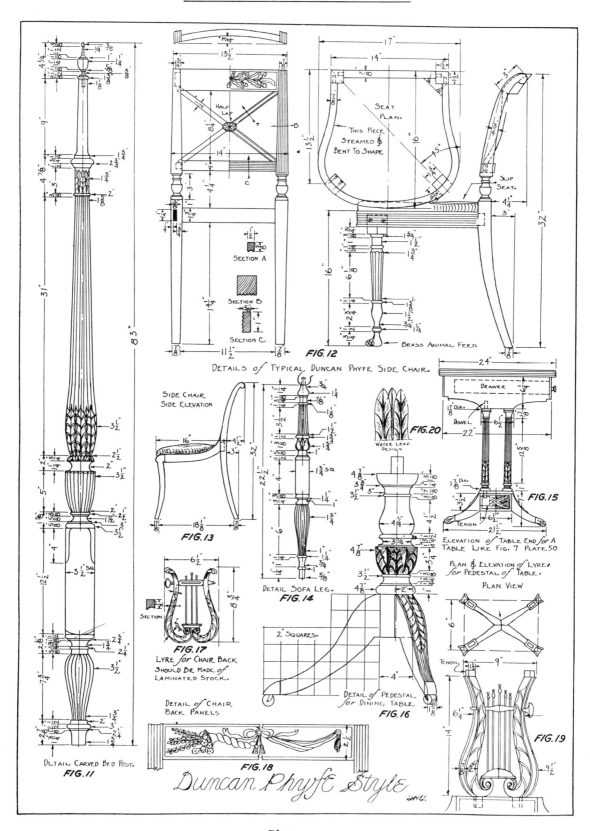

DETAILS of TYPICAL DUNCAN PHYFE SIDE CHAIR.

FIG. 12

FIG. 11
DETAIL CARVED BED POST.

FIG. 13
SIDE CHAIR
SIDE ELEVATION

FIG. 17
LYRE for CHAIR BACK
SHOULD BE MADE of
LAMINATED STOCK.

SECTION

DETAIL of CHAIR
BACK PANELS

FIG. 18

FIG. 14
DETAIL SOFA LEG.

FIG. 20
WATER LEAF
DESIGN

2 SQUARES.

DETAIL of PEDESTAL
for DINING TABLE
FIG. 16

FIG. 15
ELEVATION of TABLE END for A
TABLE LIKE FIG. 7 PLATE 50.

PLAN & ELEVATION of LYRE
for PEDESTAL of TABLE.
PLAN VIEW

FIG. 19

Duncan Phyfe Style

Plate 53.

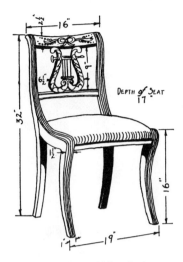

Fig. 258. Side chair
with lyre back.

ton furniture will also prove satisfactory for Phyfe pieces. A new list will, therefore, not be necessary.

SOFAS AND SETTEES

Sofas are of several types. They are, of course, in many respects similar to the chairs, as is usually the case in all styles. Figure 252 shows a settee, similar in many respects to those designed by Sheraton. It is a very handsome piece. The fine proportions, and the great delicacy of the turning and carving make this a gem. The proportions of the minor masses in the back, for example, are difficult to analyze at a glance, but the relations that exist are of such a nature as to make them exceedingly interesting. These relations prove the rule of design, number 21, given in the chapter on Proportion. On a piece of this type it is of particular importance to observe Rule 40. This is exceedingly well done on this piece.

A sofa of another type is designed more like a Roman couch (See Fig. 260). These have curved legs and other curved structural elements in the frame. The front of the frame is reeded, and other

and rounded on the front. The front of the rear leg may be reeded above the seat, or narrow beads may be carved on both edges, leaving the space between the beads lowered. Arms are curved like those shown in Figure 255. Arm supports may be turned, reeded, and carved. The construction of Duncan Phyfe chairs will be made clear by a study of Figures 24 and 259. All joints should be mortised and tenoned, for greatest strength, rather than doweled. Upholstering fabrics found suitable for Shera-

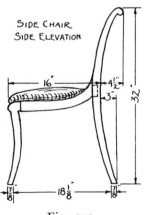

SIDE CHAIR
SIDE ELEVATION

Fig. 259.

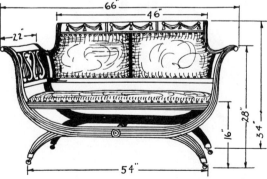

Fig. 260. Two-back settee with lyre ends.

Plate 54.

structural elements are similar to those found on some chairs in the style.

TABLES

Duncan Phyfe made many kinds of tables. These included card tables, Figure 250; dining tables, Figure 261; console tables, Figure 262; sewing tables, Figure 253; pier tables; and other occasional tables of many kinds.

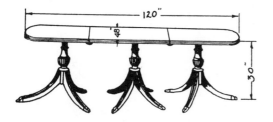

Fig. 261. Dining table in three sections.

Three types of table construction are shown on Plate 52. All tables made in the best Phyfe manner fall into one of these classes. The sewing tables and veneered sideboard represent one type, having straight, turned and reeded legs at each corner. The library table (Fig.

263), and the end of another (Fig. 264) are two variations of the second type. These are supported, at the ends, by columns, or by lyre-shaped supporting members. The third type has a pedestal base, either with a lyre arrangement sup-

Fig. 263. Library table with lyre ends.

porting the top, or with turned shafts or columns (See Figs. 250, 262, and 261). The straight, reeded legs of the first type are always delicately formed and slender. The turnings should be designed with delicate fillets, astragals, torus moldings, and coves. Notice also

Fig. 262. Console table
with veneered apron.

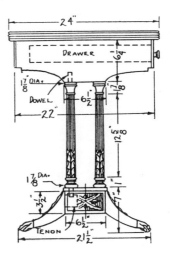

Fig. 264. Elevation
of table end.

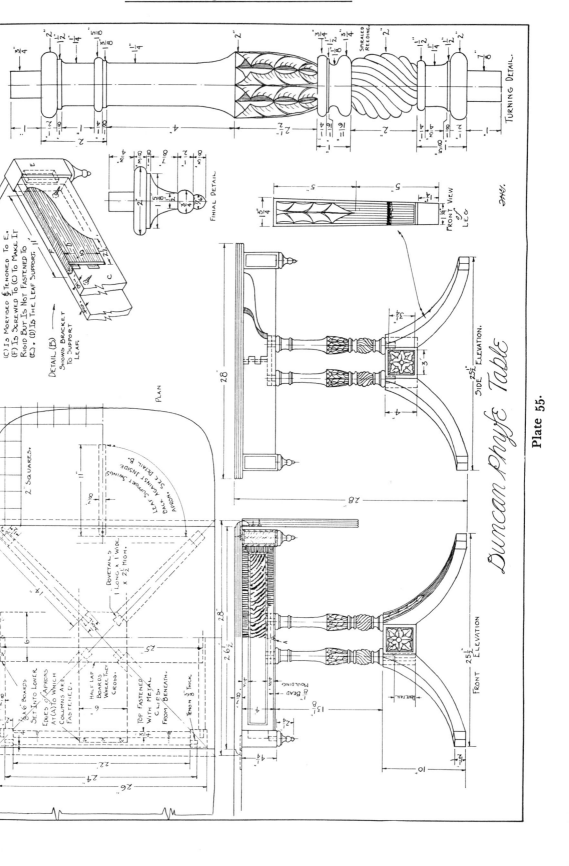

Duncan Phyfe Table

Plate 55.

the delicate swelling on the foot of the front leg of the chair (Fig. 24), a feature found on table legs as well. Other variations for treatment of turned feet are shown in Figures 251 and 253, and in Figures 254 and 265.

The fronts and aprons of these tables are often beautifully veneered, and sometimes tastefully inlaid. Drawer fronts are edged with cock beading — a narrow bead molding that is raised above the face of the drawer front, or other member, to protect the veneering and serve as an added finishing touch (See Fig. 253).

Table tops were rounded at the corners in plan, with straight ends and sides, or with ends gracefully curved, the curves being gradual and long (See Plate 55). Sometimes the ends of dining tables were half circles, as in Figure 169. Another typical shape for the design of a table top is shown in Figure 250.

The pedestal base, shown in Figure 169, may be designed with a turned shaft that is either carved or plain. Carving may take the form of reeding, and with leaf motifs as shown in many of the sketches. The curved legs are fastened to these shafts, or to the pedestal base with dovetail joints, as shown in the detail on Plate 63. It should be observed that the pedestal in the center has four feet, while those on the ends have only three feet. The construction of a lyre pedestal is shown in Figure 266. Still another type of pedestal base, and one which has especial merit, is the type shown on the design on Plate 55. The supporting structure is made up of four slender shafts, beautifully turned and

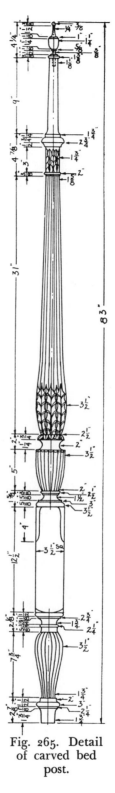

Fig. 265. Detail of carved bed post.

tastefully ornamented. The shape of the leaves is worth careful study.

PLAN VIEW

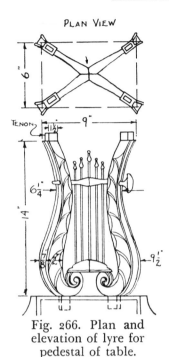

Fig. 266. Plan and elevation of lyre for pedestal of table.

Other Pieces of Furniture

The remaining pieces of Phyfe's work include small sideboards, serving tables, four-poster bedsteads, cheval glass frames, and the like. Many of these are so similar to pieces designed by Sheraton that little further comment is necessary here. He also made washstands, desks, and piano cases. Examples of pieces of this type, of authentic origin are rare, which leads one to believe that they were seldom built except to fill an important order for a good client.

Questions for Review

1. How does Duncan Phyfe rank with other American cabinetmakers?

2. What European styles influenced Duncan Phyfe's most important work?

3. What may be said for the scale and proportions of Duncan Phyfe furniture?

4. Enumerate three characteristic features that distinguish Phyfe furniture from all other styles.

5. What were the principal methods of enrichment used by Phyfe on his furniture?

6. Describe two types of chairs designed by Duncan Phyfe.

7. Describe three different types of construction commonly found on Phyfe table design.

8. What three articles of furniture constituted the greater part of Phyfe's output?

9. Name several other pieces of furniture occasionally designed by Duncan Phyfe.

Suggested Problems

1. Design a Duncan Phyfe dining table, or an entire dining-room suite.

2. Design a cheval glass or dressing-room mirror frame, in the Duncan Phyfe manner.

CHAPTER 16

THE COLONIAL STYLE
1620–1750

HISTORICAL BACKGROUND AND GENERAL CHARACTERISTICS

The Colonial, as we know it, is a composite style, having its origin in the early English styles, particularly the Jacobean and Queen Anne. All pieces made in America, up to the close of the eighteenth century, are often loosely referred to as Colonial. This is not strictly correct, because most of the eighteenth-century pieces, particularly those made of mahogany, should be classed as Chippendale or Sheraton, or be designated as American interpretations of the original English styles from which they were adapted. Nor need any furniture so designated be considered as less worthy of our esteem than the parent style by which it was inspired, for some of the finest Chippendale pieces known to us were made in Philadelphia during the eighteenth century.

In speaking of the Colonial style, we will limit ourselves to pieces made of local American woods, such as pine, maple, oak, ash, birch, cherry, and walnut. With this limiting factor in mind we will terminate the period not later than 1750. At this date, it is true, the mahogany period was already well established in England, and to some extent in America; but due to several factors, such as slowness of communication, the limited means and simple tastes of the Colonists, styles did not change so readily in America then as later.

The great appeal that Colonial furniture makes to us is due to its sturdy construction, its simplicity, and its association with the lives of a sturdy and rugged people — our forefathers. For many it holds an appeal equaled by no other style, and for adaptability to the average modest American home, no other style can quite approach it.

Although Jacobean and Elizabethan influences are strongly apparent on Colonial furniture, the style, taken as a whole, is not constructed on such a ponderous and ungainly scale as those styles were. A comparison of the pieces on Plates 56 and 57, with those on Plates 1 and 2 will bear out the truth of this statement.

The chief characteristics of the Colonial style are:

1. A sturdy construction. Legs, stretchers, and other structural members were joined together with deep mortises and long tenons, and the joints were often pinned as well. These pins were made of straight-grained hardwood, such as oak or hickory, and were roughly octagoned with a knife before being driven into a hole bored through

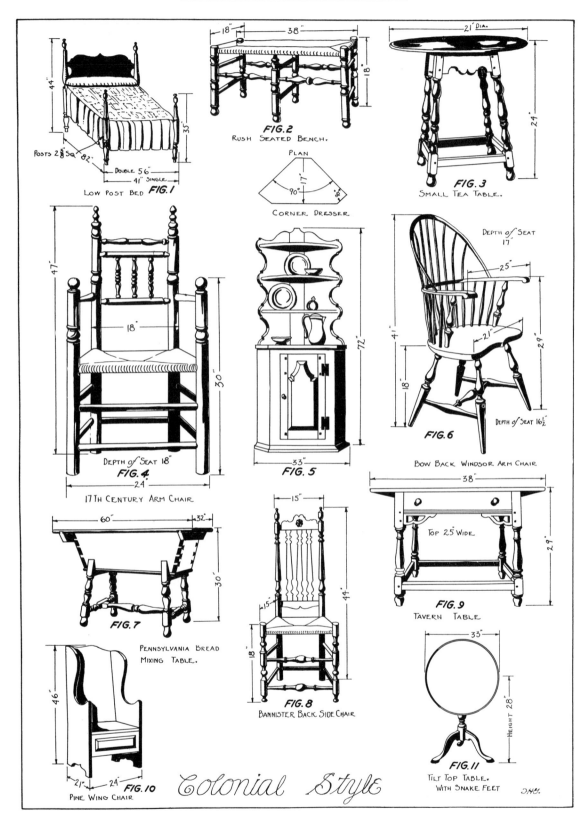

44"

POSTS 2⅜ SQ.   82"   35"

DOUBLE 56"
41" SINGLE

Low Post Bed **FIG.1**

18"   38"

18"

FIG.2
RUSH SEATED BENCH.

PLAN

17"
90"   45"

CORNER DRESSER

21" DIA.

24"

FIG.3
SMALL TEA TABLE.

47"

18"

30"

DEPTH of SEAT 18"
FIG.4
24"
17TH CENTURY ARM CHAIR

72"

33"
FIG. 5

DEPTH of SEAT
17"

25"

41"

21"   29"

18"

DEPTH of SEAT 16½"

FIG.6
BOW BACK WINDSOR ARM CHAIR

60"   32"

30"

FIG.7

PENNSYLVANIA BREAD
MIXING TABLE.

15"

15"

44"

18"

FIG.8
BANNISTER BACK SIDE CHAIR

38"

TOP 25 WIDE

29"

FIG.9
TAVERN TABLE

33"

HEIGHT 28"

FIG.11
TILT TOP TABLE.
WITH SNAKE FEET

46"

21"   24"
FIG.10
PINE WING CHAIR

Colonial Style

J.H.Y.

Plate 56.

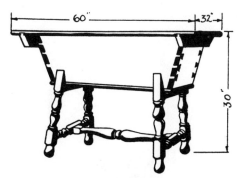

Fig. 269. Pennsylvania bread-mixing table.

set joint of modern furniture has resulted in a great loss of character for pieces of furniture on which it is found. The flush joint is more beautiful, easier to dress and clean, and just as strong as an offset joint (See Figs. 130, 270, 271, and 272).

both members of the joint. Glue being not readily available, the joints were usually draw-bored; i.e., the hole bored through the tenon member was placed about 1/16 in. closer to the shoulder than the corresponding hole bored into the mortise member. This difference resulted in the two members being drawn tightly together when the pin was driven. Dovetail joints were commonly found in drawer construction, and also on the corners of chests, etc. (See Fig. 269). Cruder joints, such as pinned or nailed butt joints, were also common.

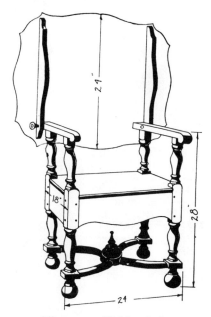

Fig. 271. Table chair.

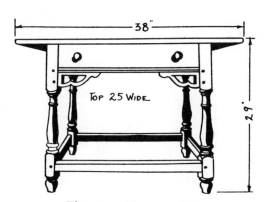

Fig. 270. Tavern table.

2. Joints were flush in nearly all cases; that is, the outside of the rail or stretcher was flush with the outside of the leg or stile where the joint occurred. The off-

3. Legs and stretchers, and other structural members were plain or turned. Outline was held to simple forms to insure the utmost practicability. Some of the turning was crude, but most generally it was excellent, both in design

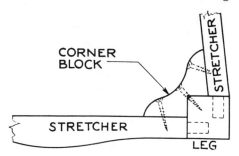

Fig. 272. Proper method of bracing a chair seat with corner block.

DEPTH AT
MOLDING 10½"

DEPTH CENTRAL
SECTION 7½"

DEPTH LOWER
SECTION 9½"

36" APPROX.

94"

21" APPROX.

20"

FIG. 13
TALL CLOCK.

20"
38"

77"

36"

FIG. 12
HIGHBOY

24"

18"

28"

24"

FIG. 14
TABLE CHAIR
EQUAL-RULE 6

20" 44"

38"

FIG. 15
CHEST of DRAWERS.

48"

60" LONG WHEN
LEAVES ARE UP

30"

FIG. 16
GATE LEG TABLE.

38"

48"

44"

LOVE SEAT **FIG. 17**

40"

43"

19"

FIG. 18
SLANT TOP DESK.

36" 72"

FIG. 19
TRESTLE TABLE.

15" 44"

TOP 30"
WIDE.

28"

FIG. 20
BUTTERFLY TABLE.

20" 48"

37"

FIG. 21
TULIP AND ASTER CHEST.

17"

DOMINANT
SEE RULE 3.

MINOR

42"

18"

21"

LADDER BACK SIDE CHAIR.
FIG. 22

Colonial Style

J.H.Y.

Plate 57.

and execution. Individual pieces show indications that the fine points of good design were either unknown or flagrantly disregarded. The use of arcs of a circle on the outline structure of Figure 21 is an indication of this. Space divisions on panels of chests and cupboards were often exactly alike, though strange as it may seem, in these very facts lies a great deal of the furniture's charm.

4. There was not a great deal of surface ornament. That which is found was often simple or crude. It took the form of applied ornament, such as split spindles, bosses, balusters, fretwork; or simple elementary types of carving, such as scratch carving, or flat-faced carving with merely the background removed. There was seldom any attempt to model the design.

5. Upholstered pieces were relatively rare, due to the great expense in securing the materials from abroad. Seats, if they were not of wood, were upholstered with oak splints or rushes, woven so they were quite comfortable and serviceable.

6. Hardware, for the few cabinet pieces and chests, was made of iron by the village blacksmith. Most of this was made in a few simple patterns, but occasionally a clever craftsman turned out designs of unusual merit. Most of the typical designs, as well as a few of the better ones, are shown on Plate 59. Brass hardware was not common, since it was imported, and only the wealthy could afford it. Turned wooden knobs were the most commonly used drawer pulls.

7. Solid wood in all of the domestic varieties was used for the furniture.

8. The finish commonly used was boiled linseed oil and wax. The wood was saturated with oil, and repeated applications of the oil and wax applied alternately. This, followed by brisk rubbing built up a kind of glazed surface on the wood. As the piece aged, the color turned to a mellow amber, and it is this amber color that we find on many of the well-cared-for old pieces today. For modern needs, especially under modern heating conditions, the rubbed varnish or shellac finishes are more lasting, and will preserve the furniture a great deal better than the oil and wax. These later finishes prevent the rapid drying out of the wood which so disastrously results in opened joints, warped tops, and the like. The old-style finish would be well enough if it were frequently administered, and the piece well rubbed, but this is seldom done.

PIECES

The pieces in common use were stools and benches; tables; chairs, both in great variety; chests, and chests of drawers; four-poster bedsteads; various types of cupboards, often with open shelves above (Fig. 21); desks, and secretaries; tall clock cases; highboys and lowboys; small looking glasses, and numerous small objects of lesser importance.

STOOLS AND BENCHES

In the early Colonial days, stools and long benches, the latter known as long forms, were seats of common use in the home. They were cheaper than chairs; they were sturdy, and easily moved about. These stools were of many kinds. There were low footstools, splay-legged

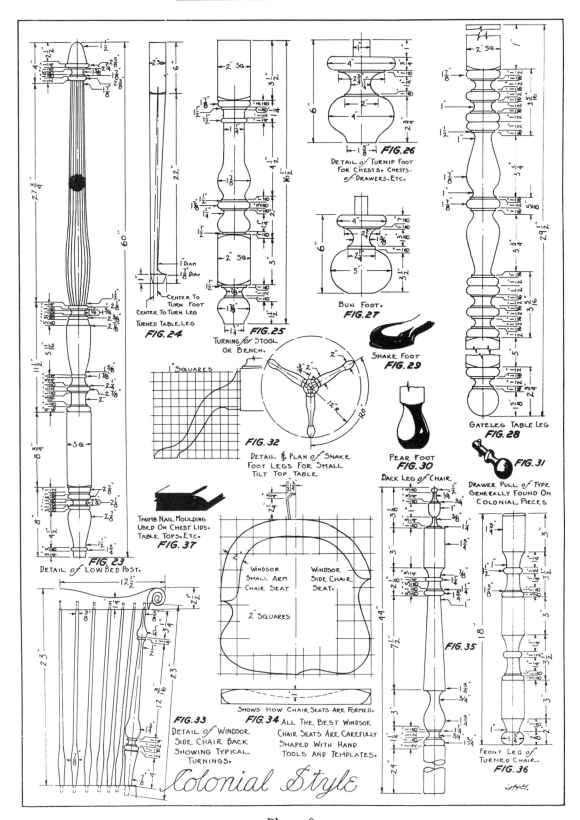

FIG. 24
Center To
Turn Foot
Center To Turn Leg
Turned Table Leg.

FIG. 25
Turning for Stool
Or Bench.

FIG. 26
Detail of Turnip Foot
For Chests, Chests
of Drawers, Etc.

FIG. 27
Bun Foot.

FIG. 28
Gateleg Table Leg

FIG. 23
Detail of Low Bed Post.

FIG. 29
Snake Foot

FIG. 30
Pear Foot

FIG. 31
Drawer Pull of Type
Generally Found On
Colonial Pieces

FIG. 32
Detail & Plan of Snake
Foot Legs For Small
Tilt Top Table

FIG. 37
Thumb Nail Moulding
Used On Chest Lids,
Table Tops, Etc.

Windsor
Small Arm
Chair Seat.

Windsor
Side Chair
Seat.

2" Squares

Shows How Chair Seats Are Formed.

FIG. 34 All The Best Windsor
Chair Seats Are Carefully
Shaped With Hand
Tools And Templates.

FIG. 33
Detail of Windsor
Side Chair Back
Showing Typical
Turnings.

FIG. 35
Back Leg of Chair

FIG. 36
Front Leg of
Turned Chair.

Colonial Style

Plate 58.

stools and benches similar to the ones shown in Figures 89 and 90. Stools and seats were rush bottomed. Some were designed with three legs; that is, tricornered, and others with six or eight legs (See Fig. 2, Plate 56). Another type of stool was the "cricket," or low footstool, which often had splayed, beautifully turned legs, similar to those found on Windsor chairs.

CHAIRS

There is a great variety of possibilities for lovely chair designs in this style. Ladder-back chairs are, perhaps, the simplest, as well as the most charming of all Colonial types. Three-slat backs are the most common. To the collector of old pieces a four-slat back is more valuable than a three-slat back, while a five-slat back is a real find. These were

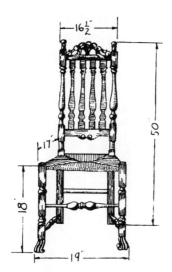

Fig. 273. Banister-back chair with Spanish carved feet.

sometimes designed as double chairs, known as love seats (Fig. 11), or with three or more backs.

The banister backs are not quite as comfortable as the ladder backs, but they are beautiful, and were popular. One is shown in Figure 57. There are many possibilities for variations of this design. Some of the finest had carved Spanish feet like the one in Figure 273.

The finest type of chair developed in the Colonial era is the American Windsor. It should not be confused with the English Windsor, as it is a much finer and more graceful chair. The English Windsor often had a pierced vertical splat in the back. The writer has never seen one that is as handsome as a number of fine American Windsors. He considers the Windsor the most important chair of this style; and it has also been

(A Wallace Nutting Reproduction)
Fig. 274. Comb-back Windsor armchair, a distinctly American invention with clean-cut lines and resilient strength.

pretty well established that this type of Windsor originated in America. It is one of the few designs to whose origin we can, with reasonable certainty, lay claim. For these reasons a Windsor armchair design has been included as an example of a typical Colonial piece (See Plate 60). This is known as a comb-back Windsor.

Fig. 275. Bow-back Windsor armchair, combining features of the bow-back and the comb-back types.

A bow-back Windsor also is shown in Figures 28 and 275. The beautiful turnings on these chairs illustrate clearly the excellent results to be obtained if design Rules 17, 18, and 19 are followed.

The wing chair was the early American easy chair. Its place was nearly always in front of the fireplace, where it protected a person from draughts on three sides, and helped to hold the heat that emanated from the hearth. Some of these were made of pine boards, and when a cushion was placed in the seat they were very comfortable indeed.

Fig. 276. Pine wing chair.

Simple wing chairs may be designed similar to the one shown in Figure 276.

Two other interesting chair designs are shown. The one in Figure 277 is now generally spoken of as a Carver armchair, it being named for one of the Pil-

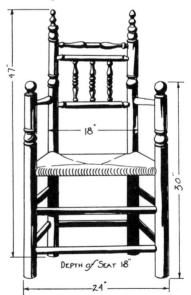

Fig. 277. Seventeenth-century armchair.

grim fathers who owned one like it. The other is a combination chair and table (Fig. 271). It is an interesting piece of furniture. These may be designed with a drawer under the seat.

TABLES

The variety of tables is greater than that of the chairs in this style. Seven different kinds of tables are shown, and seven times seven, might easily have been shown without exhausting the possibilities. Here is a fertile field for a designer, for tables are ever popular and useful pieces of furniture.

The simplest of those shown is the trestle table shown in Figure 96. The most intriguing type is the sturdy little butterfly, developed by Yankee ingenuity. A decidedly interesting one is the

The corners of the box were dovetailed together. These tables are now generally used as library tables by those fortunate enough to have inherited one.

Nearly all small rectangular Colonial tables are known as tavern tables, because they were of a type commonly found in the taprooms of taverns. There are many uses for this kind of table, and there are many ways of working up original designs for one (See Fig. 270). The small tea table (Fig. 99), offers a suggestion of the interesting possibilities for the design of many kinds of occasional tables.

BEDSTEADS

Bedsteads may be designed with high or low posts, usually turned. Many interesting designs are to be found in New

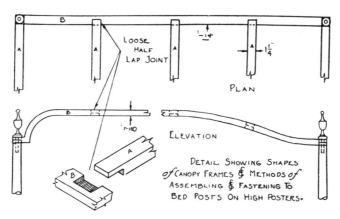

Fig. 278.

Pennsylvania bread-mixing table, shown in Figure 269. These had a bin or two to hold bread after it was baked, and to mix the dough, and hold it while it was rising. The tops were not fastened to the frame, but were laid on, so that they could easily be removed. The legs should always be turned and splayed.

England and Pennsylvania homes, and others have been collected by historical societies and museums. If high posts are used, a canopy may be added (See Fig. 278). In early times canopies had real utilitarian values, serving not only as a covering, but the frame as a means of supporting curtains that could be drawn

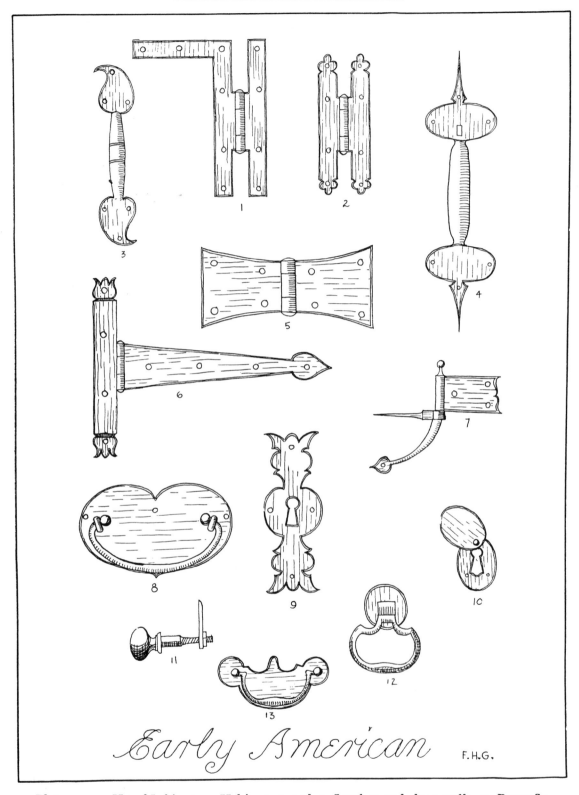

Early American

F. H. G.

Plate 59. 1. H-and-L hinge. 2. H hinge. 3 and 4. Latches and door pulls. 5. Butterfly hinge. 6. Strap hinge, tulip motif. 7. Rattail hinge for small doors. 8. Heart pattern drawer pull. 9 and 10. Escutcheon plate. 11. Door latch. 12 and 13. Drawer pulls.

clear around the bed. Occasionally it was necessary to have several members of the family sleep in a single room. Thus the need for a curtain to secure privacy is obvious. Furthermore, the rooms were cold and often draughty. This condition was somewhat alleviated by the use of curtains. Today when there is a canopy, it is usually of lace or some other material placed there for decorative purposes only.

Chests

Chests were a common article of furniture in Colonial households. There were few built-in closets. Somehow the idea of built-in closets did not seem to have found great favor with early Colonial builders. Thus it was necessary to have something in which to store clothing, blankets, etc. Nearly every room, therefore, contained, at least one chest. Many of these were made of pine boards, nailed together, or dovetailed at the corners. Others were more pretentious. The sunflower and tulip, or tulip and aster chests, are the most interesting of these early Colonial chests. These may have one or two long drawers below, or none at all. They received more than the ordinary amount of decoration, which gives us the idea that they were placed in relatively more important positions of vantage in the home.

Still other chests were designed with paneled fronts and ends, the panels being either plain, and bordered with molding, or raised or carved. The carving should not be modeled. Painted chests were numerous in Pennsylvania

(See Fig. 81). They offer opportunities to a designer to express his love of color.

We must not forget to mention Bible boxes, which were miniature chests made to hold the large family Bible. It was the most important, and often the only book, in the home of the early settler. It was read every day, both in the evening and in the morning, in many homes. Later, boxes of this type were used for other purposes, but the name persisted.

Chests of Drawers

Chests of drawers were developed from the chest, and were, in early times, an innovation. A simple design is shown

Fig. 279. Chest of drawers.

in Figure 279. Others were designed similar to the one shown in Figure 104. The more pretentious homes usually contained a highboy in the "best bedroom," or hallway. These lend dignity to a home today, quite as much as they did to the home of two hundred years ago.

Desks and Secretaries

Various types of slant-top desks and secretaries are found among the pieces in the Colonial style. The one shown in

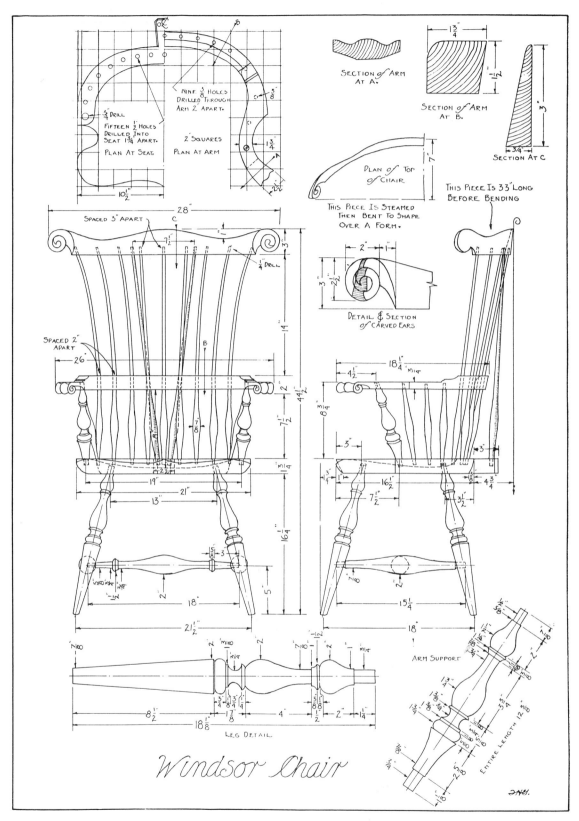

Windsor Chair

Plate 60.

Figure 280 is very plain on the outside. Many of the plain ones have beautiful interior cabinets. Bookcases may be added above, and the desk will then be-

Fig. 280. Slant-top desk.

come a secretary. Instead of drawers below, the designer may substitute a frame composed of turned legs and stretchers. The design of an interesting desk of this type is shown in a former book, *Simple Colonial Furniture.** Chests of drawers may also be designed supported on such a frame.

CUPBOARDS AND DRESSERS

A Colonial cupboard is shown in Plate 56. It is known as a dresser, because of the open shelves above which were "dressed" with shiny pewter for show. Another interesting cupboard is shown in Figure 281. There are many ways to design cupboards for this style. The hanging cupboard, made to be hung on the wall, seems to have been a popular type. It may have one or two doors, either glazed or paneled. Some were designed to hang in a corner. Tall cupboards may be designed to stand on the floor. These may have bun or bracket feet, or may be supported on

———
*Published by the Bruce Publishing Company, Milwaukee, Wis.

low frames. Such cupboards were used for clothes presses, for food storage, and for linen or china. There may be paneled doors and drawers, in the lower section, if it is divided into two parts as most of them were. Glazed or paneled doors may be put in the upper section.

A design for a cupboard will usually be more interesting if divided into two or more major masses vertically, rather than into just a single one. The reasons for this are given at some length in the first chapter on design. The upper section on many of these is removable, to

(A Wallace Nutting Reproduction)

Fig. 281. Fine early Colonial built-in corner cupboard of very best design.

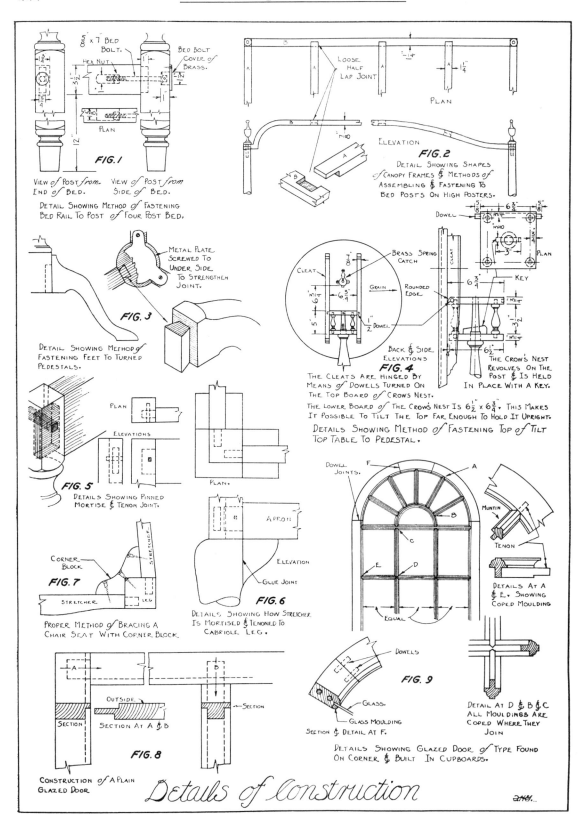

FIG. 1

VIEW of POST from END of BED.　　VIEW of POST from SIDE of BED.

DETAIL SHOWING METHOD of FASTENING BED RAIL TO POST of FOUR POST BED.

FIG. 2

DETAIL SHOWING SHAPES of CANOPY FRAMES & METHODS of ASSEMBLING & FASTENING TO BED POSTS ON HIGH POSTERS.

FIG. 3

DETAIL SHOWING METHOD of FASTENING FEET TO TURNED PEDESTALS.

FIG. 4

THE CLEATS ARE HINGED BY MEANS of DOWELS TURNED ON THE TOP BOARD of CROWS NEST.

THE LOWER BOARD of THE CROW'S NEST IS $6\frac{1}{2}$ x $6\frac{3}{4}$. THIS MAKES IT POSSIBLE TO TILT THE TOP FAR ENOUGH TO HOLD IT UPRIGHT.

THE CROW'S NEST REVOLVES ON THE POST & IS HELD IN PLACE WITH A KEY.

DETAILS SHOWING METHOD of FASTENING TOP of TILT TOP TABLE TO PEDESTAL.

FIG. 5

DETAILS SHOWING PINNED MORTISE & TENON JOINT.

FIG. 6

DETAILS SHOWING HOW STRETCHER IS MORTISED & TENONED TO CABRIOLE LEG.

FIG. 7

PROPER METHOD of BRACING A CHAIR SEAT WITH CORNER BLOCK

FIG. 8

CONSTRUCTION of A PLAIN GLAZED DOOR

FIG. 9

DETAILS AT A & E. SHOWING COPED MOULDING

DETAIL AT D & B & C ALL MOULDINGS ARE COPED WHERE THEY JOIN

SECTION & DETAIL AT F.

DETAILS SHOWING GLAZED DOOR of TYPE FOUND ON CORNER & BUILT IN CUPBOARDS.

Details of Construction

Plate 61.

facilitate moving it about. Cupboards have been designed fastened to the tops of tables. Others have turned frames supporting them. With the present-day custom of reading in bed there is no reason why a cupboard to hold books might not be built into a bedstead.

The hardware on cupboards, and for all Colonial furniture, should possess interesting and decorative, as well as utilitarian, features. Especially is this true of the hardware used on cupboards. Butter-

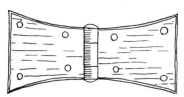

Fig. 282. Butterfly hinge.

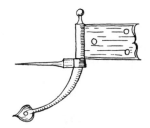

Fig. 284. Rattail hinge for small doors.

fly hinges (Fig. 282), H, and H-and-L hinges (Fig. 283), rattail hinges (Fig. 284), and many other interesting types may be used. Many of the pieces suitable for Jacobean, Queen Anne, and Chippendale furniture, especially the simpler patterns, will be found suitable to use on Colonial furniture as well. As latches for cupboards consider the interesting types shown in Figure 285.

CLOCKS

The tall clock illustrated in Figure 58, falls close to what we are pleased to call the American Chippendale era. The quarter columns and the bonnet top are indications of this. These cases, in America, were usually made of cherry or walnut wood, except in the seaboard cities where mahogany was obtainable (See Fig. 286). These stately clock cases illustrate design Rules 29, 30, and 31 remarkably well. The simple, but attractive outline structure, the well-supported superstructure, and the dignity

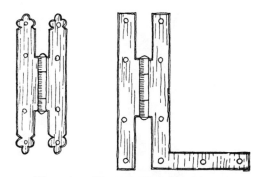

Fig. 283. H, and H-and-L hinges.

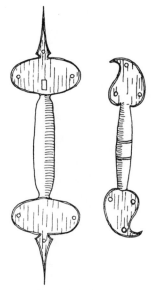

Fig. 285. Latches and door pulls.

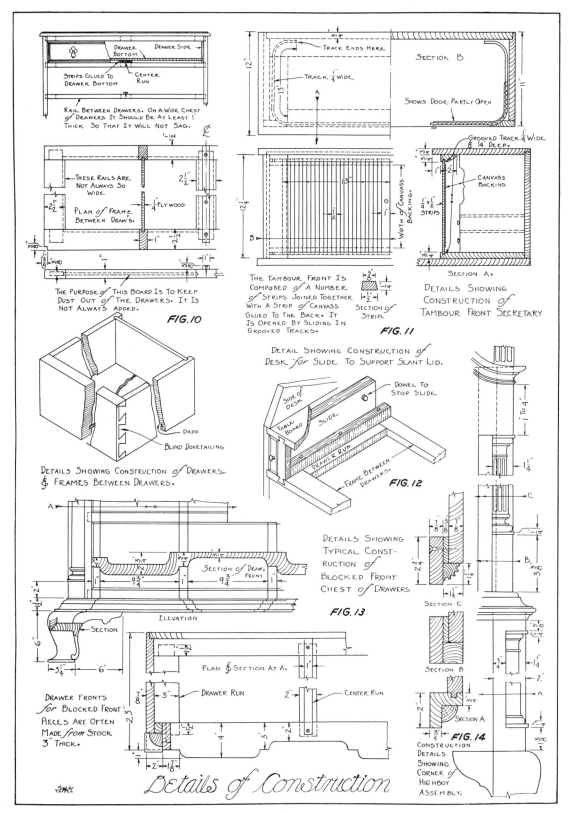

DRAWER BOTTOM
DRAWER SIDE
STRIPS GLUED TO DRAWER BOTTOM
CENTER RUN

RAIL BETWEEN DRAWERS. ON A WIDE CHEST OF DRAWERS IT SHOULD BE AT LEAST 1" THICK SO THAT IT WILL NOT SAG.

THESE RAILS ARE NOT ALWAYS SO WIDE

¼" PLYWOOD

PLAN OF FRAME BETWEEN DRAWERS.

THE PURPOSE OF THIS BOARD IS TO KEEP DUST OUT OF THE DRAWERS. IT IS NOT ALWAYS ADDED.

FIG. 10

TRACK ENDS HERE
SECTION B
TRACK ¼" WIDE
SHOWS DOOR PARTLY OPEN

THE TAMBOUR FRONT IS COMPOSED OF A NUMBER OF STRIPS JOINED TOGETHER WITH A STRIP OF CANVASS GLUED TO THE BACK. IT IS OPENED BY SLIDING IN GROOVED TRACKS.

SECTION OF STRIP.

FIG. 11

GROOVED TRACK ¼" WIDE & ¼" DEEP.
CANVASS BACKING
¼" × ½" STRIPS
WIDTH OF CANVASS BACKING.

SECTION A.

DETAILS SHOWING CONSTRUCTION OF TAMBOUR FRONT SECRETARY

DADO
BLIND DOVETAILING

DETAILS SHOWING CONSTRUCTION OF DRAWERS & FRAMES BETWEEN DRAWERS.

DETAIL SHOWING CONSTRUCTION OF DESK FOR SLIDE TO SUPPORT SLANT LID.

SIDE OF DESK
DOWEL TO STOP SLIDE
TABLE BOARD
SLIDE
DRAWER RUN
FRAME BETWEEN DRAWERS.

FIG. 12

DETAILS SHOWING TYPICAL CONSTRUCTION OF BLOCKED FRONT CHEST OF DRAWERS

FIG. 13

SECTION OF DRAW. FRONT
9¾"   9¾"
ELEVATION

SECTION

DRAWER FRONTS FOR BLOCKED FRONT PIECES ARE OFTEN MADE FROM STOCK 3" THICK.

PLAN & SECTION AT A.
DRAWER RUN
CENTER RUN

SECTION C
SECTION B
SECTION A

FIG. 14
CONSTRUCTION DETAILS SHOWING CORNER OF HIGHBOY ASSEMBLY.

Details of Construction

Plate 62.

clocks were made to be sold commercially. It was then that mantel clocks began to appear.

OTHER PIECES OF COLONIAL FURNITURE

A few other pieces of Colonial furniture are worthy of mention. One of these is the pipe box, a small box, open at the top to hold the long-stemmed pipes in use at the time, and with a small drawer below for tobacco. These were sometimes carved in homely fashion with a jackknife.

If the family possessed as many as a half-dozen sterling-silver spoons they were often exhibited on a spoon rack,

(A Wallace Nutting Reproduction)
Fig. 286. Tall clock. This reproduction of a fine clock of late Georgian influence is a masterpiece of design.

(A Wallace Nutting Reproduction)
Block-fronted chest-on-chest. A masterpiece of early American design and craftsmanship.

of these clocks suggest the matchless perfection of a column on a classic temple. No home furnished in the Colonial manner is quite complete without a tall clock to bid one welcome as one enters the hallway. Nearly all early clocks were tall clocks, because they were weight clocks. They had to be made tall in order to allow the weight to descend, thus furnishing the motive power to run the clock. It was not until late, in what we term the Colonial period, that spring

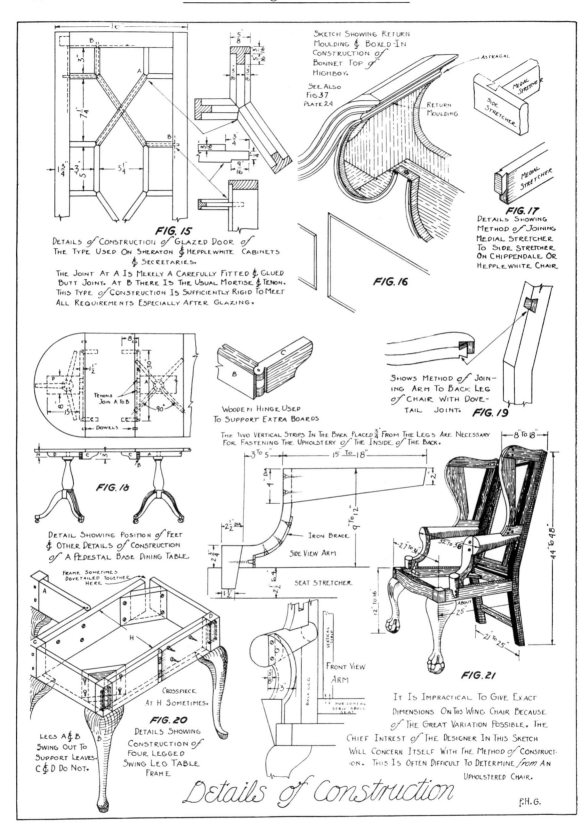

FIG. 15

Details of Construction of Glazed Door of The Type Used on Sheraton & Hepplewhite Cabinets & Secretaries.

The Joint at A Is Merely a Carefully Fitted & Glued Butt Joint. At B There Is The Usual Mortise & Tenon. This Type of Construction Is Sufficiently Rigid To Meet All Requirements Especially After Glazing.

Sketch Showing Return Moulding & Boxed-In Construction of Bonnet Top of Highboy.

See Also Fig 37 Plate 24

FIG. 16

FIG. 17

Details Showing Method of Joining Medial Stretcher To Side Stretcher On Chippendale Or Hepplewhite Chair

FIG. 18

Detail Showing Position of Feet & Other Details of Construction of A Pedestal Base Dining Table.

Wooden Hinge Used To Support Extra Boards

Shows Method of Joining Arm To Back Leg of Chair With Dove-Tail Joint. **FIG. 19**

The Two Vertical Strips In The Back Placed ¾ From The Legs Are Necessary For Fastening The Upholstery of The Inside of The Back.

Side View Arm

Seat Stretcher

Front View Arm

FIG. 20

Details Showing Construction of Four Legged Swing Leg Table Frame

Crosspiece At H Sometimes.

Legs A & B Swing Out To Support Leaves. C & D Do Not.

FIG. 21

It Is Impractical To Give Exact Dimensions On This Wing Chair Because of The Great Variation Possible. The Chief Interest of The Designer In This Sketch Will Concern Itself With The Method of Construction. This Is Often Difficult To Determine from An Upholstered Chair.

Details of Construction

F.H.G.

Plate 63.

Early American block-front chest
of drawers.

1. From what European styles was the early Colonial style in America adapted?

2. Define the term *Colonial style*.

3. What qualities constitute the greatest appeal of the Colonial style?

4. Name several important points of difference between the Colonial and the Jacobean style.

5. Describe peculiarities of construction that made early Colonial pieces more beautiful than most of the reproduced copies are today.

6. What was the principal form of ornament found on Colonial furniture?

7. Upon what did the Colonial style depend principally for its beauty?

8. What types of hardware are commonly found on Colonial furniture?

made to be hung on the wall. These racks were sometimes decorated with very simple carving.

The candle stand was a familiar and necessary piece of furniture in early homes. The best of these had the candle holders fastened to an arm, which could be raised or lowered on a vertical shaft having wooden screw threads cut on it. The base of the stands often had snake-head feet. Other candle stands were made of iron, some of them beautifully wrought in simple and tasteful designs. Many early blacksmiths were skilled artisans, and made beautiful andirons, candle sconces, candle stands, and other utensils.

Some of the most interesting of these utensils are the smoke jacks, and clock jacks, by means of which the spit rod was turned in front of the fire in the fireplace. One of the best examples of these, which the writer has ever seen, is to be found in The Wayside Inn, of Long-fellow fame, at Sudbury, Massachusetts.

A handsome chair of the American Federal period which was similar to the French Empire style.

9. Describe the original method of finishing Colonial furniture.

10. Describe the construction of stools, benches, and chairs of this style.

11. What is the most important type of chair found in this style? Describe its construction.

12. What may be said concerning the importance of table design in the Colonial style?

13. Describe the construction of a tavern table.

14. Describe the construction of chests in the Colonial style.

15. Describe the construction of desks and secretaries.

16. Why were clock cases built tall?

17. Enumerate and describe several interesting pieces of Colonial furniture, most of which are no longer of any particular utilitarian value for present-day use, but have decorative value.

18. What may be said concerning principles of design as practiced in the design of furniture at this early date?

19. When carving was used, what forms did it commonly take?

SUGGESTED PROBLEMS

1. Design a small Colonial chest or box for the storage of baby blankets and clothes.

2. Design a radiator cover or screen, using Colonial turnings for the construction of the grille.

3. Design a Colonial rush-seated chair.

4. Design a turned bridge lamp in the Colonial style.

5. Design a light tavern table to be used for playing cards.

6. Design a Colonial four-poster bed.

7. Design a Colonial mantel-clock case.

8. Design a light child's bed, with slender posts about four feet tall, and a railing composed of light turnings to prevent the child from falling out.

9. Design a set of bookshelves to be hung upon the wall.

10. Design a light chest of drawers supported upon a turned frame.

CHAPTER 17

UPHOLSTERING MATERIALS

The materials used for upholstering furniture come from all parts of the world. Besides the woven materials, in which the student of furniture design will be especially interested, there are the innumerable products that are used to build up the foundation, to which the handsome and serviceable cover material will finally be fastened. These include cotton, burlap, curled hair, moss, springs, and many other products. It is not the intention of the author to present information dealing with the sources and manufacture of products that go beneath the covering materials on upholstered furniture, since that is a subject that belongs in a book on principles of upholstery. Some knowledge concerning cover fabrics and the processes used in their manufacture is, however, essential in a work dealing with principles of furniture design.

A history of the development of the art of weaving is an exceedingly interesting study, and it is perhaps unfortunate that lack of space will not permit a more extensive presentation of the subject here. An attempt will be made, however, to put each fabric of importance into its proper family group; to point out the important qualities and characteristics of each group; and finally, to tell on what styles of furniture each

fabric, or group of fabrics, may be properly used.

Weaving is one of the oldest arts in existence, and for centuries it was carried on in very primitive fashion on simple looms. Within the last century and a half, the invention of power looms has made it possible to speed production, but the three fundamental types of weaving have not changed. All fabrics used for upholstering purposes fall into one of these three groups, which are: (1) Plain weave, in which the cloth has no figure, but is made by simply alternating the warp and the weft. The warp is the thread running lengthwise of the cloth, and the weft is the thread running crosswise. (2) The second type of weaving is twill weaving, in which the ribs of the cloth run diagonally. (3) The third type is the satin weave, in which the surface of the cloth is covered by tiny warp threads lying parallel to each other. By treating the fabrics in different ways to secure various decorative effects, many distinct textiles are produced. The first group of fabrics to be discussed include damasks, brocatelles, and brocades.

DAMASK

The cloth known as damask was given this name because ornamental silks of superior quality were woven in great quantities in the city of Damascus, during the twelfth century. At the present time some of the finest quality damasks are being woven in European countries, such as Italy, Ireland, and Germany. Irish table linen is a damask of superior qualities.

Damasks are made by weaving the figures into the cloth with the lines of the figure running in a different direction from the lines of the background. The result is a cloth with a flat pattern, showing alternately dull and lustrous, the design appearing on both sides of the fabric. Damasks are usually woven in one or two colors. There are many interesting designs, and they are particularly well suited to furniture of the Georgian periods, such as the Chippendale and Brothers Adam styles, and for all of the French styles treated in this book. When only one color is used, as in the weaving of fine table linen, the contrast of the weave makes the pattern. When two colors are used, both the colors and the pattern of the weave form the contrast of the figure with its background.

Damasks are woven of cotton, silk, linen, or wool, or combinations of these materials. For upholstering purposes it is usually sold in strips 50 inches wide.

BROCATELLES

Brocatelles are produced by using a binder warp, and by the application of a second filler of linen. This gives the cloth an embossed appearance, because the coarse weft threads throw the satin figures into bold relief on the twill ground. This weave makes bold effects possible, the cloth having a raised and sculptured aspect, and therefore brocatelles are suited to furniture of the Jacobean, Carolean, and Spanish styles, in which we find bold carving and contours. They are not so well suited to the more refined scale of the Brothers Adam or late Georgian styles.

BROCADES

Brocades differ rather sharply from the two fabrics just discussed. They are richly colored, but are not reversible, because the embroidery-like effects are obtained by a floating weft; that is, by crosswise threads that appear on the surface to form the design. The delicate figure of the design shows up like fine Chinese embroidery on the rich ground. Here are found the stripes, the love knots, the delicate floral sprays, of the Louis XV and Louis XVI styles. Exquisite patterns and lovely color schemes are woven into these beautiful fabrics. The colors in the figures are often beautifully shaded in two- or three-tone effects, giving them a richness seldom equaled by other fabrics. Brocades are suitable for use on Louis XV, Louis XVI, Chippendale, Hepplewhite, Sheraton, and Brothers Adam furniture.

VELVETS AND VELOURS

Velvets have always been associated with royalty. "Velours," is the French word for velvet, and so the two terms mean practically the same thing. The yarn for weaving velour is made from long, staple fiber. The pile of velvets and velours is made by using wires, over which the warp is looped. These wires

Fig. 47. A print in soft, well-blended colors, used on Jacobean furniture.

Fig. 49. Brocade. The quaintness of this motif is in perfect accord with the spirit of the Queen Anne style.

Fig. 48. William and Mary and Carolean print. Also may be used on Chippendale pieces.

Fig. 50. Damask suitable for Chippendale pieces.

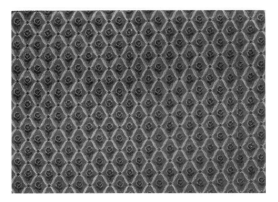

Fig. 51. Velde Gênes material used on Hepplewhite furniture.

Fig. 52. Sheraton and Louis XVI striped damask.

Fig. 53. Louis XIV style damask. Note scale of pattern. Scarlet background and gold design.

Fig. 54. Beautiful brocade suitable for Louis XV and Louis XVI styles.

Fig. 55. Georgian silk damask also suited for eighteenth-century Italian and French furniture.

have a cutting edge on one end, and as the wires are removed these cutting edges sever the loops, leaving the very short, soft bristles. Plain velvets are woven face to face, the backs out, and the pile between. The two pieces of cloth are separated by a sharp blade that follows the shuttle, and this method of weaving makes it possible to dispense with the wires.

After the goods has been woven it is dyed and sheared. The pieces are drawn through the dye in the form of a rope, which is constantly revolved to secure a uniform color. After being dyed, the cloth is brushed, and then sheared to make the bristles uniform. If brocade effects are desired the pile is burned, thus forming a background lower than the design. Sometimes the velour is woven in various patterns on a Jacquard loom.

Velvets and velours may be made of silk, cotton, linen, or mohair. Velvets having a satin ground are known as Velours de Gênes, the name originating with famous fabrics manufactured in Genoa, Italy. Velvets and velours may be used on Spanish Renaissance furniture, and are suitable for William and Mary, Carolean, Louis XIV, and Louis XV styles. The cloth is woven in pieces 50 to 54 inches wide.

Mohair

Mohair for furniture fabrics is woven from the fleece of the Angora goat. The cloth usually has a cotton or a wool background.

Mohair fabrics are very lustrous, and are of such fine quality that the natural luster of the fabric is not destroyed by either wear, sunlight, or dampness. The pile is woven in loops, and these are cut after being woven, causing the pile to stand upright. Various interesting effects are obtained by subjecting the cloth to different finishing processes. To secure a brocade effect the pile is burned or sheared to form a background lower than the design. It is one of the most durable of fabrics, and is therefore highly prized for the seats of automobiles, and other places subjected to hard wear. Its greatest drawback is that it attracts moths which quickly destroy the cloth once they get into it. It is greatly prized for overstuffed furniture, but may be used wherever velvets and velours are proper.

Tapestries

Tapestry weaving has been practiced for a very long time, but the most famous tapestries came from the Gobelin looms in France. These reached their finest degree of perfection under the patronage of Louis XIV and Louis XV. Gobelin tapestries are produced, and remain famous to this day. Not only were large wall hangings woven, but rugs, and upholstery fabrics for furniture.* Great artists and designers worked upon cartoons for these masterpieces of the weaver's art. The work was carefully supervised by trained experts from beginning to end.

There have been three great schools

---

*Louis XVI presented George Washington with a beautiful rug for Mt. Vernon. This was woven on the Gobelin looms.

of tapestry weaving: (1) The Gothic, in which the figures were flat in effect with clearly defined outlines. The designs were not shaded, but the colors were applied in flat tones, and clearly outlined with other colors. (2) The Renaissance brought into being a second school of tapestry weaving, in which the fabric was treated much as a painting. Figures were more rounded, and the weavings showed a perspective not found in Gothic tapestries. (3) The third great school of tapestry weaving is the one in which we are principally interested, because during this period tapestry for furniture took on an importance that had never been known before. Naturalistic motifs, pictures, pastorals, classical subjects, all-over patterns, and many more interesting designs were used. The whole range of the color scale, with all its hues and tones was brought into play. Famous painters, such as Watteau, Le-Brun, and Boucher designed cartoons for these tapestries. Cartoons for earlier tapestries were designed by Raphael, Rubens, and other famous artists.

Tapestry is an ideal material for upholstering furniture, because it wears very well. It, therefore, is commonly used by upholsterers. Its interesting texture, brought about by a crosshatching effect of the weave, makes possible a depth of perspective and a variety of color tones impossible in other fabrics. Tapestry may be used on nearly all styles of furniture, and it may be woven in special designs to fit chair backs or seats. It usually comes in rolls 50 inches wide (See Figs. 223 and 226).

CHINTZES AND CRETONNES

Chintzes and cretonnes are printed fabrics. In modern usage of the terms, cretonnes are somewhat heavier fabrics than chintzes, and the design is somewhat more pronounced.

Chintz is prepared by beating the cloth to make it smooth. Originally the colors were painted on the cloth. Others are dyed by covering the parts of the cloth to be left in the original color with wax, and then dipping it. The cloth is then finished by subjecting it to heavy pressure. The result is the glossy fabric which is so suitable for Colonial and provincial furniture. Glazed chintzes are very appropriate for French provincial styles.

Toiles de Jouy are printed chintzes originally made in France. They became famous at the end of the eighteenth century, because they were designed by some of the most talented artists of the period. They often depicted legends and historical events.

Glazed chintzes are produced by treating the surface, and then hot calendering; that is, rolling between steam-filled rollers which burnish the surface.

Chintzes and cretonnes may be used as substitutes for more expensive fabrics, on almost all styles of furniture. Their greatest service is as coverings for chairs to brighten them up and keep the material underneath clean.

PLAIN FABRICS

Plain fabrics have no pattern. They are made in many interesting ways to give them interesting textures. Differences in yarn, in direction and spacing of thread, and in color, make numerous textures and effects possible.

QUESTIONS FOR REVIEW

1. Name some of the sources from which upholstering materials come to us.

2. Name an important improvement in weaving that has made it possible to manufacture upholstering materials of good quality cheaply.

3. Name the three types of weaving.

4. Describe the method of weaving damasks.

5. How many colors are usually found in damasks used for upholstering?

6. Upon what styles of furniture may damasks be used?

7. Describe the method of producing brocatelles.

8. Describe the method of weaving brocades. How do they differ from damasks?

9. For what styles are brocades suitable as upholstering material?

10. Describe the manufacture of velours. Upon what styles of furniture may velours be used?

11. Describe the fabrics known as Velours de Gênes.

12. What special quality is possessed by mohair that makes it valuable for places subjected to extra hard wear?

13. Enumerate the three schools of tapestry weaving, and give brief descriptions of each one.

14. Tell why tapestry weaving was developed to such a high degree of perfection in France during the seventeenth and eighteenth centuries.

15. For what styles are tapestries suitable as upholstering materials?

16. Define the terms *printed fabrics, plain weave, toiles de Jouy.*

————

NOTE: Most of the material for this chapter was made possible by the courtesy of F. Schumacher and Co., of New York, and is by their consent taken from literature published by them.

CHAPTER 18

THE MECHANICS OF FURNITURE DESIGN

Having studied the principles of design, together with characteristics of all the important furniture styles, the designer will now be prepared to put the knowledge he has gained to some practical use.

It is assumed that he is familiar with the principles of mechanical drawing; that he is able to do some freehand drawing; and that he is reasonably familiar with most of the materials in common use in the furniture industry. A knowledge of construction based upon actual experiences in the trade of cabinetmaking will be of the utmost value. A study of architectural principles is strongly urged.

When one wishes to design a piece of furniture, such considerations as the style in which it is to be designed, the purpose it is to serve, the space it is to occupy, the height of the room in which it is to be placed, the character and temperament of the people who are to use it, the amount of light in the room, and similar factors must, if they are known, be given due consideration. It is well to have proper objectives before beginning a design. These will help intelligent planning.

When the style has been selected, and some of the other above-mentioned con-siderations have been determined, a list should be made consisting of all essential requirements, utilitarian and otherwise. Drawbacks, such as too much underbracing on a gate-leg table for dining purposes, too low an apron on a dressing table to give adequate knee room, and other important details, should be anticipated to avoid mistakes in the final drawing. Preliminary planning of this nature will save a great deal of trouble when actually drawing the plans.

When this list has been made it will be necessary to make sketches of the piece and some of its important details. Thus ideas will begin to take concrete form. The sketches may be made very roughly at first, then as ideas take more definite form, more careful sketches should be made. It is at this point of the work that the shaping of an apron, for example, or a turned leg, or the idea for a distinctive pediment may cause some trouble in its solution; but by experimenting with various ideas, and using what knowledge has been acquired of styles and principles of design, the designer should finally arrive at a satisfactory solution of the problem.

It is always best to check up for authenticity of style characteristics at this time. Some of the gravest mistakes made by designers of furniture are directly due to carelessness in this matter. For example, to be authentic, a Jacobean chest of drawers should not be designed with quarter columns. Not that it cannot be done, but if authentic style characteristics are desired one must be careful to select only proper details. Quarter columns were not used until Chippendale's time. After checkups of this kind have been made, and the designer feels that he has come pretty close to having the design he has hoped for, the important dimensions may be added. It will be necessary to change many of these later when the scale drawing is being made, but they will materially help in working up a scale drawing.

The scale drawing comes next. First draw the outlines of the primary mass. It will be well to do this with a three-view drawing, showing the plan, front, and side elevations. It is here that the designer will wish to experiment considerably with proportions, and the division of masses. Proper care at this point will be well repaid in the final result. Much thought should be given to the division of the major and minor masses; their proportions, and the interrelation of these proportions.

Moldings, carvings, inlay, and all other decorative details should be carefully planned, first on the scale drawing itself, then in greater detail at full size. A convenient scale to use on furniture drawings is 3 in. equals 1 ft. Almost any piece of furniture, except very tall pieces may be drawn at that scale on a sheet of paper measuring 19 by 24 in. This is a very common standard-sized sheet of drawing paper.

In many furniture factories it is the custom to make full-sized drawings of whole pieces of furniture. From these, patterns of wood or cardboard may easily be made. For cabinet furniture, "rods" are made; that is, full-sized details and cross sections are laid out on a board or stick, called a rod. This is then used by the cabinetmaker in laying out his work. It saves guesswork and mistakes on the part of the workman, because he may measure distances, and take off exact shapes from the rod. Large factories have layout men who do nothing but make patterns and rods from the designer's sketches and specifications. This is especially true in establishments where large quantities of work are turned out, and where the designer has very little to do with determining the details of construction, his work being more in the nature of artistic representation. Where only one piece is to be made from a drawing, it will hardly pay to make full-sized drawings of the entire piece. Full-sized drawings are unwieldy, and except for important details of which separate patterns may easily be made, they are no more necessary than is a full-sized drawing of a house.

All dimensions should be added when the drawing has been completed. In checking the drawings these should be complete to such an extent that it will be possible to make out a bill of material from the drawing without having to take a single measurement from the drawing with a rule. In checking a drawing the designer should ask himself constantly, questions of this kind: "How far is it from this place to this other place?" or "How long, how wide, and how thick must this piece be?" He should mentally go over the construction of the furniture from beginning to end, so that no dimension may be left to guess, and so that all mistakes may be rectified.

If a good drawing is desired, or if the drawing is to be shown to a client, a final drawing should be made. The old drawing will probably have many erasures, may not be clean, and need not necessarily be inked. The final scale drawing should be inked, should be well arranged on the paper, and should in all respects be a work of art. It may also be well to make a picture drawing, a pen and ink sketch with proper shading, or a sepia tint, rendering, to submit to a client (See Plates 28 and 32). Drawings of this kind are necessary because there are comparatively few who are able to understand a working drawing, or to get a clear image of what the finished piece will look like.

Questions for Review

1. What are a few of the things in which a designer should show some proficiency in order to do satisfactory work?

2. What are some of the factors that should be taken into consideration before beginning the drawing of a piece of furniture?

3. What is the first step in making a drawing for a furniture design?

4. Why is it important to determine authenticity of details?

5. What step will follow freehand sketches in the design of a piece of furniture?

6. What is a convenient scale to use in making the scale drawings for a piece of furniture?

7. Is it necessary to make a full-sized drawing of an entire piece of furniture?

8. Of what details should full-sized drawings be made?

9. Describe a "rod."

10. What is the final step in the drawing of a design for a piece of furniture?

GLOSSARY

abacus, the slab crowning a column or pillar. See Fig. 37, Plate 24.

abstract design, design originating from geometric sources. See Chapter 4.

acanthus leaf, a naturalistic form of ornament of Classic derivation. Any leaf with an irregular edge. For furniture it is used in various conventionalized forms.

acorn finial, a turned member resembling an acorn, found on tops of chairs, or at the intersection of X-stretchers on William and Mary pieces.

Adam, the surname of four brothers who became famous as architects and designers of furniture during the latter part of the eighteenth century.

Adelphi, a trade name adopted by the Brothers Adam, the term being of Greek derivation.

almery, cupboards originally intended as receptacles for doles for family retainers.

amboyna, a beautifully figured wood grown in the East Indies. It was used by Chippendale, Hepplewhite, and later designers for veneering purposes.

analogous harmonies, a term referring to color harmonies in which all hues are related to one major hue in the group. See Chapter 5.

anthemion, a conventionalized ornament of Classic origin representing the honeysuckle. See Fig. 26, Plate 41.

antiques, a term loosely applied to all old furniture. It should be confined to periods ending with Sheraton's style in Europe, and with Duncan Phyfe's in America.

applique, a term given to applied ornament, such as carvings, turnings, lozenges, etc., which are tacked or glued to a surface rather than cut from the solid wood.

apron, a narrow strip of wood, or shaped element, such as the horizontal cross member under a table top, chair seat, or lowboy.

arabesque, a Saracenic form of ornament, usually composed of naturalistic ornament twined about a rod or stem. See vertical end panels, Fig. 11, Plate 40. Originally as employed by Mohammedan designers, no animals were ever represented in an arabesque. The motifs were restricted to flowers, foliage, fruits, and figures of geometric design.

arcade, a series of arches supported by turned columns or spindles. See Fig. 1, Plate 48.

architrave, that part of the entablature, or part of a cornice, which rests immediately upon the columns.

armoire, a cupboard for storing clothes, arms, or armor.

arm support, the member supporting the front of a chair arm.

arrow foot, a term applied to the turning found on the foot of New England Windsor chairs, which come to a narrow point at the floor. See Plate 60.

artificial objects, a group of objects from which important design motifs are taken, such as vase forms, musical instruments, etc.

aster, a favorite motif for early Colonial chests. It took the form of a conventionalized type of flat-faced carving on the panel, Fig. 21, Plate 57.

astragal, a small, convex, half-round, beaded molding. See Fig. 16, Plate 63.

bail, a brass drawer pull consisting of plate and handle. See Fig. 12, Plate 38; Fig. 8, Plate 26.

ball and claw, a carved foot found mostly on Chippendale designs. It is a form of ornament originating in China, and is supposed to represent a bird's claw grasping an egg.

ball foot, a turned foot for chests or chests of drawers, usually quite large in diameter, and found on early styles.

baluster, a turned spindle or column, such as a split baluster on a banister-back chair. See Fig. 13, Plate 2.

bamboo turning, a type of turning formed to simulate bamboo, and used by Chippendale for chairs. It is also sometimes found on early American Windsors.

banding, a narrow band of veneer, applied around the edges of drawer fronts. See Fig. 9, Plate 33.

banister, See baluster.

barefaced tenon, one that has a shoulder on one side only.

baroque, a name sometimes applied to rococo ornament. See Fig. 5, Plate 47.

barrel chair, a chair which in appearance resembles a barrel with the upper front half cut away. They are usually upholstered. See Fig. 21, Plate 23.

base mold, the heavy molding around the base of cabinet furniture. See Fig. 5, Plate 39.

bead, a narrow half-round convex molding, its surface being either flush with the adjacent surface, or raised above it. See Section A, Plate 31.

bead and reel, a carved molding of Classical origin, in which the ordinary bead is interrupted at regular intervals.

bed bolt, an iron bolt used to fasten the long horizontal rails to the posts of a four-poster bed. See Fig. 1, Plate 61.

bed-bolt cover, a small brass ornament used to cover the head of a bed bolt. See Figs. 10 and 11, Plate 38.

bedside table, a small light table having a drawer or two, and occasionally a shelf near the floor, placed by a bed to hold a lamp or toilet articles.

beech, a cabinet wood, sometimes substituted for maple.

bench, a seat without a back, large enough to accommodate at least two persons.

bergere, a French term for an upholstered armchair. See left-hand unit, Fig. 6, Plate 43.

bevel, a 45-degree angle, planed or chiseled on the edge of any surface.

bisymmetric balance, balance of a design secured by making design units exactly alike on both sides of the vertical center line. See Chapter 4.

block front, a term applied to the unique type of construction for fronts of early American chests of drawers and chests-on-chests; consisting of a concave, but flattened, recession at the center, and two convex, but flattened, swells on the ends. It is a type of construction supposed to have originated with John Goddard, a famous cabinetmaker of Newport, R. I. See Fig. 13, Plate 62 and the illustrations on pages 227 and 229.

blocked foot, a bracket foot on which the blocking is carried to the floor. See Fig. 13, Plate 62.

blunt arrow, a turned foot found on Pennsylvania Windsor chairs. It greatly resembles Fig. 26, Plate 58.

bombe, an outward-swelling kettle-base construction for chests of drawers and secretaries, found on the Chippendale and Louis XV styles. See Fig. 7, Plate 22.

bonnet top, the covered tops or pediments found on Queen Anne or Chippendale highboys, in which the swanlike necks of the cyma curves ended with a carved scroll, in some cases. See Fig. 16, Plate 63; Fig. 37, Plate 24.

boss, a circular or oval convex ornament applied to surfaces on sixteenth- and seventeenth-century furniture. See Fig. 58, Plate 5.

Boucher, an artist who designed cartoons for tapestries for Louis XV furniture.

Boulle work, a form of ornament consisting of inlays composed especially of tortoise shell and precious and semiprecious metals. It was named for its originator, Andre Charles Boulle, a French designer of the time of Louis XIV. See Chapter 13.

bow back, a term applied to the rounded top of a Windsor chair. See Fig. 6, Plate 56.

bracket, a supporting member found at the junction of legs and stretchers on chairs, tables, etc. These may be plain, carved, or pierced. See Fig. 9, Plate 56.

bread-mixing table, a Pennsylvania German type, used to knead dough and hold it while rising. See Fig. 7, Plate 56.

break, a term applied to the opening found at the center of a pediment or a bonnet top on a highboy or secretary. See Fig. 24, Plate 11.

brocade, a type of woven upholstering material in which the design is raised and resembles fine Chinese embroidery. See Chapter 17.

brocatelles, an upholstering material of embossed appearance, resulting from coarse weft threads which throw the satin figures into bold relief on a twill ground. See Chapter 17.

broken arch, similar to bonnet top. See Fig. 24, Plate 11.

buffet, the French term for a sideboard.

bulbous turning, a heavy turning commonly found on Elizabethan and Jacobean refectory tables and court cupboards. See Fig. 25, Plate 3.

bun foot, a Dutch foot similar to a ball turning, but the ball is usually greater in diameter than height. See Fig. 12, Plate 11.

bureau, the French term for a writing desk with drawers below, but in America it has come to mean a chest of drawers.

burl, a figured veneer secured from a tree at a place where an abnormal growth of some kind has produced a figure of unusual beauty in the grain.

burlap, a material used in upholstering to hold the filling. It is woven from jute yarn, and produced mostly in India.

butterfly hinge, a hinge made of iron and resembling a butterfly. It is found on early American furniture. See Fig. 5, Plate 59.

butterfly table, a small table, the leaves of which, when opened, are supported by winglike brackets, the whole resembling a butterfly with its wings spread. See Fig. 20, Plate 57.

butt hinge, a square or rectangular hinge of brass or iron, the two leaves of which are connected by a pin. See Detail of Rule Joint, Plate 31. This particular type of hinge having one leaf longer than the other is known as a back flap.

butt joint, the term refers to a joint on which the squared end of one member is butted against the side or end of another member.

cabinet, a piece of furniture having compartments, such as drawers, doors, shelves or other divisions built into a case.

cabochen, a plain convex or concave surface, round or oval, surrounded by carved ornament. Found on grotesque Queen Anne style. See also Fig. 52, Plate 5.

cabriole leg, a cyma curved leg that swells outward at the knee, and turns inward at the ankle. It is used on Chippendale, Queen Anne, and Louis XV furniture principally. See Fig. 39, Plate 24.

camber, a hollowed arch or surface. See Fig. 22, Plate 11.

camel back, a term referring to the arching at the top of a sofa back. See Fig. 2, Plate 39; Fig. 8, Plate 22.

canape, a French term applied to a sofa or couch.

candle stand, a small light table or stand usually with turned pedestal, supported upon three short legs, these being either of the cabriole type or turned.

caned, the woven mesh found on chair seats and chair backs, made of split reed, and found especially on Carolean, Louis XIV, and sometimes on later furniture. See Fig. 40, Plate 4.

canopy, the frame or tester over a high four-poster bedstead, with or without its covering material. See Fig. 2, Plate 61.

capital, the enriched top of a column, found on all orders of architecture. See Fig. 7, Plate 22.

carcass, the frame or body of a piece of cabinet furniture.

card table, a table used for gaming. They usually have a swing leg at the back which supports a leaf of the double top. See Fig. 12, Plate 34.

Carolean, furniture of the Charles II period in the Jacobean style. See Plate 2.

cartoon, a term applied to the original design for a piece of tapestry.

cartouche, a carved ornament based upon an unrolled scroll, the central part of which is often used as a field for painted devices or inscriptions.

carved, in other words modeled, by cutting and shaping on wood with chisels of various shapes.

Carver chair, an early turned chair of local American wood, having turned vertical and horizontal spindles in the back. It was named after a Pilgrim governor of Plymouth who owned one. See Fig. 4. Plate 56.

caryatid, a conventionalized human figure or bust, carved at the tops of posts, chair legs, and similar members, especially on seventeenth-century or earlier furniture, and sometimes on cabriole legs of the grotesque Queen Anne or early Georgian types before Chippendale.

caster, a roller, first used on furniture about the beginning of the nineteenth century. See Fig. 7, Plate 38.

caul, a form made of wood or metal, used with clamps to hold veneers in place on shaped surfaces while the glue sets.

cavetto, of Latin derivation, meaning a cove molding. See cove, Fig. 29.

cellaret, a container for wine bottles, also used as a cooler.

chair table, a combination piece of furniture

which may be adapted to serve either purpose. See Fig. 14, Plate 57.

chaise longue, See daybed. Fig. 6, Plate 43.

chamfer, See bevel.

chandelier, originally a candle holder, but more recently applied to lighting fixtures hung from the ceiling.

chaneling, a carved border the ornament of which is composed of a series of short flutes. See Fig. 51, Plate 5.

Charles LeBrun, a French designer of the time of Louis XIV. See Chapter 13.

chasing, incised decoration on hardware. See Fig. 5, Plate 21.

check, a crack, split, or similar defect in lumber, caused by improper drying conditions.

chequered, veneer or inlay composed of differently colored squares.

cherub, an angelic or fairylike figure usually found painted on panels during the Louis XVI period. See Fig. 23, Plate 45.

chests, boxlike receptacles of wood with hinged lids. See Fig. 1, Plate 1.

chest of drawers, a cabinet piece of furniture in which the compartments are composed of drawers. See Fig. 3, Plate 1.

chest-on-chest, a chest of drawers divided into two sections by a prominent horizontal molding. See page 227.

cheval glass, a mirror which swings between vertical supports. A tall dressing mirror which stands upon the floor.

Chinese Chippendale, a type of furniture in which the structural members were made to simulate bamboo, or with fret carved stretchers, or with members having other Chinese characteristics. See Fig. 23, Plate 23.

chintz, a printed fabric, sometimes glazed by hot calendering. Used as a hanging or for upholstering purposes. See Chapter 17.

chip carving, carving in geometrical patterns done with a sloyd knife. See Fig. 3, Plate 48.

Chippendale, refers to the style originated by Thomas Chippendale, an English cabinetmaker, and one of the four greatest furniture designers of the eighteenth century.

chroma, a color term having the same meaning as intensity. See Chapter 5.

cinquefoil, a five-pointed ornament of Gothic tracery, found on very early furniture using Gothic motifs. See upper drawer, Plate 50.

clamp, a tool used for applying pressure when making a joint, or to hold work in place while it is being formed.

Classical or **Classic,** referring to forms of ornament or structure originating with the ancient Greeks or Romans. See Plate 41.

cleat, a narrow border or batten joined to the ends of table tops, or desk lids to hide end grain and provide added strength and finish to the member. See desk lid, Plate 27.

clock case, the cabinet used to hold the works of a clock. See Fig. 13, Plate 57.

club foot, a term referring to poorly formed feet on Queen Anne furniture.

clustered column, a term referring to bedposts carved with heavy reeds which appear to be separate members clustered together to form a single shaft or column. See Fig. 24, Plate 24.

cock beading, a narrow raised beading surrounding the edge of a veneered surface as a form of protection and finish. See Fig 6, Plate 52.

coffer, originally an Italian chest, but usually refers to small boxes or chests used to store valuables.

colonnette, a column in miniature. See Plate 50.

comb back, refers to the top of a Windsor chair which resembles a high comb. See Plate 60.

commode, a term applied to a low cabinet, often used under a mirror in a hallway or boudoir. They may be straight fronted, but are more often semicircular or semielliptical in shape. See Fig. 7, Plate 39.

complementary colors, colors which when mixed together tend to neutralize or gray each other. See chapter on Color.

composite, an order of architecture composed of Corinthian and Ionic ornament.

compound curve, one which changes direction more than once. See Fig. 32, Plate 58.

concave, a hollowed surface, the opposite of convex.

concentric, refers to a number of circles having one common center. See Color Chart, Chapter 5.

Connecticut chest, a term often applied to chests having tulip and aster carved panels. See Fig. 21, Plate 57.

console, originally a large bracket supporting a shelf, but in furniture parlance it refers to any group consisting of a table or cabinet with a mirror hung above it. See Fig. 8, Plate 40.

constitution mirror, a mirror having a convex glass and a circular frame, gilded and decorated with balls and a carved eagle. A design invented about the beginning of the nineteenth century.

contour, the outline or profile of an object.

contrasted harmonies, color harmonies brought about by combinations in which complementary hues are used. See Chapter 5.

convex, an outward curve, the opposite of concave.

convolute, rolled upon itself, or in the form of a Classic scroll. See detail of carved ears, Plate 60.

core stock, the soft, well-seasoned wood forming a foundation upon which veneer may be applied. It is often laminated, or built up of wood that is not easily subject to warp.

Corinthian order, a style of architecture in which the capital of the column is composed of acanthus leaves clustered about a central core. It is also the smallest order in scale.

corner block, a bracket used to reinforce the joints of chair seats and similar structures on the inside. See Fig. 7, Plate 61.

corner cupboard, a cupboard which is triangular in plan, so made to be placed in a corner. See Fig. 5, Plate 56, also Fig. 281 in text.

cornice, a protruding architectural structure found at the tops of buildings, and on cabinet furniture. It is composed of moldings, plain or decorated surfaces, and occasionally dentils. See Fig. 7, Plate 44.

court cupboard, a cupboard set upon a frame. The term originated from the French word *court* meaning short. See Fig. 4, Plate 1.

cove, a concave molding.

credence, a sort of sideboard, used in early times as a kind of serving table.

cresting, the carved or ornamental decoration found on the upper horizontal member of early chair backs. See Fig. 31, Plate 4.

cretonne, a printed upholstering fabric, similar to chintzes but somewhat heavier. See Chapter 17.

Cromwellian, furniture of Cromwell's time, or the middle period of the Jacobean style.

cross stretcher, a stretcher composed of two intersecting members, somewhat in the form of an X, found on William and Mary and Louis XIV furniture as underbracing. See Plate 13.

crotch mahogany, referring to the interesting figure of the grain produced on that wood at the place where a limb of the tree is joined to the trunk.

crown, the carved top of an early chair, or a molding found at the top of a cabinet. See Fig. 7, Plate 44.

crow's nest, two square boards joined together with four colonnettes, to form the support for a pie-crust or tilting table top. See Fig. 4, Plate 61.

C scroll, a Flemish carved scroll resembling a C. See Fig. 61, Plate 5.

Cupid's bow, refers to the shaping of the rail in a chair back or other member in which two cyma curves are combined to resemble the bow staff usually carried by a cupid. See Fig. 19, Plate 23.

curled hair, the best filling material for upholstered furniture. It is manufactured for this purpose from horse tails and manes, cattle switches, and hog bristles.

curly maple, maple having a grain which when finished produces the effect of rippling water. See inset veneer on chair leg, page 151.

cyma recta, an ogee molding, one of the simple moldings. See Fig. 29.

cyma reversa, the reverse of cyma recta. See Fig. 29.

dado, a square groove cut with or across the grain of the wood. See Fig. 10, Plate 62.

dais, a raised surface or platform.

damask, an upholstering material in which the lines of the design are contrasted with the background by running them in a different direction. See Chapter 17.

daybed or **chaise longue,** a kind of couch with a head that may be raised or lowered. Also refers to French upholstered couches. See Fig. 6, Plate 43.

deal, an English cabinet wood similar to our pine.

dentils, rectangular shaped blocks with narrow spaces between, found on architectural structures arranged in rows under cornice moldings. See Plate 36.

Derbyshire chairs, small side chairs similar to the Cromwellian type, with carved cresting and two or three vertical spindles in the back. See Plate 9.

diaperwork, an all-over pattern consisting of repeats carved or inlaid over a comparatively large surface. See Fig. 16, Plate 45.

Directoire, the early part of the French Empire period.

dish top, a round table top having a raised rim. See Fig. 11, Plate 56.

dolphin, a marine animal, the head and body of which is carved as ornament on the feet or chairs of rich Chippendale or Louis XV furniture.

Doric, the second order of Classic architecture, also one of the plainest, the capital having little carving.

double complementaries, a color harmony brought about by using two adjacent hues found on the complementary color chart and their complementary hues in a color scheme. See Chapter 5.

dowel, a plain turned member used to join two pieces of wood together. See Fig. 9, Plate 61.

dower chest, a hope chest or marriage chest. See Fig. 81.

dovetailing, a method of joining two members together by cutting away triangular shaped pieces from the edge of a board and joining it to another on which the same thing has been done. See Fig. 10, Plate 62, and Figs. 17, 19, Plate 63.

drake foot, a three-toed foot found on Queen Anne furniture. See Fig. 15, Plate 17.

draw bore, a method used for drawing two members of a mortise-and-tenon joint together by driving a pin through two holes, the one on the tenon member being closer to the shoulder than the hole on the mortise member.

dresser, a structure having open shelves set upon a closed cupboard. See Fig. 5, Plate 56.

dressing table, a light table having one or several drawers, and a mirror hung on the wall above it or fastened to it. A lowboy. See Plate 14 and Fig. 126.

drop finial, a turned ornament fastened to the bottom edge of a lowboy or highboy apron. See Fig. 1, Plate 16.

drop leaf, the leaf of a table top which may be dropped to a vertical position. See Plate 31.

Dutch style, a term referring to William and Mary and Queen Anne styles.

dynamic, a term referring to the onward motion produced by ornament on a band or border. See Fig. 4, Plate 51.

ears, a term applied to the enrichment found at the ends of the upper rail on a comb-back Windsor chair. See detail and section, Plate 60.

ebony, an oriental wood which is black in color.

egg and dart, a carved Classic molding. See Fig. 16, Plate 41.

ellipse, an oval.

Empire, the French style originating during the time of Napoleon.

enamel, a paint used as an overglaze, made of finely ground pigments and varnish.

endive, a form of water leaf, carved on furniture. See lower detail, Fig. 4, Plate 39.

entablature, the superstructure supported by columns in architecture, such as the cornice. See adaptation, Plate 36.

entasis, a slight swelling found about one third of the way up on a well-proportioned column. See Plate 36.

escritoire, a writing desk with drawers and other compartments. A small secretary.

escutcheon, a brass plate surrounding a keyhole; sometimes also made of bone or ivory. See Figs. 15 and 16, Plate 38.

evolute, a mathematical curve or recurrent wave motif. Opposite direction of involute.

façade, the front of a building — also applied to the front of cabinets.

fauteuil, a French carved and upholstered armchair, open under the arms.

feathered, describing figured grain on mahogany or other valuable woods resembling a feather. See oval panel, Fig. 12, Plate 29, and Fig. 11, Plate 29.

featheredge, a term applied to the edges of panels where they are thinned for joining to stiles or rails. See Section A–B, Plate 7.

Federal, American furniture between the period when American independence had been won to about the beginning of the nineteenth century.

festoon, a wreath or garland of leaves or flowers. See Fig. 37, Plate 41.

fiddle back, a vertical chair splat somewhat resembling the back of a violin and found mostly on Queen Anne chairs. See Fig. 26, Plate 18.

filigree, a term applied to the decoration on mirror frames of the type designed by the Brothers Adam. Plaster or composition ornament was molded upon a network of wires, the whole being known as filigree. See Fig. 8, Plate 40.

fillet, a flat narrow band used as a connecting member for curves of moldings and turnings. See Fig. 29.

finger joint, a joint used to connect the swinging bracket, or apron, to a table frame. It is a wooden hinge resembling the fingers of both hands when they are interlocked, hence the name. See Plate 31.

finial, a turned or carved decoration used at the tops of chair posts, in the break of pediments, and similar terminations. See Figs. 30, 31, Plate 24.

fire screen, a term usually applied to a small screen fastened to a shaft on three short legs, and used for the purpose of shielding the eyes from the glare of the sun or candlelight. See Fig. 4, Plate 39.

flame, the carving on a finial resembling the flame of a torch. See Figs. 30, 31, Plate 24.

flat carving, a type in which the background only is lowered, leaving the design flat. See Fig. 45, Plate 5.

Flemish scroll, a carved scroll in which the continuity of the figure is broken by an angle. See Fig. 40, Plate 4, and Fig. 62, Plate 5.

fleur de lis, a national emblem of France, carved or painted as ornament on furniture of the French styles.

fluting, a series of semicircular grooves or channels cut into a flat or turned surface. See Plate 36.

foliated, ornament in which leaves form the chief decoration.

free ornament, ornament which is not bisymmetrically balanced. See Fig. 2, Plate 47.

French foot, commonly applied to a slender flared-out bracket foot found especially on Hepplewhite chests of drawers; though the term may apply to a large number of other feet commonly found on French furniture. See Fig. 8, Plate 29.

fret work, the sawing or carving out of backgrounds to form tracery of flat geometric patterns. Found especially on Chippendale furniture. See Fig. 155.

friction catch, a small bullet-like catch used to hold small doors closed on desks or other places. It has a spring which holds a ball in contact with a plate, though this connection may be easily released.

frieze, the plain or decorated section under the cornice mold. See Fig. 5, Plate 39.

fruit wood, cabinet woods of fruit trees such as pear, apple, lime, cherry, etc.

gadroon, a carved molding also known as nulling. The short flutes or reeds are sloped. See lower edge of apron on Fig. 4, Plate 22.

gallery, a raised rim of pierced metal or wood, or a railing supported on turned colonnettes, and found on table tops or the tops of sideboards. See Fig. 6, Plate 16.

gate-leg table, a type of table on which the leaves are supported upon framed gates made to swing out from the frame of the table on either side. The frame of the tables is usually turned. See Fig. 8, Plate 16.

gesso, a substance made of plaster and glue, which may be molded into ornament of various shapes, and which is usually painted or gilded.

Gibbon, Grinling, a famous wood carver of the seventeenth century, who did some of the most elaborate wood carving ever attempted.

gimp, a woven ribbon used in upholstering to cover the heads of tacks on a piece of furniture.

girandole, a candle branch attached to a mirror frame.

glazed chintz, See chintz, Chapter 17.

Gobelin, the name of a famous tapestry works in France, where the finest tapestries ever made were produced, especially during the seventeenth and eighteenth centuries.

Gothic, furniture motifs or entire pieces derived from the Gothic style of architecture. See Fig. 15.

grandfather's clock, a tall weight clock. See Fig. 13, Plate 57.

griffin, a chimerical beast whose head and wings resemble those of a large bird, and whose body is like that of a lion. See Fig. 8, Plate 40.

grille, a term applied to ornament composed of turned spindles, decorative wrought iron, or pierced carving, used as a screen over an opening. See Plate 50.

gros point, a type of needlework in which the stitches are comparatively large.

grotesque, usually said of carved ornament representing chimerical beasts, or masks of horrible aspects. See Fig. 10, Plate 54.

guilloche, carvings, the curved figures of which are interlaced. See Fig. 44, Plate 5.

Hadley chest, an early American type on which flat-faced carving completely covers the surface.

hair cloth, cloth woven of horsehair, used on nineteenth-century furniture.

half column, an architectural column split in half, and fastened to edges of highboys, cabinets, and secretaries, in the same manner as a pilaster. See Plate 36.

harewood, See sycamore.

harmony, a term applied to design when there is a natural and seemingly correct relation between several of its members, or elements.

harmony by analogy, See analogous harmonies, Chapter 5.

harmony by contrast, See contrasted harmonies, Chapter 5.

haunch, a short projection on the tenon member of a joint, found at the top edge of tenon or on its side. See Section A–B, Fig. 8, Plate 61.

heart and crown, a motif frequently found on banister-back chair tops.

Hepplewhite, one of the four greatest cabinetmaker designers of the eighteenth century in England. See Chapter 10.

herringbone inlay, a band of veneer on which the figures of the pattern cross each other obliquely. See Fig. 26, Plate 35.

highboy, a tall chest of drawers supported on high legs or on a frame. See Fig. 2, Plate 22.

Hitchcock chair, usually a painted chair, of a provincial Sheraton type.

honeysuckle, See anthemion. Fig. 26, Plate 41.

hood, the semicircular tops found on William and Mary cabinet furniture. Fig. 8, Plate 10.

hoop back, See bow back.

hope chest, See dower chest. Fig. 81.

H, and H-and-L hinges, hardware the members of which are in the form of those letters of the alphabet. See Figs. 1 and 2, Plate 59.

horizontal division, a term used in design to denote the division of areas in a horizontal direction with vertical lines or elements. See Chapter 1.

horseshoe seat, chair seats resembling a horseshoe in shape. Used mostly by Duncan Phyfe. See Fig. 12, Plate 53.

hue, a term meaning the same thing as the word *color.* See Chapter 5.

husk, a drop inlay, usually the cornflower motif. See Fig. 20, Plate 30.

hutch, a chest built like a cupboard, with doors. An early form.

imbricated carving, a type of all-over pattern resembling the scales on a fish.

inceptive axis, a real or imaginary line about which design elements are grouped to form a design unit. See Chapter 4.

intarsia, inlays on solid wood, composed of colored wood, tortoise shell, bone, ivory, and precious or semiprecious metals.

intensity, a color term denoting the brilliance or purity of a color. See Chapter 5.

intermediate triads, a color term relating to harmonies that are brought about by combinations of intermediate colors. See Chapter 5.

inverted cup (inverted bowl), a turned element resembling a cup turned upside down, and found on William and Mary turnings. See Fig. 11, Plate 11.

Ionic, the order of Classic architecture following the Doric, a feature of which is the Ionic scroll.

Jacobean, the English style which followed the Elizabethan. It is composed of the furniture built during the reigns of James I, Charles I, Cromwell, Charles II, and James II.

japanning, See lacquer.

joint stool, a stool joined together with mortise-and-tenon joints. See Fig. 10, Plate 1.

kapok, a silk floss, manufactured from a fiber adhering to the seeds on trees growing in the East Indies. It is a valuable filling material used for upholstering, especially to fill pillows.

kas, a large wardrobe.

Kauffman, Angelica, a celebrated artist who painted panels on Brothers Adam, Hepplewhite, and Sheraton furniture.

keepers, a clasp of brass or iron used to hold two sections of a large dining table together. See Fig. 18, Plate 54.

kettle base, See bombe.

key plate, See escutcheon.

kneading trough, See bread-mixing table.

knee, the upper part of a cabriole leg which swells outward from the frame.

knee-hole desk, a flat-topped desk having an opening in the center for knee room, with rows of drawers, or doors on either side. See Fig. 7, Plate 29.

lacquer, an oriental process of painting furniture, in which repeated coats of coloring material alternated with rubbing, builds up a perfectly sealed surface, and on the best work, raised figures in the design. It is a process invented by the Chinese and brought to a high degree of perfection by the Japanese. See Fig. 7, Plate 10.

ladder-back chairs, chairs on which the backs consist of a number of horizontal slats resembling a ladder. See Fig. 19, Plate 23.

laminate, the process of building up wood in three or more layers, the grain of each alternate layer running at right angles to that of the preceding layer.

laureling, carved or painted ornament using the laurel-leaf motif. See Fig. 30, Plate 41.

Lazy Susan, a form of dumbwaiter similar in construction to a tilt-top table, but with several galleries placed above each other. See Fig. 9, Plate 22.

lectern, a standing reading desk, used when delivering a speech.

linenfold carving, a type of carving found on Gothic furniture, in which the design resembles folds of cloth.

link, a term used in design to denote minor elements used as connecting links between two more important design elements. The dart in Fig. 16, Plate 41.

lip mold, a quarter-round molding surrounding the edges of drawer fronts and used to prevent dust from entering the drawer opening. Lid and drawers of desk, Plate 27.

livery cupboard, an early type of cupboard used to hold food, with grilled doors to provide a circulation of air. See Fig. 4, Plate 48.

long form, a long bench in which the frame is mortised and tenoned together. See Fig. 9, Plate 1.

Louis Quatorze, another name for Louis XIV.

Louis Quinze, another name for Louis XV.

Louis Seize, another name for Louis XVI.

low relief, modeled carving on which the background is lowered not more than $1/8$ in.

lozenge, an applied ornament similar to a boss but diamond shaped. See Fig. 57, Plate 5.

lunette, a semicircular ornament found in carving on borders. See Fig. 53, Plate 5.

lyre, a structural and ornamental feature resembling the musical instrument of that name, and found on Duncan Phyfe furniture especially. See Fig. 17, Plate 53.

mahogany, a tropical wood having a richly figured, somewhat open grain. It is the king of cabinet woods, having a rich red color, medium hardness, and when once correctly dried holds its shape remarkably well. The fine grain is easily worked with edge tools and is neither too hard, too soft, nor too brittle.

major mass, a term applied to the largest division of a primary mass. See Chapter 1.

mantel, a shelf.

maple, a hard, fine-grained, close-textured wood, valuable for cabinetmaking. It is greatly prized in America for this purpose. It is light in color, and figured boards such as curly, mottled, or bird's eye, are used as veneers or in the solid.

marquetry, marqueterie, similar to intarsia, but distinguished from it by the fact that it is done upon veneered surfaces.

Martha Washington chair, See Hepplewhite Chapter. Fig. 6, Plate 29.

mask or **masque,** a carved face, often grotesquely executed. See Fig. 10, Plate 54.

medallion, a round, oval, or rectangular ornament, usually carved, and applied near the junction of two members as chair legs where the stretchers join it. See Fig. 35, Plate 41.

medial stretcher, a stretcher joining two other stretchers, at or near the centers as a brace. See Fig. 17, Plate 63.

miniature, small copies of larger objects.

minor mass, a term applied to the minor divisions of a primary mass.

miter, an angle cut on the end of a molding or other member, to form a joint with an intersecting member.

modeled surface, a surface that is shaped or formed, or otherwise than flat. See Fig. 78, and Fig. 14, Plate 54.

module, a unit of measurement used in architectural design.

mohair, a kind of upholstering material similar to velvet, and made from the fleece of the Angora goat. See Chapter 17.

mold, molding, a molded band used to decorate furniture and to form gradual junctions between two masses.

monotony, referring to design elements that are exactly alike, or so similar as to lack interest. See turnings, Fig. 8, Plate 1.

mortise, the cut-out element of a joint to which a tenon is joined. See Fig. 5, Plate 61.

mosaic, a pattern or design formed by geometric figures. Panels on chest, Fig. 3, Plate 48.

moss, a stuffing material made from hanging moss which grows on trees in Louisiana. It is an air plant, and must be prepared especially for the purpose. It is a cheaper substitute for curled hair.

mother of pearl, an inlay made of seashells.

motif, motive, the guiding, controlling, or dominant feature or detail on a design.

mounts, a term applied to hardware such as drawer pulls.

muntin, the molding or wooden divisions between panes of glass in a door or window. See Fig. 9, Plate 61.

naturalistic motifs, designs whose sources are elements taken from nature.

needle point, a handmade tapestry of needlework used for upholstery.

nest of tables, a group of small tables that may be placed under each other, each being reduced sufficiently to go under its larger mate.

neutral, colors which may be used in any color scheme, these being, gray, white, black, gold, and silver.

neutralize, the process of graying a color by adding some of its complementary color to it.

niche, a semicircular recess into which busts or other ornaments are placed.

oak, one of the most durable of all cabinet woods. There are several species, white oak being the best for cabinet work. The wood is hard, tough, and open grained, and has a distinct and fairly large scaled figure. Used where solid and substantial construction, and bold effects are desired.

occasional table, any small table that may be used for a number of purposes as convenience dictates.

occult balance, a balance secured in design by placing heavy masses closer to the vertical center line than lighter elements which balance it on the opposite side of the center line. See Fig. 5, Plate 47.

ogee, same as cyma recta.

ormolu, brightly gilt furniture mounts composed of brass and zinc.

overstuffed, furniture in which the frame is thickly padded and stuffed under the upholstery material.

ox-bow front, a serpentine form of cabinet construction found on the fronts of Chippendale chests of drawers, in which the center is concave, with convex swellings on either side. See Fig. 38, Plate 24.

oystering, a form of veneering in which the figure of the grain is suggestive of an oyster, because of irregular concentric rings. It is sliced from ends of small limbs. See Fig. 4, Plate 10.

pad foot, a foot found on Queen Anne furniture, having a disk resembling a pad under the foot proper. See Fig. 14, Plate 17.

painted furniture, any furniture having painted designs as decoration. See Fig. 81.

palmated, leaves in the form of a palm branch, painted or carved. See Fig. 25, Plate 41.

panel, a board set into a frame composed of rails and stiles, mortised and tenoned together. It may be plain or ornamented. Also a surface set off from its surrounding surface by a band or border, either painted, inlaid, or otherwise separated. See Fig. 21, Plate 57, and Fig. 8, Plate 33.

parcel gilt, ornament partly covered by gold leaf or gold paint.

parrot back, a term applied to Queen Anne chair backs which have a contour resembling two parrots facing each other. This result is brought about by outline enrichment between the splat and the back legs. See Fig. 39, Plate 19, and Fig. 23, Plate 18.

pastel, a term sometimes applied to colors lighter than middle value.

patera, an elliptical, circular, or oblong ornament, carved, painted or inlaid. See Figs. 28, 29, Plate 41.

patina, a unique tinge resulting from aging, polishing, or seasoning of the finish or surface of a piece of wood. Ordinarily a natural process as the result of age.

pear foot, a foot turned to resemble the shape of a pear. See Fig. 30, Plate 58.

pedestal, a column or shaft used as a supporting member for a table top. See Fig. 16, Plate 53, and Fig. 9, Plate 52.

pediment, the triangular-shaped top of a classic building. It is a motif adapted for the tops of important cabinets and secretaries. The bonnet top is also spoken of as a pediment, it being a variant of this type of superstructure. See Fig. 6, Plate 33.

Pembroke table, a small light table with drop leaves. It got its name from the Countess of Pembroke who is said to have had one made to her specifications. See Plates 31 and 32.

Period furniture, that which belongs to a definite style.

petit point, needlework embroidery of a fine slanted stitch, used on Queen Anne and later styles.

Phyfe, Duncan, the most famous American cabinetmaker, doing work in the Sheraton and Empire styles about the beginning of the nineteenth century.

pie-crust table, a tilt-top table, the raised edge of whose top resembles a pie crust. See Fig. 165.

pierced work, See fretwork.

pier glass, a narrow mirror hung above a table but not attached to it.

pier table, a table used under a mirror.

pigeonholes, compartments in the cabinet of a desk or secretary, which are open in the front, and are used to hold letters or papers. See Plate 27.

pilaster, a flat architectural column, fastened to a wall or cabinet. See Fig. 7, Plate 22.

pile, the term applied to the soft bristles of velvet, velours, and mohair.

pine, an American softwood, the best of which, for cabinet purposes, is white pine. It is very light, soft, but not spongy, and close grained; and does not warp easily after being seasoned.

pipe box, a small box to hold long-stemmed pipes, usually hung upon the wall, and with a small drawer to hold tobacco.

plain weave, a fabric into which no figure is woven.

plinth, the base of a column or pedestal. See Fig. 9, Plate 52.

points of concentration, positions on a design to which special attention is directed by placing there the most striking elements of a design.

polychrome, ornament or surfaces decorated with more than one color.

powder stand, a small cuplike container for face powders.

press cupboard, a cupboard similar to the court cupboard, but enclosed with doors below as well as above. See Fig. 86.

primary colors, colors which cannot be further broken up into component parts. They are red, yellow, and blue.

primary mass, the largest division or element, comprising all the units of a design. See Chapter 1.

primary triad, a harmony in which the primary colors are used to form a design. See Chapter 5.

Prince of Wales feathers, three feathers or plumes used together as carved ornament, especially by Hepplewhite. An emblem adopted by the Prince of Wales as an insignia. See Fig. 1, Plate 29.

proportion, the comparative relation of one element to another, such as the ratio of the length to the width of an object. See Chapter 3.

quadrant, a support in the form of a quarter circle for a desk lid; made of brass and found on Sheraton pieces in particular.

quarter column, the fourth of a column, usually placed into a niche at the corner of a lowboy or the base of a highboy of Chippendale design. See Figs. 35 and 36, Plate 24.

quartered oak, a distinctive grain secured by quartering a log, and sawing each quarter exactly parallel to the medullary rays of the wood.

quatrefoil, an ornament formed by Gothic tracery, having four foils or points. See cinquefoil.

Queen Anne style, a style named after Queen Anne of England, which follows immediately after the William and Mary.

rabbet, a groove or step cut on the edge of a board. See section in Fig. 37, Plate 19.

radial line, a part of a circle. See Rule 43, and Fig. 78.

rat's ball and claw, a slender ball-and-claw foot. See Figs. 9 and 10, Plate 22.

rattail hinge, a hinge made of iron which has a tail resembling a rat's. See Fig. 7, Plate 59.

recess, a niche or hollow.

reeding, a carved ornament found on chair legs, stretchers, or columns, composed of convex molds resembling a bunch of reeds tied together. Lower section, Fig. 16, Plate 35.

refectory, a long rectangular table braced near the floor with rails. See Fig. 5, Plate 1.

relief carving, a form of ornament in which the figure is in relief by lowering the background and also shaping the design itself. See Fig. 40, Plate 4.

Renaissance, the period when there was a revival of learning and of all the arts and sciences. It came about during the fifteenth and sixteenth centuries.

return mold, a molding running from the front to the rear of a cabinet. See Fig. 16, Plate 63.

reverse curve, a cyma curve — one which turns in the opposite direction from its beginning. See Plate 16.

rhythmic curve, a curve that is attractive to the eye because it unfolds gracefully.

ribbon back, a type of chair back in which the carved ornament resembles ribbons and knotted bows. A favorite motif of Chippendale's.

rocaille, See rococo.

rococo, a carved form of ornament of naturalistic origin, in which the motifs consist of rock-and-shell forms from which sea water is supposed to be dripping. See Fig. 1, Plate 47.

roll edge, a method of upholstering the front of a chair seat to form a large roll which prevents the cushion from slipping forward.

rosette, a medallion carved with a flower ornament. See Fig. 48, Plate 5.

rosewood, a hard, brittle, red wood used solid or for veneering purposes on fine furniture. It has distinct markings that make it valuable for this purpose.

rule joint, the joint on table leaves in which a cove molding on one leaf slips over a quarter-round molding on another. This construction prevents an open space when the leaf is dropped. See Detail, Plate 31.

rush seat, a seat woven from dried bullrush leaves. See Fig. 6, Plate 48.

saddle seat, a dipped seat, or in other words one that is hollowed in the center. See Fig. 1, Plate 29.

saltire, a form of X-stretcher, but the members are curved instead of straight. See Fig. 1, Plate 43.

satin weave, one of the three types of weaving in which the surface of the cloth is covered by tiny warp threads lying parallel to each other to produce a satin finish. See Chapter 17.

satinwood, a deep yellow silky wood with a beautiful figured grain that makes it very valuable for veneering purposes. It was in great demand for this purpose on the fine cabinet work of the eighteenth century. Beautiful effects were produced by using it with woods of other colors, particularly mahogany. The wood grows in India.

sausage turning, turning on which the long segments resemble sausages connected end to end.

Savery, William, a famous Philadelphia cabinetmaker, who worked in the Chippendale style.

scale drawing, a working drawing on which a fraction of an inch represents an inch or a foot. See Chapter 18.

sconce, a wall bracket for a light. See wall lights, Fig. 8, Plate 40.

scotia, a hollow molding of refined design. See Fig. 30.

scratch carving, carving in which the figure is formed by lightly incised lines. Panel, Fig. 1, Plate 1.

scrutoire, a French name for a writing desk.

secondary colors, colors produced by mixing two primary hues. They are green, orange, and violet.

secondary triad, a color harmony produced by using secondary colors in a color scheme.

secretary, a desk with a cabinet or bookcase above, and drawers nearly to the floor. See Fig. 7, Plate 22.

serpentine, descriptive of a form of construction in which a series of alternate concave and convex curves resemble the form of a serpent in motion. See Fig. 38, Plate 24.

serrated, zig-zag carving. See Fig. 50, Plate 5.

settle, settee, a seat having a back and arms like a sofa, but not as fully upholstered as a sofa. See Figs. 242 and 252.

sewing table, a small light table with one or two drawers, and sometimes a silk bag suspended beneath. See Fig. 6, Plate 52.

shade, a hue which is darker than middle value.

Shearer, Thomas, an English cabinetmaker and designer, said to be the originator of the Sheraton-type sideboard.

shell ornament, carved ornament resembling various seashells, found especially on Queen Anne, Chippendale, Louis XIV, and Louis XV styles. See Plate 49, and Fig. 15, Plate 17.

shell top, refers to the ceiling of china cabinets which were carved to resemble cockleshells. See Fig. 281.

Sheraton, the last of the great English furniture designers. Many authorities say he was the greatest of them all.

shield back, referring to a chair back, the

outline of which resembles a heart-shaped shield. A favorite motif of Hepplewhite. See Fig. 2, Plate 29.

sideboard table, a high table used as a sideboard, and distinguished from a sideboard by the fact that it has no drawers. See Fig. 4, Plate 22.

side chair, any chair without arms. See Fig. 1, Plate 52.

skirt, See apron.

slant front, as on a desk, the lid of which slants upward, toward the back. See Plate 28.

slat back, See ladder back.

slip seat, an upholstered seat slipped into a rabbet in the chair seat frame. See Fig. 12, Plate 53.

snake foot, properly a snakehead foot, from its resemblance to the head of a serpent. See Fig. 29, Plate 58.

sofa, an upholstered settee. See Fig. 2, Plate 39.

soffit, the underside of an arch or cornice. See Fig. 7, Plate 44 (Molding Detail).

spade foot, a square tapered foot resembling a spade. Found on Hepplewhite furniture. See Fig. 17, Plate 30.

Spanish foot, a unique type of ribbed foot having scrolls on two sides. See Fig. 33, Plate 4, and Fig. 2, Plate 48.

spindle, a light turning. See turnings, Plate 60.

spinet, an old type of musical instrument similar to a piano, but much smaller.

spiral, a screw-like ornament carved around shafts and columns. On Jacobean furniture the spiral is convex, resembling twisted wood. On Spanish furniture, which has Moorish and Gothic influences, the spirals are often concave. See Fig. 26, Plate 3, and Plate 50.

splat, the vertical central member in a chair back, so called if it is a single piece. See Fig. 12, Plate 16.

splay, the rake or slant of a leg or chair back, etc. See legs on Windsor chair, Plate 60.

spline, a thin piece of wood glued into grooves for joining two members together, especially the ends of mitered joints. See Plate 8.

split complementaries, color harmonies resulting from taking a primary hue and the two hues found on either side of its com-

plementary color on the complementary color chart. See Chapter 5.

spool turning, a form of turning on which the segments resemble a number of spools joined end to end.

spoon back, a chair back the side elevation of which is curved like the handle of a table spoon. See Queen Anne furniture. See Fig. 36, Plate 19.

spring seat, upholstered seats into which coiled springs are placed under the stuffing and covering material.

squab cushions, a loose upholstered cushion, generally flat and square. See Fig. 16, Plate 2.

steaming, a treatment to which wood is subjected prior to bending it into shapes such as those found at the top of Windsor bow-back chairs or on horseshoe seats. After steaming the wood is placed into forms for drying.

stile, the vertical member of a door or panel frame. See left-hand door, Plate 7.

strapwork, carved ornament resembling interlaced straps. See guilloche, Fig. 47, Plate 5.

stretcher, any turned, straight, or carved horizontal bracing member on a chair, table, or cabinet frame. See Fig. 17, Plate 63.

Stuart period, the Jacobean period with the exception of the Cromwellian style.

sunburst, a circular or elliptical ornament having carved or inlaid ribs or segments, and resembling the risen sun. When only half of it appears it is sometimes called a sunrise carving. See Fig. 32, Plate 24.

sunflower, another name for the aster carved on Connecticut chests. See Fig. 21, Plate 57.

swag, a festoon of flowers, fruit, or similar ornament. See Fig. 37, Plate 41.

swan neck, See bonnet top. Fig. 37, Plate 24.

swell front, a front of a cabinet swelled out with a single convex curve. See Fig. 8, Plate 29.

swing leg, a leg fastened to a short apron, which is pivoted on a finger joint from the table frame. See Fig. 20, Plate 63.

sycamore, a soft redwood sometimes used for veneering or inlaying purposes by European cabinetmakers.

tabouret, a stool with a wooden top.

tall boy, See highboy.

tambour, a sliding panel found on late eighteenth-century desks. It is made by gluing narrow strips vertically to a canvas back, so it may slide on a curved track. See Fig. 11, Plate 62, and Fig. 10, Plate 29.

tapestry, a woven upholstery material. See Chapter 17.

tavern table, a small rectangular table of a type found in the taprooms of taverns. They usually have a frame composed of turned members, and a drawer. See Fig. 9, Plate 56.

tea table, a small low table used for serving tea or coffee to guests. See Fig. 6, Plate 16.

template, a pattern of wood, metal, or cardboard for testing curves.

tenon, the male member of a mortise-and-tenon joint. See Fig. 5, Plate 61.

tertiary colors, the three hues resulting from mixing secondary colors. They are olive, citrine, and russet.

tester, See canopy. Fig. 2, Plate 61.

three-part division, the division of a mass into three parts either vertically or horizontally, by means of moldings, borders, or other members. See Chapter 1.

thuja, a colored wood used by Hepplewhite for inlay.

thumb-nail mold, a refinement of the quarter round. See Fig. 30.

thunder bolts, ornament of Classic origin, composed of a bundle of diverging arrow-headed reeds. See Fig. 3, Plate 52 (Top Panel).

tilt top, a small round-topped table, the top of which may be tilted to a vertical position. See Fig. 11, Plate 56.

tint, a hue lighter than middle value.

toiles de Jouy, printed chintzes originally made in France. See Chapter 17.

torchere, a French term for a carved or decorated tall candle stand.

tracery, fret work, or Gothic carving consisting of concave bands, arches, etc. See Fig. 15.

transitional, descriptive of a piece of furniture which has elements commonly identified with two periods that follow each other. See William and Mary table, page 82.

trefoil, similar to cinquefoil, but with only three points.

trestle board, a table, the understructure of which is a trestle upon which a top is laid to form a table. See Fig. 19, Plate 57.

triads, harmonies of color secured by using hues in combinations of three.

triglyph, applied ornament in groups of three, arranged in series, and found on the frieze of the Doric order of architecture. It is used as a decoration for early chests and cabinets being applied to posts, etc. See Fig. 46, Plate 5.

triptych, a carved or painted three-part picture or panel. Often the sides are hinged to the central portion, which in most cases is larger than the sides. Found in the Gothic styles.

trumpet turning, a leg turned to resemble a trumpet, and a distinguishing feature of the William and Mary style. See Plate 11.

trundle bed, a low bed that was made to fit under a larger bed when not in use to conserve space.

Tudor rose, a conventionalized rose form carved in the manner of a rosette. See Fig. 48, Plate 5.

tufting, a form of upholstering in which buttons are sewed to the covering material at regular intervals and drawn tight. The raised pads that result form soft cushions. The method is seldom used on furniture except nineteenth-century pieces.

tulip, a conventionalized carving representing that flower. See Connecticut chest. Fig. 21, Plate 57.

turnip foot, a turned foot resembling a turnip, used mostly on early American chests. See Fig. 26, Plate 58.

Tuscan, a simplified Doric order of architecture. The simplest order.

twill weave, a type of weaving in which the ribs of the cloth run diagonally.

two-part division, a term used in design to denote the division of a mass into two parts either horizontally or vertically, by some decorative or structural element.

unity, said of a design in which the elements are harmonious.

upholstering, the woven material used to cover furniture, or the art of applying covering material to furniture.

urn, a vaselike ornament of Classic origin. See finials, Plate 36.

utility, relating to the usefulness of an object, or a piece of furniture.

value, a color term relating to the quality by

which light hues are distinguished from dark ones.

vargueno, a Spanish desk of a unique cabinet type. See Fig. 1, Plate 48.

velour, a velvet upholstering material. See Chapter 17.

Velours de Gênes, a velour of a type made famous in Genoa, Italy. See Chapter 17.

veneer, usually made of a thin layer of beautifully grained wood, applied with glue to a core stock of softwood or laminated stock. Veneer of extra fine quality runs from a thickness of 1/28 in. to thicker sizes. It is generally cut in sheets from the outside of a log by rotating the log, which has first been soaked in water, in a giant lathe. Various figured effects are secured by slicing it from the butt end of a log or from the sides of the log.

vermilion, a cabinet wood, of vermilion color, used for inlay.

vertical division, a term referring to the division of a mass in a vertical direction by horizontal elements such as moldings, etc. See Chapter 1.

volute, the spiraled scroll found on the capital of an Ionic column. It has been adapted successfully for a large variety of ornamental purposes on furniture. See Plate 28.

wainscot, a form of paneling found on Jacobean chair backs. See Fig. 56, Plate 5.

walnut, the most valuable native American cabinet wood. The finest quality black walnut grows in Pennsylvania it being of superior hardness and dark color. Figured walnut such as Circassian, which has a lighter brown color with a very flashy figure, is imported.

warp, the curl or twist on a board or plank caused by improper seasoning. The threads running lengthwise of the cloth on woven material.

water leaf, a leaf with a regular outline used for carved ornament. See Fig. 20, Plate 53.

Watteau, a French artist of the eighteenth century who designed cartoons for tapestry.

webbing, strong bands used as supports for spring in seat frames and chair backs. It is tacked to the frame and the coil springs are sewed to the strips with twine. It is manufactured from jute fiber.

weft, the threads running crosswise in woven materials.

Welsh dresser, a dresser originating in Wales, England. See Jacobean style, Fig. 103.

wheat ear, a motif found carved on Hepplewhite chair backs. See Fig. 67.

William and Mary, a style of furniture following the Carolean. See Chapter 7.

window seat, a long bench, usually upholstered. See Fig. 6, Plate 39.

Windsor chair, a light chair composed of slender turned spindles. See Colonial Chapter, Fig. 6, Plate 56.

wing chair, an upholstered armchair with wings on each side. These were originally intended as a protection from draughts of cold air. See Fig. 21, Plate 23.

Wren, Sir Christopher, a famous English architect who designed beautiful Classic interiors during the latter part of the seventeenth century, in addition to other noteworthy artistic and scientific achievements.

wrought iron, the iron from which early American hardware and ornament for Spanish furniture is formed. The best grade is known as double refined iron. See Plate 59.

X-stretcher, See cross stretcher.

Yorkshire chair, a design of the Jacobean period originating in Yorkshire County, England.

zoning, a principle of design in which interest and variety are obtained by means of a series of receding planes or design elements. See Plate 28.

INDEX

In this index italic numerals indicate illustrations and the Roman numerals indicate text matter.